Homesteader

Homesteader

A Prairie Boyhood Recalled

James M. Minifie

Macmillan of Canada,
Toronto

ISBN 0—7705—1037—X

This edition first published 1973

Author's photo by Robert C. Ragsdale

Printed in Canada by The Alger Press Limited
for The Macmillan Company of Canada Limited
70 Bond Street, Toronto M5B 1X3

dedicated to my wife,
Gillian Wadsworth Minifie

Acknowledgements

The author gratefully acknowledges the assistance of the Canada Council, which made it possible to research materials for this memoir, and the invaluable help of Archivist Allan R. Turner and his staff of the Provincial Archives Branch, Regina, Saskatchewan, in directing attention to and making available the remarkable land office records preserved there. Identity of the earliest settlers in the Vanguard region was furnished by an autograph manuscript written by Winnifred Turner, one of the early teachers in the district, in the possession of her son, Allan R. Turner, who kindly made it available to the author.

Assistance was also received from early prairie settlers in Manitoba, notably Mr. and Mrs. J. D. Wiens of Winnipeg, who volunteered recollections and photographs when this project was announced.

The demanding task of retyping under pressure of deadlines a manuscript skilfully revised by Kenneth McVey of The Macmillan Company of Canada Limited, and of integrating it with my pencilled notes, was conscientiously performed by Miss Beverley A. Hall, of Victoria, British Columbia, and by my wife.

To all of these friends, and to the many others who have made a contribution, the author gives his thanks.

JAMES M. MINIFIE
Victoria, British Columbia

Homesteader

Chapter One

In 1909 my father, Philip Richard Minifie, decided to emigrate from England to Western Canada. The decision was not a sudden one, but had been maturing for some time. He was the descendant of sturdy yeoman farmers and strong in the determination to be his own master — not easy to do in the conditions of Edwardian England. But the decision could not have been a simple one for a man who was then thirty-five years of age, married, and the father of two small children.

Why did he select Canada rather than Australia, where his elder brother Jim was already established and reported to be "doing well"?

I think he originally contemplated going there, but his older sisters, twins, lobbied against the Antipodes as too remote. He was a posthumous child, reared by these sisters. Having no offspring of their own, they filled the void with the child they had raised, and resolutely opposed his departure to the ends of the earth. My mother was equally reluctant to break so utterly and irrevocably with the Northern Hemisphere. These pressures paralleled my father's own reluctance to be beholden to his brother, and his desire to be independently successful on his own merits.

These factors were reinforced by powerful promotional campaigns waged by interested parties, official and unofficial, to attract immigrants to Canada. Lavish promises were scattered of free land, fortune, and no taxes, which were decisive for many who later complained, not without some reason, that they had been misled.

The settler was promised from the federal government, for a fee of ten dollars, 160 acres of land for his homestead, provided he resided on it for three years, cultivated 30 acres of wild prairie, and built a house worth at least three hundred dollars. He was also allowed and indeed encouraged to pre-empt an adjoining 160 acres to be paid for within three years at four dollars an acre.

These offers appear minute compared with the allotment to the Canadian Pacific Railway of 25,000,000 acres for building a railroad across the virtually empty plains, and to the Hudson's Bay Company of 1,120 acres out of every 23,040 acres (or one and three-quarter sections — a section is 640 acres — out of every thirty-six sections) of surveyed prairie land between the Great Lakes and the Rocky Mountains. In addition to these insatiable cormorants, there were Canadian and American land speculators who bought up large blocks to retail to land-hungry immigrants who poured into the "Golden West". These grants and block purchases drastically limited the choice and location of free land to the legitimate settler without limiting official inducements.

Thus, in 1901 the Hon. G. H. V. Bulyea, then Commissioner of Agriculture for the Canadian North-West Territories, sponsored a 72-page booklet entitled:

The Canadian North-West Territories
An Official Handbook
containing reliable information
concerning their resources.

This booklet went at some length into the system of government and taxation, implying, without actually promising, full freedom from personal taxes and presenting a glowing picture which lured many to the prairies.

Bulyea's "reliable information" assured would-be immigrants

> ... each quarter section of land ... is taxed to the extent of $2.00 to $2.50 per annum. The only other

tax levied is that for schools. The total tax for all purposes on a quarter section — 160 acres — seldom ex-
ceeds $7.00 to $8.00 per annum, and in those portions
of the country where the settlers have not yet decided
to form school districts, the total taxation per quarter
section is only from $2.00 to $2.50 per annum.

My father contended that this and similar assurances entitled him
to decline to pay more than eight dollars per quarter-section per
annum. When this view was rejected by federal and provincial Min-
isters of Finance alike, he fell back on that universal refuge of the
victim and the voter, cursing all politicians as liars, swindlers, and in
general "a bunch of grafters", to take only the mildest of the popular
epithets of the day.

The Bulyea pamphlet was backed up by another blurb of official
origin, a production called "The Last Best West, issued by direction
of Hon. Frank Oliver, Minister of the Interior, Ottawa, Canada".
This last-chance hard sell introduced a question-and-answer section
designed to push the hesitant or timid headlong into the water.

Question #4: Are the taxes high?
Answer: No. Having no expensive system of
              municipal or county organization, taxes
              are necessarily low. Each ¼-section of
              land, owned or occupied, is taxed to the
              extent of $2.00 to $2.50 per annum.

It repeated the Bulyea pamphlet's claim that total taxes, even in
organized school districts, seldom exceeded eight to ten dollars.

Another question dealt with rainfall, which was critical because
the atlases of the day represented southern Saskatchewan and
Alberta as a northern continuation of the Great American Desert.

Question: Is there sufficient rainfall?
Answer: Speaking generally, yes. A sufficient supply
          can be relied on. The most rain falls in May
          and June, just when it is most needed.

The immigrant would never have suspected from this that searing winds in June and July might shrivel the standing grain or that the stooks of wheat might be hidden by snow in September.

After making allowances for exceptional years, the federal government must be faulted for misrepresentation in the booklet issued in 1912 by direction of Robert Rogers, Minister of the Interior. It was entitled "Canada, the Land of Opportunity". It reprinted a letter said to have been written by a settler from Ireland on Jan. 10, 1910, from Edgerton P.O., Alberta, Canada. It went into raptures over the crop, and continued: "And the taxes are very light; I just had to pay 8 s [shillings] each year [then about equivalent to $2.00] these last three years. The land is worth £600, and all I had to pay for it was £2 to file on it."

The publicity material issued by private land speculators was not less enticing and often even more misleading than the government brochures.

There was a pamphlet from the William Pearson Co., which had land to sell in the Last Mountain section of Southern Saskatchewan. Percy A. Maxwell, a hard-headed sceptic who nevertheless had been cozened by this "Gull's Hornbook", later wrote: "You needn't believe all that Pearson's book says about Last Mountain. It says that 'water of the clearest and purest is obtainable anywhere'. So it is — in the months of April and May, when the snow melts, but unfortunately neither we nor the horses can drink enough in those two months to last out the other ten."

Mr. Maxwell continued: "There are lots of fellows about who can work the willow witchery business, but I haven't much faith in it, and I will get a machine to bore us a well as soon as I can."

His letter is filed in the Saskatchewan Provincial Archives, but there is no record of the results of his boring machine.

The Americans moved in for their share of the loot.

McGraw and Co., giving their address as "on 40th Street, East of Broadway, New York", weighed in with a 24-page brochure which concluded with the pledge: "Our lands are all open prairie, free from bush or stone, and ready for the steam plow."

Obviously anticipating some scepticism, McGraw and Co. insisted that "Every statement we make in this booklet is founded on FACTS."

It buttressed some very unfactual statements by calling in such unlikely authorities as President Taft; James J. Hill, a rival land purveyor who was also president of the Great Northern Railroad; W. C. Brown, identified as president of the New York Central Railroad; and a Mr. E. S. Bayard, described as "a famous breeder of Aberdeen Angus cattle".

Mr. Hill made a sound point by predicting that "the world will go to bed hungry in 20 years." He did not, however, add that most of the hungry would be rice-eaters, nor did he promote the Canadian prairies as rice-growing areas, actual or potential. McGraw and Co. were less happy in their selection of other "facts", including these items which their brochure listed:

1. The soil is almost inexhaustible
2. The climate ripens grain very quickly
3. There is ample rainfall
4. Cyclones never occur
5. There are no personal taxes; land taxes are 10 cents per acre
6. There is utter absence of rust
7. Insect foes are unknown.

Rust is a fungus disease that seriously reduces the yield of any grain it attacks. Serious crop damage was caused on the prairies by a heavy attack in 1896 and another in 1904 which was widely reported to have "robbed farmers (both American and Canadian) of 100,000,000 bushels of wheat". There is no excuse for these lies about rust and insects, depredations of both being of acute national concern in both countries.

But the publicity material, from both commerical and government sources, was designed to attract settlers, not to present a factual picture of the realities of prairie settlement. It was overwhelmingly successful. Immigrants from eastern Canada, the United States, Great Britain, and Europe flocked to the western plains in the early years of this century.

An important element in this influx was the tremendous advance in milling techniques about the time my father was born. Previously, hard wheat, which was becoming the staple prairie crop, was poorly regarded by millers. With traditional processes, using two millstones, the gluten could not be separated from the flour, which was by consequence lumpy and off-white. It had high baking quality, but the colour was unattractive. The same defect characterized the hard wheat from the Hungarian and Russian plains.

Then a Lancashire man named Wilkinson and a Swiss named Sulzberger discovered that by using steel rollers instead of the traditional millstones, the gluten could be removed, leaving a white flour which was perhaps not as nutritious, since the wheat germ was removed with the gluten, but was in demand both by bakers and by the public. This was the first significant advance in milling in nearly two thousand years, and it was of dramatic consequence for the fortunes of the Canadian prairies. The millers first experimented with hard wheat from the plains of Hungary, from which this method became known as the Hungarian roller process; it proved equally successful with the refractory hard kernels from Saskatchewan. The first mill to use Hungarian rollers was established by Ogilvie in 1871 at Glenora, Ontario. Its success confirmed the economic importance of the Canadian prairies as the successor to Central Europe, until then the bread-basket of the world.

Interest in this historical development was further stimulated by the evolution, under patient selection and breeding, of wheat maturing early enough to avoid the frosts lurking on the fringes of the short prairie summer. They had been the bane of the farmers in the Red River Valley. The Selkirk settlers relied on Old English or Irish strains and Norway white, Assiniboine, Black Sea, Prairie du Chien, Scotch Fife, Club, Golden Drop, and later White Russian and Odessa Red. Out of these sturdy wheats from the Russian steppes, Dr. William Saunders and his sons developed Preston, Stanley, and Early Triumph, much later to be renamed Red Bobs after Lord Roberts, who had galloped to fame in the Boer War.

Red Fife was introduced into the Red River Valley from the United States in 1843. It was selected by David Fife for its high milling and baking qualities which made it popular in the British market. By 1870 it had superseded the varieties used by the early settlers. It was well established when Winnipeg merchants advertised for wheat for cash in 1879. Its fame reached Britain with the first all-Canadian shipment of wheat to Glasgow in 1884. A variant known as Early Red Fife came on the market in 1908, followed in 1910 by Prelude and in 1911 by Marquis 10-B, that noble wheat which was the ancestor and foundation stock for all the great line of Marquis wheats and their successors, world champions from 1911 to

1918. The new wheats and the advanced milling processes generated an enthusiasm for the Canadian prairies and a rush of interested parties anxious to cash in on it both in England and in eastern Canada.

Foremost among these was the Canadian Pacific Railway. The C.P.R. had a triple interest. First, it sold the immigrant cheap passage. The competing Canadian Northern met this by offering third-class accommodation from Antwerp to Montreal for $100. No Australian fares could meet this competition. Once the immigrant reached Canada, the C.P.R. was interested in selling him land. It issued a brochure deprecating his natural hunger for the free land which the Canadian government offered as bait. This free land, the C.P.R. explained ingenuously, was likely to be a long way from the railroad, often thirty miles or more. The C.P.R. did not explain that the main reason for this was that the C.P.R. itself had gobbled up half the free land closer in when it took over its 25,000,000 acres of land grant received for building lines across the empty prairies. Understandably, it passed lightly over the circumstance that its own land grants carried subsoil rights but the acreage it resold to immigrants did not. Ultimately the subsoil rights became so profitable that they were transferred to a C.P. holding company, lest they jeopardize the railroad's demand for higher freight rates and render it liable to standard taxation. C.P.R. sold land it had received free for eight to ten dollars an acre, one-twentieth cash, the rest in nineteen annual payments at six per cent interest.

My father found irresistible the appeal of free land, no taxes, low fares, and the new hard wheat (contrasting so favourably, to a miller, with the soft Australian varieties). The combination lent overwhelming force to the appeals of my father's twin sisters in favour of Canada. Another factor added to the pressure. Time was running out. The best lands were being snapped up fast. As conditions improved, and letters home grew more glowing, the stream of emigrants from Europe attained flood proportions. The last, best West was filling up fast; my father determined to get in while he could. He closed down his business and decided to go as far west as his money would take him and bought a ticket for Calgary.

Thus it was that on a bright spring day in 1909, I stood at our garden gate with my mother and my brother Dick, three years younger, waving good-bye. My father waved back from the top deck of a tram which was taking him to the railway station. He was wearing a brown cloth cap, tweed jacket, and knee breeches. Shiny brown leather leggings with straps encased his shanks, fitting over ankle shoes. On the seat beside him he steadied a small leather portmanteau. As the tram clanged around the corner, the lonely figure on the back platform waved again and was borne out of sight.

Chapter Two

I was born in Burton-on-Trent, England — a brewing borough in the Midlands — on June 8, 1900, the eldest son of Philip Richard and Frances Marion Minifie, née Eglington. A few days before, the South African town of Mafeking, long besieged by Boer commandos under Cronje, had been relieved. The patriotic revelry this occasioned was so extreme as to lodge the word "mafficking" firmly in the language. My mother yielded to none in patriotic enthusiasm, but she resisted the urge to call me Mafeking and compromised on the general commanding the relief column, Sir Hector MacDonald. She nodded to my father's family by adding the name of his favourite elder brother, James, who had emigrated to Australia some years before.

My birth certificate described my father, with the inadequacy inherent in official documents, as a corn factor, which meant that he dealt in hay and feed. It did not disclose that he had been a prize scholar in Latin at Bridgenorth Grammar School, Shropshire, or that his upbringing on the farm in the tradition of a long line of yeoman ancestors had fostered in him an independent spirit which brooked no man as his master.

Once his apprenticeship to a Brownhills miller had been fulfilled, my father looked around for a likely opening to set up a business for himself. He lacked capital for purchase of a flour-mill, which would have been his preference, but he thought that capital might be built up gradually in a hay and feed business in a nearby centre such as Burton-on-Trent, where flourishing breweries transported their wares on drays drawn by massive Clydesdale horses with prodigious appetites. There was plenty of hay grown in the area, and my father knew good hayricks when he saw them. So he proposed to buy ricks in the surrounding countryside, bale the contents, and retail it to the brewers' big horses, while he looked around for a small flour and grist mill.

Bins of birdseed, maize, and sunflower seeds, and sacks of oats and linseed, filled his shop. The front window displayed a heated chicken foster-mother which had to be watched unflaggingly, lest the brood inconsiderately die under the very eyes of potential customers. A loft behind the shop was filled with bales of hay. Occasional knot-holes thrust into the darkness rods of sunlight along which motes gyrated and danced; one shaft provided a rudimental sundial, the hours of which I marked on the floor with stones. It was my intro-duction to astronomy.

This became an enduring passion; but for unfortunate chance it might have become a profession. My interests were fostered by my mother, who longed to move herself and her family from the rather dingy little hay and feed shop into more socially acceptable sur-roundings. She had met my father at a horse show near Brownhills. She was keen on horses and spent some of the happiest months of her youth in Dorset, where one of her brothers was a veterinarian in Cerne Abbas.

An equine crisis at the Minifie farmhouse at Coton in Shropshire provided the opportunity for my mother to accompany her brother when demand for his professional services brought him up from Dorset.

Everything at Coton delighted her; it was an old-fashioned farm-house, with red-tiled floors, an open fireplace with a settle beside it, and a roasting-spit in the kitchen where black oak beams criss-crossed the ceiling. All the bedrooms smelled of lavender plucked from the garden and hung in posset-bags. My father's mother wore her hair in ringlets and on her bosom a locket with a curl of her husband's hair; he had been found dead of a heart attack in a field a few weeks before my father's birth.

My mother rode to hounds locally, while my father followed the chase on foot, as many local farmers did who disliked crashing horses through their own or their neighbours' fences. Father was a good shot and provided plenty of game as the encroaching scythes drove rabbits and partridges out of the wheat. Only friction between my father and his eldest brother, William, marred these gracious bucolic surroundings.

In these pleasant circumstances, and under my grandmother's approving eye, the friendship between my father and my mother quickly matured, and my father was soon in Bridgenorth shopping for an engagement ring.

They were married in Hammerwich Church, near her home, in 1898 soon after my mother's return from Coton. After that she divided her interests between the physically unattractive Black Country, where her family had established themselves in leather and harness bright-ware, bits and so forth, and the bustling borough of Burton-on-Trent, twelve miles away, where my father was setting up his hay and feed business. There I was born, my brother Dick following three years later.

My mother agitated for better housing, and ultimately induced my father to move our living quarters away from the shop into a pleasant semi-detached villa with an attractive garden, about half a mile away. My mother's small industrialist kindred in the Black Country did not hide their view that she had done poorly for herself socially by marrying a small-town tradesman in a not very socially eminent or successful business. They too were in business, to be sure, but highly profitably. They maintained horses; my father fed them. They made harness; my father bought it, which put him in a very different category.

Economic change ignored these social distinctions. The horse was on its way out, taking with it harness and bright-ware equally with hay and feed. My uncles tried to postpone the inevitable by exporting to Mexico, where the passion for cut-rate glitter consumed quantities of a tarnish-proof near-silver my uncles had developed, but the First World War, that confrontation with Germany they had long desired, destroyed their hopes. The government rationed their metal but not their sons. They had nothing to export but their children and they sent them to Flanders. The Americans devoured their markets. Field-Marshal Haig devoured their sons. Small industrialists and small tradesmen found equality in ruin. But my father by that time had bowed to the inevitable and gone to "the colonies".

Tears coursed down my mother's face as my father disappeared from sight on that spring morning in 1909 and we turned back into the new garden where neat lawns ran up to a rockery glowing with London Pride, backed by tall lilacs and a trellis supporting rose bushes. Behind the trellis was a back garden with a line of plum trees on one side and rows of kidney beans, peas, and potatoes down the centre. A tall laburnum and ground cushions of gaillardia added colour. Our end of the semi-detached house was covered to the roof with ivy. In this tranquil setting my parents delighted to pass the long summer evenings, reclining in deck chairs. My mother read the *Daily Express* while my father worked through last Sunday's *News of the World*. It had been forbidden to me as soon as the authorities realized that I read too well for my own good.

Denied this diversion, my brother and I clambered up the sycamore trees in the front garden, chasing the gossamer-winged green insects whose tranquillity, along with our parents', we had destroyed. On Sunday the pattern altered. Lounging on the lawn, considered too close to enjoyment to be practised on the Lord's Day, was transferred indoors. However, it was considered unobjectionable in the eyes of the Lord for me to take an over with my cricket-bat to my brother's bowling on the back lawn. I was never able to determine whether this dispensation was a recognition of the inherent nature of cricket as a duty rather than a pastime, or a tribute to W. G. Grace, a paragon of cricket in our day and a hero of my father's, whose favourite reading was Grace on cricket. On Sunday my father divided his attention indoors between Mr. Grace's observations and the *News of the World*, while my mother played the piano in the drawing-room. This was a pleasant, light room, with a gay carpet, bright chintz-covered chairs, pots of viviparous ferns hanging from a bamboo tripod, and a healthy aspidistra.

The piano was considered an amusement in terms of the Lord's Day, but this could be mitigated by restricting playing to "sacred music", to wit, some of the gloomier hymns and anthems approved by the Church of England, but fortunately including Mendelssohn's

"Songs Without Words". I objected to these on the grounds that there could be no such thing as songs without words; tunes without words, if you like, but songs, no. My mother met this essay into linguistic purism by pointing out that the German title was *Lieder ohne Wörte* and that *Lieder* might mean tunes or songs. This reconciled me to Mendelssohn and to Sunday in the drawing-room. But it confirmed the impression I shared with the British public, that the imprecision of the language reflected the tricky character of the Germans, who obviously were not to be trusted.

In her youth my mother had been sent off to a "finishing school" in Germany at Stuttgart. In those days it was the fashion to send young ladies to finishing schools in Paris, where they were supposed to learn French and pick up the current graces; but as the century wore on, solid middle-class English parents began to wonder whether a smattering of French and deportment was worth the exposure to the exquisite temptations with which Paris was believed to abound.

It was credibly reported that these were doing the Prince of Wales no good, and that Queen Victoria, to whom Midland manufacturers looked for guidance in everything from finishing schools to handling chicken bones, was not amused. These factors were strengthened by the consideration that Germany was less expensive — a term they preferred to "cheaper", which had a connotation of second-rate. The royal connection with Saxe-Coburg furthered German claims to fashion. These considerations, coupled with an extensive and profitable business carried on through Hamburg, overcame the family's deep-seated dislike and distrust of "Made in Germany", and my mother was duly packed off to a young ladies' Akademie on the Hasengebirge, just outside Stuttgart, for three years. There she was taught to write and play the piano, German fashion. She was taken to the opera, where Wagner was in high favour, and observed *opera buffo* in the round when Kaiser Wilhelm II, who was also in high favour, made a triumphant entry into the capital of Württemberg-Baden on a spirited charger, favouring his withered left arm but looking dramatic and operatic in splendid uniform, medals and orders and ferocious upturned moustaches. My mother and her young lady companions allowed themselves not to be impressed — except the German *fräuleins*, who shrieked with delight. My mother returned to England with a healthy disdain for all things German, except their composers. This attitude rather disturbed her brothers, whose export business through Hamburg was so thriving that they had sent one of their sons there as manager of a branch office.

My mother's agitation as we turned back into the garden may have been aggravated by a presentiment that my father's departure marked the end of a happy era in more ways than one. Her own life, like the world, would never be the same again. It meant an abrupt termination of the struggle for social acceptance which her family's attitude towards "trade" as distinct from the export business had imposed on her.

One episode in this struggle had been to persuade my father to rent a pew in our parish church, St. Modwen's. My father disliked the idea, and reacted negatively to injudicious pressure from the Vicar. He compromised at length on sharing a pew with the Fergusons, who were in beer, not trade. All the best people in Burton were in beer, or malt. Mr. Bass, indeed, used his brew and a substantial contribution to the Unionist Party to move into what passed locally for nobility as Baron Burton, and Mr. Gretton, of Bass, Ratcliffe, and Gretton, obtained the Queen's commission as Colonel of Yeomanry, a low-calorie substitute for the Horse Guards, which used to execute weekly in Manor Croft dashing charges in the style of the Light Brigade. As the Yeomanry were prime customers of my father for hay, feed, and bedding and Manor Croft was a fief of St. Modwen's, my father's opposition was eroded. It disappeared when he reflected that St. Modwen, whose symbol was a swan, appeared to be an Anglican variant of the classical Leda, with whose character and career my father had become acquainted at Bridgenorth Grammar School. Without mentioning this to Vicar, my father made no further protest, but marched to church on Sunday morning in frock coat and topper. My brother and I went to an abbreviated session called the Children's Service, and sat quietly in the Minifie-Ferguson pew, understanding little and caring less, but itching to have done with it.

Another rung in the social ladder was my enrolment in Miss Gorton's Kindergarten. This was conducted privately by a plump, kindly maiden lady in a small, gloomy room rented from St. Modwen's, on Friar's Walk, which skirted the graveyard from the church to the Y.M.C.A. Our schoolroom could not be said to look out on the graveyard, since a high brick wall cut off all view and most light. We chanted the arithmetic tables every morning, went through a spelling routine, discussed a variety of natural phenomena such as volcanoes, whales, and comets in the afternoon, and sewed perforated cards with coloured thread. We were drilled in the counties of England and Wales, their rivers and county seats, and the countries of Europe with their capitals and the rivers on which they were situated — France, Paris, on the Seine; Germany, Berlin, on the Spree; Russia, St. Petersburg, on the Neva, etc. We were encouraged to copy world maps on Mercator's Projection, with British possessions coloured red. History was satisfied by learning the dates of the Kings of England from the Norman Conquest. I did not realize how thorough Miss Gorton's indoctrination had been until I met others my age who were surprisingly deficient in these fundamentals. I can still align world events by reference to the accession of King Edward III, Henry VIII, or George III, and my picture of continental Europe has survived the vagaries of half a century of politics and modernized spelling. Unfortunately Miss Gorton's mathematical curriculum was less impressive. It was mostly business arithmetic — pounds, shillings, and pence, plus troy and avoirdupois weights and measures. Decimals were adequate, but the study of fractions was limited by their tendency to become vulgar, improper, or both. It was years before I could handle them easily, and this blunted both my progress in astronomy and a kindred fondness for physics.

An immediate result of my father's departure was my removal from Miss Gorton's. The expense had been high, but socially unrewarding, partly owing to my tendency to establish friendships with children I liked, sons of butchers and carpenters, rather than with the scions of wealthier parents. Strict economy now demanded my transfer.

I was inducted into a secondary Council School, as likely to be less expensive, though less desirable socially, than Burton Grammar School, which was just around the corner. I was aware of the inferior social standing of my new school, but this bothered me less than my poor grasp of fractions. All my class-mates handled them with an assurance which left me gaping, while the masters spoke a mathematical language which might as well have been Chinese. My resentment at this was fed by a growing conviction that they lacked historical perspective as well as intuitive pedagogical minds.

One of them, who flaunted a red tie and radical views, said openly that the British Empire, on which at that time the sun never set, was no more likely to enjoy this immunity forever than its ephemeral predecessors of Rome, Greece, and Persia. This same master, however, taught me the rudiments of botany, which were immensely valuable and an enduring delight later. He was the first of a long series of devoted teachers whom good fortune sent my way.

However, I think my report on school radicalism convinced my mother that the sooner I was removed from this corrosive influence the better. She gave this more weight than social considerations, because, for all her normal feminine desire for recognition, my mother was a nonconformist socially. If Trade was scorned by Beer, she would publicly embrace Trade. She rented a long-abandoned garden next to the Manor Croft, where she kept a score of hens and a goat. This creature terrified me. I never entered her compound but she laid aside all feminine gentleness, lowered her head, and prepared to butt. I do not know her economic justification, unless it was to deter thieves from the hen-run. She certainly deterred me.

My mother collected the eggs herself and sold them, fresh from the nest, to select customers for one shilling a dozen. It was my task to deliver them. I trudged twice weekly along Lichfield Street to the Whitehalls, the Blackhalls, and the Bubbs with a straw basket and instructions to look where I was going and not smack the eggs against a lamp-post. For this duty I received 3d a week. I laid it out for sweets only after agonizing indecision, torn between the extravagance of French nougat at 1½d an ounce and the lush but tasteless general assortment at four ounces a penny. Occasionally I dodged decision by opting for a penny dreadful, which surprisingly included a penny-a-line version of the Persian Wars and the battles of Thermopylae, Marathon, and Salamis. My pronunciation of Xerxes would have surprised Herodotus, but these penny dreadfuls fired my interest in Greece. They may not have been the orthodox approach to the classics, but they stimulated my curiosity; I longed to know more and to find out for myself. Greek fascinated me as Latin never did, partly perhaps because of the erratic aspect of the Greek alphabet, but chiefly because of the impact of the penny dreadfuls, and, when I got around to them, the superiority, as a narrator, of Xenophon over Caesar and Thucydides over Tacitus.

Chapter Three

About the time my interest in Greece began, my maternal grand-mother suffered a stroke. Uncle Ted, who had been managing her affairs, came to the rescue. He engaged a nurse and proposed that my mother run the household in return for a modest stipend plus board and lodging for herself and her two sons. My mother agreed and we all moved to my grandmother's house at Muckley Corner, near Lichfield. This seemed a reasonable arrangement, although a sick bay was not the ideal atmosphere in which to raise boys.

My grandmother's position in the community was a substantial one, despite her ailment. Across the way was the mission church she had founded and still supported, after a fashion. It was a modest chapel, but it enjoyed the services of curates from Lichfield Cathe-dral Close, who employed themselves afterwards in trying to seduce the amateur organist who manipulated the harmonium.

Following the afternoon services, I used to slip out of the vestry to a bush outside the choir window which afforded an unobstructed view of what went on in the chancel. I associated this exercise with our headmaster's bashful identification of the David-and-Bathsheba episode as seduction — a concept which we Third Formers amplified by recounting among ourselves what was alleged to go on along the canal banks between soldiers from Whittington Barracks and local girls. This, together with selected passages from Genesis, was the extent of my sex education until I appeared on my father's prairie farm, when the facts of life were profusely illustrated by everything that moved.

My contribution to the redemption of the local sinners, most of them valued patrons of the Red Lion Inn at the corner, was to sing in the choir. Both my choral career and my initial sex education terminated when I destroyed the solemnity of the Harvest Festival by stumbling over the fruit and vegetables piled around the pulpit, sending a cascade of vegetable marrows, apples, and tomatoes (including Grandma's prized yellows) tumbling down the aisle, to the intense delight of the villagers. Most of them worked in the collieries at Cannock Chase, and tended their gardens with what leisure and enthusiasm they could muster after their long bicycle-ride from the pits and a look-in at the Red Lion. They resented the advantages Grandma enjoyed.

One of these was her gardener-coachman, appropriately named Palfrey, who lived in a small cottage near by, and in the morning tended the garden, the greenhouses, and the stable. In the afternoon he dressed up in a threadbare black tail-coat and topper; looking like an incarnation of Sam Weller, he mounted the box of the frayed black Victoria and took Grandma for her outing, driving cautiously through country lanes whose tranquillity was beginning to be disturbed already by the horseless carriage. The horse shied conscientiously when one of these monsters thundered by in a frenzy of dust, while Grandma wondered what the world was coming to.

"No good, mum," Palfrey returned, "if you asks me."

"Ah, it's all the fault of that horrid Mr. Gladstone and his income tax," Grandma vouchsafed. She identified Gladstone as the Seven-headed Beast of Revelations, and could cite chapter and verse for her views at a moment's notice. Palfrey, who had had his retainer nibbled down on the excuse of economies necessitated by that nefarious tax, seconded Grandma's views. Using that curious case inversion common in the Midlands at that time, "Ah," he said, "us don't find nowt in it for we." With that he whipped up the horse and turned in at Grandma's eldest son's house. Uncle Ted thought even less of Mr. Gladstone than did either Grandma or Palfrey. He was all for tariff reform and Joey Chamberlain. To mark his support he had instructed *his* gardener to compete with Palfrey for the first flower from a basket of epiphyte orchids which his eldest son had sent back from Mexico, where he had been dispatched to beat the Americans to the market for bits, spurs, buckles, and similar equine bright-ware.

Uncle Ted was as Victorian as Fair View, his suburban villa. At his father's death he had accepted his duties as head of the family, carrying them out over the years with exemplary fidelity. When a younger brother and sister-in-law died leaving a baby daughter, Uncle Ted at once adopted the orphan, although by that time he had four children of his own. He brought up Marjorie as his own daughter. He also took over the management of his father's business, becoming one of the first commuters in the county. He induced the London & Northwestern Railway to build a tiny station at Hammerwich, half a mile from his house, where a morning train could pick up passengers for Walsall, a manufacturing town four miles or so away where his business offices were located, while an evening train returned them home in time for dinner.

Every morning, summer or winter, he rose at 6.30, took a turn around his garden to examine his roses and sweet peas with loving solicitude, and after a hasty breakfast caught the train for Walsall. His dark suit was of rich but conservative cloth and cut, his waistcoat was bordered with white piping, and his butterfly-wing collar was set off by a conservative four-in-hand tie. He was a vestryman of Hammerwich Parish Church and contributed conservatively to the slender stipend of the Rev. Teddy Froissard, the French Protestant curate. His two sons sang in the choir.

He married youthfully a Miss Ashmall from a local family which claimed relationship with the more conspicuous Ashmole clan, celebrated for their Museum of Antiquities. The Ashmalls were prosperous farmers. Between them Uncle Ted and Aunty Lucy gave impetus to the Church, the choir, the Institute, the Cottage Hospital, the Flower Show, the Sewing Circle, the lending library (by kind permission of W. H. Smith & Sons), and the curate (by kind permission of the Bishop of Lichfield). Aunty Lucy was warm-hearted and enjoyed her position as leader of the village's activities, but she was not noted for tact. During a tea-party she was giving for a young lady about to marry a very junior bank clerk, Aunty Lucy suggested that she "go and sit by Teddy Froissard's wife and learn how to keep house on nothing a year"! Her house was always full of flowers, which Uncle Ted grumbled about, saying that she plundered his roses and sweet peas by injudicious cutting and clipping, thereby impairing his chances of carrying off any trophies at the Flower Show, even though it was held under a marquee on his own lawn.

But naturally my own life centred around school. I was entered at Lichfield Grammar School, to which I had been fortunate enough to win a scholarship on a written examination, thus beginning a long career of instruction at the expense of others whose ability to acquire wordly goods had exceeded my parents' and my own.

Every morning, rain or shine, I cycled three miles to school, and after a weary day pedalled painfully back to Muckley Corner. The winter's chill induced burning chilblains on my toes, which made school a misery. I strove to bear it "like a man" but finally broke down, and was ignominiously carried out, sobbing, over the headmaster's shoulder.

He advised my mother that the affliction was probably caused by frostbite, and suggested warmer footwear.

Once the agony of winter chilblains was over and I had swallowed my spring spoonful of brimstone and treacle to thin my blood, I was healthy and reasonably cheerful. I tramped the neighbouring commons in search of birds' nests; I dangled a float in the canal, and on one happy occasion connected with a school of perch, from which I drew six small fish before the survivors took fright. This triumph supported me through hundreds of unproductive forays; half a century would have to pass before I hooked another fish. This was above all the era of the model aeroplane. Our interest at school had been stimulated by the arrival of the French aviator de Lesseps, son of the builder of the Suez Canal. We were marched to a field just outside the city to see this wonder, which the headmaster rightly judged to be a phenomenon of historical importance. It turned out to be a fragile little monoplane, one of Blériot's earliest, built of bamboo and canvas held together with piano wire; but it had already won a prize of £10,000 for flying across the Channel from France to England. We were all duly impressed and lost our caps when the engine started up. After a short run over the bumpy field the fragile dragonfly took to the air, circled, and headed north.

The occasion added realism to my collection of cigarette cards, which had moved from regimental colours of the British Army to aeronautical types. Sets of these cards were in great demand. They presented a documented history of aerial navigation, from the Mont-golfier fire-balloon, through Lilienthal's wings, to the latest triumph of the French or the Wright Brothers. A lively trade in doubles went on in the playground. I was under a handicap, inasmuch as none of my family smoked, but I had a compensating advantage in a Tetnall pear-tree in the meadow beside Grandma's house. I used to take bulging pocketfuls to school for barter against anything desirable, such as marbles (in the season Big Ring and Little Ring were both popular) or cigar-boxes. These were essential construction material for model planes. With a penknife, a propeller could be fashioned from any handy scrap of wood. Elastic bands were switched from use as catapults for paper-wads to power-plants for model aero-planes, a change which brought profound relief to the teaching staff and taught us something of the essentials of torque and bearings along with elementary aerodynamics. Every bicycle had to carry a home-made propeller wired to the handle-bars.

I had another asset which eased my social status at school; our house was surrounded by horse-chestnut trees, which produced an abundance of conkers. These were old nuts threaded on a string, knots on which tallied the number of victories rung up when an opposing nut was smashed by a well-aimed swing. The victor took as his prize the number of victories claimed by the conquered. Baking or otherwise hardening the nuts was ruled out, and it was a matter of individual honour to keep reasonably clean accounts of victories. With the inexhaustible supply at my command I could afford to be honest, so I was considered an ornament to the playground and my quaint anti-frostbite leggings were ignored. This caused my morale and my work to look up, although not to the point where I might be considered a "grind". This would have been bad form. Another rule I observed carefully was never to take a swallow's egg; they were considered very unlucky. On the only occasion I took one from the mud nest in our boat-house by the Grand Union Canal, I spent so much time avoiding alarming the swallow that there was no time left to do my homework, which was to memorize that horrible jingle of Browning's: "How we brought the good news from Ghent to Aix". Consequently, when called on to recite it next morning, I bogged down and was ordered kept in the following Saturday afternoon to learn the piece. I regarded this as a perfect and unquestionable demonstration of the validity of the legend of ill-luck attaching to removal of swallows' eggs. A similar attribute shielded robins' nests from plunder. I was careful not to put this to the test, but accepted the taboo without further question on the basis of my unhappy experience with swallows' eggs.

These precautions taken, life at Lichfield Grammar School was amusing, and occasionally instructive.

My younger brother was less fortunate. Dick had been put to board and study at an establishment run by three maiden ladies, the Misses Barry, who were old school-friends of Mother's. I do not think that either his mind or his body was nourished as well as a growing boy's should be; certainly he had none of the elements of Latin, French, and science drilled into him as painstakingly as I had at the Grammar School. I did not see much of him either, since he was immured at school during term, so we grew up rather remote from each other.

My mother's duties permitted her to keep up modest social contacts in the neighbourhood, with her brothers and sisters and their families, and with fringe associates like the Misses Negus, whom I remember as prim antiquities sheathed in black silk, with jet jewellery and lockets containing a curl of faded hair. They regretted the decadence of the times, and particularly the ill-repute into which the universities were falling, possibly an echo in the puritanical provinces of the scandals occasioned by the writings and deportment of Swinburne and his coterie. It was strong enough to cause Uncle Ted to deny his sons' desire to go up to Oxford; Walsall and the business would be quite good enough for them. This was odd because his two daughters had taken matters into their own hands and decided that they would climb up into the university world. In those days this called for great daring and a skin thick enough to shake off the slings and arrows of outraged society. They dared and did as they thought fit, and in time both the world and the universities accepted women's presence.

Uncle Ted's four children and his adopted daughter were my greatly revered senior cousins, from whom I inherited equipment, books, advice, and much affectionate solicitude. In turn, I think I communicated a halo of glamour resulting from my imminent departure for the wild, romantic West, where infinite spectacular adventures undoubtedly awaited Pieface, as they teasingly nicknamed me. Pieface breaking broncos, Pieface fighting Indians, Pieface returning at length loaded with wealth and honours; all these visions my cousins swathed me in while they tried to make me choke with giggles over arcane jokes at the breakfast table. I returned their affection with intense fervour, following their careers with admiration and, ultimately, heartbreak, and from an increasing distance.

Chapter Four

During the time we lived at Muckley Corner, the *ancien régime* glowed in bright, autumnal colours. My mother, having her bicycle and the use of Grandma's horse and trap, was mobile, and could enjoy the gentle distractions of tea with the Neguses, "at homes", church bazaars, Institute gatherings, and the Flower Show. As a result of three years spent at the finishing school in Stuttgart in the less sophisticated atmosphere of German provincialism, she found English provincial landed and commercial gentry a receptive and congenial milieu.

Its attractions were enhanced as my father's letters, despite their infrequency, gave a glimpse of a harsher world with few of the values which my mother had learned to cherish. Her enthusiasm for emigration fell so low at one point as to alarm me, and I urged the claims of my father and the pioneer spirit with insistence. In this, although I did not know it at the time, I was supported by Uncle Ted. When my mother sought counsel of him, he reminded her that her place was at her husband's side. Some time early in 1912 she made the fateful decision to leave, strongly approved by Uncle Ted.

My father's description of the rigours of prairie climate dictated spring as the preferable season for reunion with his family; his assurance that the shack he had built was as nearly complete as it was ever likely to be combined with Uncle Ted's reminder of my mother's duty to urge departure as soon as blankets, clothing, and other paraphernalia could be assembled and crated.

My father's letters gave a minimum of instruction about household trimmings; he appeared to regard as effete and superfluous many accessories which he could not have done without in England, such as mahogany furniture, a tantalus, a hard but durable horsehair sofa, or W. G. Grace on cricket. Hence his letters were uninformative on household matters; my mother had no idea what to take with us or leave behind.

Her dilemma was not solved by Uncle Ted's dictum, that the main thing was to get there, and buy what was needed on the spot.

To take some of the sting from this austere advice, Uncle Ted outfitted my brother and me in splendid new cloth overcoats for the journey, dark grey, with black velvet collars, knitted woollen gloves, and new caps. My brother's cap was dark blue with his school badge in metal; mine was the standard Lichfield Grammar School pattern: navy blue with a ring of yellow ribbon. My straw sailor with H.M.S. *Majestic* hatband was discarded as unsuitable for an emigrant.

With this outfit there was no further excuse for delay. Passage was secured on the Canadian Pacific twin-screw steamship *Lake Manitoba* scheduled to sail April 15, 1912, from Liverpool for Montreal. However, on April 14 the White Star liner *Titanic* sank with great loss of life after colliding with an iceberg. The Board of Trade immediately suspended further Atlantic sailings until substantial additions had been made to the number of lifeboats and rafts provided for passengers and crew. This held up *Lake Manitoba*'s departure for ten days. We waited fretfully at home, saying an infinity of last good-byes, which made more acute my mother's distress at leaving known associations and the social habits and connections of a lifetime. We said good-bye to Uncle Ted, who added his best walking-stick to our blanket-roll. We took a last long look at Hammerwich Church, glowing red in the afternoon sunshine. We said good-bye to Uncle Tom, who pressed half a sovereign into my hand and a small archery bow and some arrows into the blanket-roll. We said good-bye to Uncle Arthur, who presented a snaffle-bit calculated to tame the wildest horse and a watch with a gun-metal case. We said good-bye to Lichfield Grammar School, where I traded two heavily endowed conkers to "Pony" Moore for a perpetual calendar. We said good-bye to the Misses Barry, who wept over losing my mother. And in the end Palfrey drove us down to Hammerwich Station and loaded us and the bric-a-brac into a train for Lichfield Trent Valley, where we should catch the boat-train for Liverpool.

There could be no drawing back now. I had my perpetual calendar, a penknife with six blades and a pearl haft, and my new watch in my waistcoat pocket; my bird's egg collection had been disposed of for a packet of air-gun pellets; the bow and arrows, the air-rifle, the walking-stick, my cricket-bat, and a carriage-rug had all been strapped into the blanket-roll. We were stowed in comfortable third-class seats in a long corridor train with the blanket-roll in the rack overhead. The tidy English fields, contained by hedges and supervised by church steeples, hurried by. The tidy English telephone poles slipped past so fast that they looked like a picket fence. I soon tired of gazing at pictures of Conway Castle, Crewe Junction, and other glamour spots on the L. & N.W.R. system, and devoted myself to calculating our speed by timing the telephone poles with my new watch. Forty to the minute gave an estimated speed of sixty miles per hour. I was vastly excited when the express picked up speed after Crewe and, by my calculations, touched ninety. The bogies clattering over rail-joints and points hammered out a new refrain: "Going to Canada!" "Going to Canada!" "Going to, going to, going to Canada!"

My mother sat silent and melancholy. She was saying good-bye to everything she knew and loved, to face unknowns which my father's recent letters had described as harsh and uncertain. She lacked the resource of trying to calculate our speed which was my refuge; she saw only the hedges shot with green, the fields bright with cowslips, and the woods, obvious coverts to be drawn by an alert hunt-master. We were all thankful when the train drew up at the embarkation pier and we scrambled out to look for the *Lake Manitoba*. We soon discovered her sitting, squat and black, out in the river. There would be no easy boarding; we should be taken out by tender.

We found the tender just as it was about to leave, and we were soon huddled against the vast black hull of the liner. We watched apprehensively as luggage, recognizably our own, as well as the blanket-roll, dangled overhead in a rope net, to be swung inboard and dumped on the liner's deck. On board we gasped incredulously when we found everything stowed in our cabin, to which we had been led by a polite young officer, who professed flattering interest in my perpetual calendar, which, he said, every ships's navigator should have. I chose not to believe this rather than hand over my most prized possession, but was assured that if I met him on the top deck at noon tomorrow, he would show me how to "shoot the sun". This reception wiped out the unfavourable impression made by the tender, and we settled down easily to stow ourselves on the two bunks and the sofa under the porthole.

The *Lake Manitoba* was listed as a one-class vessel, which meant you paid first-class fare for second-class accommodations. But even these were so superior to "steerage" that visits between the two communities were discouraged. Through the influence of the Navigating Officer, however, we not only glanced at the steerage quarters, which were crowded and dark and smelled of paint, oil, and stew, but we even descended to inspect the engine-room and the propeller-shaft. The mysteries of radio-communication were explained to me by "Sparks", and by the time we moved into an ice pack after four uncomfortable days of rolling and pitching, I felt competent to take care of either the ship or my family in any emergency. We were awakened with a start one night by a sudden reversal of engines, which the Navigating Officer confided had been occasioned by the appearance, uncomfortably close, of an iceberg. The intelligence was supported by a gleaming mountain of ice on our starboard beam (I was getting on to nautical terms) and a mottled scum of broken ice surrounding us. We nosed through it cautiously, reassured by the Navigating Officer's estimate that we should sight Newfoundland in less than two days. While appreciating the information, I felt, however, that the Navigating Officer was waiting far too assiduously on my mother, so I insinuated myself into every tête-à-tête until I was driven off with a rap on the head and a request to make myself scarce. I did, but I kept a sharp eye on the officer for the rest of the voyage.

The *Lake Manitoba* was under no compulsion to make speed, so the chances of collision with an iceberg were reduced. She nudged cautiously through the icefield, giving the bergs a wide berth, and in due course made the St. Lawrence, halted briefly at Quebec, then plodded up to Montreal, where I felt grass and earth under my feet for the first time in what seemed an eternity. Before we were allowed to land we were subjected to inspection and classification. Medical inspection consisted of looking under my eyelids. The rest of the ceremony, conducted in the main lounge, was a long interview with Mother answering as well as she could a variety of awkward questions about why we were coming to Canada and what we were going to do there. A polite official noted the answers and sent them on to Ottawa, to get lost.

The journey west from Montreal was a long tale of discomfort and novelty. We left Friday evening. My mother, my brother, and I shared an upper berth. A family of four shared the lower half. There was a kitchen, tiny and crowded, at one end of the colonist car where my mother did some rudimentary cooking. We were unused to the violent jumps and jerks with which Canadian trains got under way — so different from the almost imperceptible slide of English trains. The track compared poorly with English "permanent way", and there were constant alarms and excursions when jugs and mugs upset. We were possessed by an agony of longing to be done with this monstrous train. All things were different, starting with the yard or so of tickets. To the young to be different is to be wrong.

The telegraph poles along the right of way, for instance, were saplings, bent and crooked, so different from the stalwart Scandinavian poles alongside English tracks and roads. The very brooks which foamed with the spring melt were the colour of tea — iron ore stains, we guessed correctly. The gaunt tamarack poles had a special beauty which was difficult for a stranger, particularly a young stranger, to appreciate. Youth is intolerant. My mother took her cue from our strictures. Even the prairies, once we reached them after the interminable lakes and rocks and tamarack, were not the green, flowery meadows we were used to, but dun-coloured plains stretching to the horizon, dotted with ponds where wild ducks disported themselves.

Odd people lived in this region. We were confused by changes of hour, so I jumped down at Broadview, Saskatchewan, to ask the time. I selected a tall man in blue overalls. He could not understand me. I found this disturbing, but he must have found me just as odd. I was wearing what was then called an Eton suit: striped trousers, black jacket and waistcoat, across which dangled my precious watch-chain of linked skeletons, with a metal skull. A white starched wide collar and the school cap — blue with a thin yellow ring — completed the picture of an English schoolboy, Edwardian vintage. I suppose this vision contributed to the strangeness of my North-Midland accent to make my question unintelligible. However, at length he dragged at a piece of tarred string and hauled out a splendid gold watch, which he returned to his pocket after briefly announcing the Mountain Standard Time. I reported the incident in detail. It confirmed our impression that adjustments would be needed if we were to fit into the new environment. At the time, however, we thought the environment should adapt to us.

We tumbled off the train at Morse, Saskatchewan, terrified lest the monster leap forward and carry us on to Herbert, the next station.

For one anguished moment I feared there might have been some mistake after all. I remembered my father as the neat figure in tweed jacket and leather leggings whom I had last seen on the upper deck of the tram in Burton. There was nobody answering that description on the wooden platform at Morse that morning. The panic feeling of having detrained at the wrong place persisted until a figure in blue overalls, very like the man with the watch at Broadview but swathed in a sheepskin jacket with buckles instead of buttons, materialized and moved a few paces towards us. My mother rushed up and hugged him. My brother and I, benumbed by panic and the inhibitions of English schoolboys, met this romantic occasion with shy hand-shakes, but as my father turned to walk away, I fell into step, while my brother tagged along behind. Turning to me, my father asked if I was a Boy Scout. I replied briefly, "No, I took gym," and silence followed.

My reverie was broken by my father: "Well, boy," he said, "this is the great North-West!"

There was a note in my father's voice which moved me. Without being able to analyse my reaction, I was aware that, whatever this great North-West might be, he was proud of it, proud to be part of it. I responded to the ring of triumph; I too felt proud to be part of this great North-West, although it was not what I had expected. I had envisaged forests and mountains. I had the fixed idea that we were all going to Alberta to settle, and I wondered why this plan had been changed, and why the clear, bright hills of Alberta, as I had imagined them, had been given up in exchange for this dun, treeless plain.

It took me years to put the story together bit by bit, for my father was not given to anecdote, and information had to be dragged from him piecemeal.

Chapter Five

In the spring of 1909, on the immigrant train west-bound from Winnipeg, my father struck up a conversation with a man who told him that Alberta was too dry to farm without irrigation, and that all free land within thirty miles of the railroad had already been taken up by the C.P.R. "You bet your life they grabbed it fast," the man told my father. "So there's no homesteads left in the good land for you and me." However, he had heard that new areas of good land in Saskatchewan near this very region through which they were travelling at that moment were to be opened up for homesteads soon, and it would be well to be on the spot, before it was all gobbled up.

"It's not too dry here?" my father asked.

"You see them sloughs?" the man replied. The train was rolling through the eastern parklands, dotted with tree-fringed sloughs, each with its quota of water-fowl. My father's informant continued: "That means plenty of snow, and water in the ground. Where trees will grow, wheat will grow. Anyway, you can check on the rainfall at the Government Experimental Farm at Indian Head. They'll give you the figures and tell you all about it."

My father consulted the conductor, who came by just then. He suggested that, since Indian Head was the next divisional point, my father could get off there and obtain a refund on the remainder of the trip to Calgary. But he added the point that if my father was looking for farm work, it would be better to drop off at a smaller place, "like this here Sintaluta, coming up now," the conductor said. "It's good farming country; lots of fellows unload here, and there's always farmers coming in with loads of grain. If you want to get off, I'll open the gate. Sinta-luta!!"

Sintaluta! The name meant nothing, but the conductor's assurances and the visual appearance of good farming country meant much. Heavy wagons crept along the trail beside the track, with horses straining at the traces. Elevators flashed by; brakes began to squeal; the conductor opened the gate with a crash; having no time to weigh the pros and cons, my father gathered up his bags, said goodbye to his friendly informant, and swung to the platform as the train shuddered to a halt. "Good luck!" the conductor called after him as he handed him his two portmanteaus. The platform was bare. Bits of cottonwood fluff floated by. The conductor shouted "All aboard!", and my father was half tempted to comply, but that would have been humiliating, a loss of face. While he hesitated, the engine bell clanged, and the train jerked into motion. My father watched it pull out with what he later admitted was a sinking heart as the loneliness seized him. However, the sun was shining, a gentle breeze fluttered the leaves of poplar trees planted around the depot, and on a post near by, a bird with a yellow vest with a big black V on it trilled indomitably.

Pleasant as they were, the bird and its song added to the loneliness. It was not the familiar melody of thrush or blackbird with which a man from Shropshire could feel at home, but something more colourful: the meadow lark — beautiful . . . but different.

Fighting off a feeling of panic, my father recalled the livery barn he had seen from the train window. That, at least, would hold familiar sounds and scents in this totally unfamiliar land. He wanted something familiar, something he recognized by sight, sound, and smell. So he stowed his luggage in the ticket office and walked down the street. The owner of the livery barn handed him a pitchfork and told him to "load up the stone-boat".

The fork was unfamiliar — three tines instead of the two my father was accustomed to. The "stone-boat" turned out to be a sled, squat as a toad, hitched to an ox. But the rest was familiar, and my father put his back into loading the stone-boat with horse droppings and wet straw, enjoying the familiar, pungent smell of ammonia. He reflected that in England the task would have been given to an ostler, or to the stable-boy. However, since the owner of the livery barn did not consider himself above it, but pitched in with my father, the pair of them worked steadily through a week's accumulation of horse droppings, my father thankful enough that it wasn't cow-dung, too. Then he bedded the stalls down with clean straw, and filled the mangers with hay and green oat bundles. My father, who had pitched many a load of English timothy hay in his time, thought poorly of the Western hay, and said so.

"You're green," said the liveryman, "and you've got plenty to learn. First of all, get yourself some overalls and horsehide shoes, like mine. Don't soil those good Old Country togs with work like this." Overalls were better than tweed, he said, because denim cuts the wind, and you could wear two pairs if you needed them; also denim did not pick up burs and seeds the way tweed did. He went on, "This slough-hay may not look good to you, but it's the best we've got. It ain't really grass at all. It's a sort of rush, I guess. But the cattle like it better than prairie wool, because there are no hay-needles in it. Watch out for hay-needles! They'll give your cattle lump-jaw, raise lumps on your dogs — and on you, too, if you get them in your clothes." He picked out a bent from a pile of "prairie wool", pointing out the characteristic twisted awn, and the sharp tip of the grain with its slanting hairs which enabled the tip to work into the flesh of man or beast.

My father appreciated the kindly spirit which prompted this lesson on what to avoid on the prairies. He was ready to learn their ways, but he did not fancy a long-term post as stable-boy. This one morning had shown him that there was much to be learned; even the harness was different. Bits, cruppers, martingales had all developed from standard English types to meet new conditions. Worst of all, the horses did not understand plain English.

"It ain't you," said the liveryman, noticing my father's concern. "They don't understand me, neither. I bought them from Dutch Schwartz, and they don't understand nothing but German. But they'll soon learn. You just go talk to them and teach them Haw and Gee; they pick up real fast." A post as instructor in elementary equine English seemed too specialized to offer much future, so my father asked about the prospects for employment as a hired man with some farmer from whom he might learn good western practice before taking up a farm of his own.

Partridge would be the man, the liveryman said; he was in a fight with the C.P.R. and the elevator companies, so he needed help on the farm. The liveryman said he would drive my father out there in return for the work he had done in the stable that morning.

They drove out along a winding trail full of puddles from a recent rainstorm. On either side clumps of brushwood, aspen and willow, and chokecherries were bursting into leaf; the air was heavy with the vanilla-perfume of saskatoon-berry bushes in flower. "Wonderful in pies, they are," the liveryman said, "but this bush is a damn nuisance; you either have to burn it down or tear it up or plough around it."

"Pretty good for duck-shooting," my father replied.

"Yes," the liveryman agreed, "and in the fall those damn ducks creep along the sheaves, shelling out the ears; they don't eat it for the most part, they just shell it out where it lies and leave it there. They're a worse pest than the hunters, and that's saying plenty. A hunter shot one of my cows last fall, and then one of the silly beggars shot himself. So his friend piled him in the back of the wagon, and when those nosy Mounties came along to check his bag and asked him what he had in the wagon, the fellow said, 'Two ducks and one damn fool.' The Mountie looked over the wagon-box, and sure enough that was it. So he arrested the guy for exceeding his bag; but the judge threw it out."

With such anecdotes they beguiled the time until the liveryman drew up before a two-storey white house with green trim, flanked by a big red barn with white trim. It looked attractive, and my father was drawn to the prospect of working for E. A. Partridge, who had been described by the liveryman as a leader in the farmers' fight against what he called "the interests" for better treatment and prices for their crops. My father, however, was disappointed: Partridge was not too anxious to have a greenhorn on his hands, who would need constant supervising. He needed a clear run at his own work of persuading, organizing, and marshalling farmers, always individualists and unaccustomed to co-operating. So he made a minimum offer of twenty dollars a month, with room and board, plainly hoping that it would be rejected. My father took the hint and walked out, climbed back into the buggy, and asked the liveryman to try another place.

"Bird's," he said. "He's been looking for someone."

They drove to an almost identical cluster of house, barn, and granaries, and to my father's great relief Bird offered him a job and invited him to go out with him for a shoot. My father was a good shot and they soon came back with three brace of prairie chicken and an established friendship. Bird's offer was no better than Partridge's, but it was made without reservations and since it seemed to be the going rate, my father accepted it and settled his bags, prepared to stay until he had learned the ways of the west. Bird fitted my father out with overalls and horsehide gloves, sent to town for rawhide shoes against his first month's pay, and set out to teach him the rudiments of agriculture as understood in the West.

This was virgin soil, Bird explained, so rich it would never need fertilizer. The newly turned prairie sod was a three-inch layer of turf bound tightly by the roots of grasses, dwarf roses, buffalo willow, yellow bean, and similar low surface cover. It was too tough as turned over to grow wheat, so for the first two years the new breaking was sown to flax. This was a tougher plant, able to fight successfully for food and water from the sod, which it broke up in the process. The yield per acre of flax was smaller than wheat or oats, but the price was higher. However, the thin, wiry stalks returned little fibrous matter to the soil, on which, like all oil-producing plants, they made great demands; consequently two crops of flax were all that the soil should be subjected to.

The great secret was: plough deep, then break up the turf with flax and tilling. My father accepted this readily, and took pride in turning over a regular, five-inch unbroken sod. His English farming experience seemed to bear out the merit of this method, but he did not take into account the different condition which the method was designed to deal with. English land culture was designed to create a well-drained, warm seed-bed out of very wet soil which received heavy rainfall during the growing season. When that wet-culture was applied to farming on the dry, windy prairies, the results were disastrous. Bad principles were reinforced by working large fields unshielded by hedges to cut the wind, and by running the plough east and west across the narrow width of most half-section farms. This gave the prevailing westerly winds a full sweep at the dry topsoil, creating vast damage as the soil began to drift.

I often wondered why so many homesteaders had selected their quarter-sections on a north-south rather than an east-west axis. There were few exceptions to this north-south pattern, which in turn practically dictated east-west breaking and cultivation — a habit that endured for more than a quarter of a century. The answer which most farmers gave my inquiries was a shrug and: "It just seemed the natural way to do it. We didn't know anything about drifting soil in those days, and if we'd known about prevailing westerly winds, we'd still have cultivated east and west, to avoid a cross-wind, which tugs on the reins and is hard on your arms as well as the horses' mouths."

The stimulus to assembling quarter-sections on a north-south axis appears to have been supplied by the great Torrens survey of 1884. In prairie areas west of Manitoba, which would be incorporated in 1905 as the provinces of Saskatchewan and Alberta, this survey laid out the land in "sections" one mile square, each containing 640 acres. East and west of each section the survey laid out a "road allowance" one chain wide, which of course ran north and south. These north-south roads were linked every two miles, along the northern boundary of every second section, by an east-west road allowance, thus creating an oblong block running north and south, twice as long as wide. When filing on land, farmers generally followed this pattern, choosing for pre-emption the quarter-section adjoining the homestead for obvious reasons of convenience, and selecting where possible a quarter-section to the north or south, thus duplicating the pattern set by the Torrens survey and taking advantage of the bordering road allowance.

In Manitoba, the east-west road allowances were run every mile instead of every two miles, thereby creating a square pattern which is clearly visible from the air, and recognizable as a signature when the provincial boundary has been crossed. This system would have been advantageous in the territories to the west as encouraging smaller fields, but in Manitoba the rainfall was much heavier, and there were numerous natural aspen and willow copses sheltering open fields from the wind, so that the problems besetting the other two prairie provinces never became acute in Manitoba. In these circumstances the survivors of the "dirty thirties" in Saskatchewan and Alberta tasted the full irony of the decision by the bulk grain dealers to change the classification of premium wheat from "No. 1, hard" to "No. 1, Manitoba".

These factors were hidden in the future when my father had to make decisions which would be controlling not only for his own life, but for his descendants. Unfortunately much of the information available to him came from tainted sources, and led him into decisions based on faulty information which he might have avoided had he relied on his instincts. But he suppressed his instinctive English dislike of large, unsheltered fields, without hedgerows, and accepted local custom with the decent modesty expected of a newcomer. He also accepted the then ruling dogma of clean fields. This, too, turned out to be mistaken, and after thirty years and a dust-bowl had left their mark, "surface trash" began to be welcomed as a treasure, valuable for hindering soil drifting. New slogans were circulated: "Don't break up the clods! Don't burn the trash! Diversify and cultivate strips running north and south." However these things had to be learned by years of heart-break and ruined land.

At the time my father came to the West there had been a series of good crops, the sloughs were full of water, and the rushes had not yet been crowded out by worthless grasses such as foxtail or sweet-hay. The Bird family was prosperous. There were clouds, however; chief of these was the problem of selling the crop at the most favourable price. Prices were set by the Winnipeg Grain Exchange. Country elevators bought wheat from the farmer and stored it until it could be shipped east to the lakehead, either Fort William, Ontario, or Duluth, Minnesota, depending on where the better price could be obtained. The country elevators, however, rarely met the full Grain Exchange price, and often docked extravagantly for weed seeds in the load. They set their own standard of quality, and gave the farmer Number One or Number Two as they saw fit. If he did not like it, he could do little, for the banks were pressing for payment on their advances for the crop season, and the implement firms wanted their cash, too.

There was trouble, also, about boxcars, which were in short supply when a big harvest had to be moved. Freight rates were set by law, but the C.P.R. complained that they were too low to be profitable. With this excuse they adopted a carefree attitude towards the elevators' demands for boxcars, which were more profitably employed on hire to railroads in the United States.

Wheat moved slowly, and with every day's delay the price fell a few cents, until by the time the crop reached the consumer it had fallen below the profit level. The eastern papers complained that low freight rates were a subsidy to farmers which the country could ill afford. But they screamed to high heaven at any suggestion that they forgo the subsidy afforded to newspapers by low postal rates for printed matter. It depended on whose ox was being gored — or into which manger the alfalfa went.

These factors combined to build up resentment among farmers against the elevators and the Winnipeg Grain Exchange, as well as the railroads, the eastern newspapers, the banks, and the implement companies, all of which seemed to be linked in an unholy conspiracy to buy farm crops cheaply and sell goods and services dear.

Meditating these matters on his farm near Sintaluta, E. A. Partridge felt that this resentment could be used to break the chains with which eastern and foreign financial interests had shackled the farmer. But he was well aware of the independent spirit of farmers, and of the tight organization needed to secure any semblance of united action. No help could be expected from the press, which favoured *laissez-faire*, or from the pulpit, whose credo was summed up in the refrain:

> *Work and pray,*
> *Live on hay,*
> *You'll get pie*
> *In the sky,*
> *When you die.*

The conclusion was inescapable that the farmer would have to work out his own salvation; this meant long conversations and discussions with like-minded settlers. Since there were no telephones connecting farms in those early days, all discussions took place in person; this meant interminable journeyings to and fro, and an unending round of visits, at which the ceremonial ritual of a cup of coffee and a biscuit had to be observed as rigorously as an ecclesiastical liturgy. All this took time, but it had to be maintained, lest a touchy farmer and his touchier wife should feel that they had been slighted, and that their shack, their kitchen, and their cooking were not considered good enough for these fine folks ... who might already be getting — could it be? — too big for their britches. To avert this suspicion, Partridge often took my father along with him on these visits, and my father went conscientiously through the routine, sitting endlessly silent on uncomfortable kitchen chairs until the propitiatory cup of coffee had been downed, when the topic could be broached, grievances aired, and relief planned. Partridge urged that a strong farmers' selling agency be created, with officials at Winnipeg and the Lakehead capable of investigating losses of wheat in transit, either by theft or by leakage, for which the C.P.R. stubbornly refused responsibility. Partridge said (as he later reported to the Twelfth Annual Convention of the Saskatchewan Grain Growers Association, of which he was to become a director) that he had known a car of wheat reported at Winnipeg as loaded two inches above the grain line to be reported at Fort William as loaded six inches below the grain line. Under such conditions, he pointed out, without a check on the C.P.R.'s reports, there was small chance for the shipping farmer to prove claims for shortage.

In the farmers' shacks around Sintaluta there was talk of the alternative of easing the loading situation through establishment by the Dominion government of interior storage elevators. Partridge felt that drying plants should be installed in these elevators to handle crops which might get caught in early snowfalls. My father felt that this would be a useful move, but he and his fellow farmers had little faith in the Dominion government, whom they regarded as "a bunch of grafters". The feeling of resentment stirred up among the neighbours by discussion of their treatment by the "big interests" (everybody from the Dominion government down to the local bank manager) was aptly summed up some years later by the *Regina Leader* in an editorial which warned that:

> the masses of the Canadian people are on the verge of revolt against this conscienceless, cold-blooded, grafting, profiteering aggregation of Big Interests, puppets, styled the [Borden] Government, and which is now endeavoring, with might and main by flag flapping and similar devices to delude the people ... into voting to keep these task masters over them whip in hand.

With slight changes in topical references, this editorial, to be written in 1917, would accurately describe the reaction my father noted in his visits with Bird and Partridge to the farmers in the neighbourhood of Sintaluta in 1909.

With some like-minded neighbours they worked out a bold scheme to get up a farmers' sales agency, which would dispose of grain at top prices and return the profits to the growers instead of to the horde of middlemen who were then skimming them off. The scheme drew the full fire of the vested interests. They used all media to oppose it; in the press they represented the grain growers' leaders as dangerous radicals, a general slur much in favour before the Communists provided the privileged class with their convenient all-purpose smear. They took a cue from the rabid American editorialists; sheets which called themselves "The Farmers' Friend" shouted that the radicals would destroy society (by which they meant special privilege), ruin the country, and tear down everything the Fathers of Confederation had built up (by which they meant the vested interests — banks, railroads, and international grain speculators).

Chapter Six

My father, although he was aware from his experience in England of the fate of the little man who got in the way of "the interests", eagerly supported Partridge's plans and became an early member of the Grain Growers Association. This brought him in touch with other farmers in the district, like-minded men of similar background and experience. They came, for the most part, from Ontario, where they had worked in lumber camps on the fringe of the white pine forest, or eked a scanty living from stump meadows. As the forests retreated the lumbering industry dropped its teamsters and peewee loggers, whose thoughts turned to the Western prairies, with their promise of 160 acres of free land, with none of these damn stumps to be pulled, burnt, or blasted out before a crop could be planted. They crowded onto the railroads' harvester specials, which dumped them anywhere west of Winnipeg to find a job in the fields or starve. In good crop years, work was not hard to find for those willing and able to work twelve hours a day, six days a week, for food, board, a dollar a day, and find your own overalls. Many of the harvesters were bitten by the land fever, and filed on land for themselves once the harvest was over. Good land, however, was already becoming hard to find. As the eastern prairies filled up and poor farming methods impoverished the soil and multiplied weeds, land-hunger drove the restless still farther west: immigration has always moved west. Russia is the exception to prove the rule. The southwestern sector of the recently created Province of Saskatchewan was about to open up. Mennonites were pouring in, sniffing out the best land. An entire block was occupied by settlers from Wales who had moved on from an unsuccessful attempt to found a Welsh-speaking community in Patagonia. When they too talked of moving farther west for free land, it became apparent that land and time were running out.

My father's interest in the Grain Growers Association brought him into touch with the Ontario group around Sintaluta. They sent two men to the southwest to look over an area spotted on the map as 50 degrees north latitude by 107 degrees west longitude, and on the Torrens survey the six-mile-square block of Township 12, Range 9, west of the third meridian. The Torrens survey of the prairies had run range lines north and south every six miles, with township lines east and west also six miles apart; the townships blocked out were divided into thirty-six numbered sections of one square mile, or 640 acres, each.

From the iron marking post left by the surveyors, a settler could pace off with fair accuracy the 880 yards to establish the limits of the 160-acre quarter-section of his free homestead, to which he would, if possible, add another adjoining quarter-section of pre-emption north or south of his homestead, for which he would pay four dollars an acre.

The two scouts returned to report that the area was good rolling prairie, no visible alkali patches or washouts, good grass, no trees, ready for the plough. There were a few low hills but no sand dunes. A few miles south there was a small creek, identified on the map as the Notokeu or Old Man River. The C.P.R. main line ran forty miles to the north.

On May 6, 1910, my father, armed with this information, drove to Indian Head with Bird, determined to file on a homestead and pre-emption, sight unseen, before all the land between the C.P.R. main line and the United States border was taken up. At the Dominion branch office he studied a detailed map of the area. Up to that time the region had been used for grazing, leased to the Turkey Track ranch.

The map on which my father had based his selection described the area as "prairie". It had been issued a few months earlier by the Department of the Interior, on the authority of the Dominion Lands Act, 1908. It specified that "all unoccupied, surveyed agricultural lands, whether odd-numbered or even-numbered sections, that are not reserved or that have not been disposed of, are open to entry for homestead." "Under Clause 27 pre-emptions are authorized in the area enclosed by red shading," the map advised. This restricted choice, since only about one-fifth of the surveyed land fell within that area. But an extra 160 acres, to be obtained on easy terms and adjoining the 160 acres of homestead, was most desirable, for even at that time it was becoming clear that one quarter-section of 160 acres would not support a family farm. The map was drawn to a scale of twelve and a half miles to one inch. It traced rivers, lakes, the larger sloughs, and railway lines. It marked towns, villages, and Indian reservations; it gave the number of vacant quarter-sections in each township of thirty-six sections. It also described the surface — "some timber, good soil, hilly in parts, prairie, rough in parts, good soil and water", etc.

My father felt that this was a reasonable guide to the area and that he could safely file on land, sight unseen. So he declared on oath that he was a British subject, that his previous occupation had been farmer, and that he had not previously received a homestead patent. He undertook to reside on his land for three years, build a house worth three hundred dollars and break thirty acres of prairie. My father selected a quarter-section adjoining section 11, which was reserved in every township for financing and building a neighbourhood school. The scouts had reported that the centre of this section was taken up by a large slough, flanked by low hills with a generally northerly slope and a good clay loam without alkali or sand. Alf Annis, an ex-logger from Gravenhurst, and Frank Boyd, who had come in to the Land Office with them, filed on homesteads near by. Annis, who had four children, took a half-section, the east half of section 12, immediately east of the school section; Boyd joined my father in filing on section 2, taking the east half, my father having secured the west half, adjoining 11 on the south side. My father paid the ten dollars registration fee and walked out into a spring thunderstorm, feeling like one of the landed gentry. Boyd had another reaction. Setting his felt hat askew, he said, "The gummint just bet me ten bucks against a half-section that I can't stand this climate for three years!"

"Bet your life we'll do it!" my father returned.

"That's the stake all right," Boyd declared, sticking a bent of grass between his teeth. "And it looks like the odds are on the climate." A binding flash of lightning accompanied by crashing thunder startled them as they came out on to the street. Torrential rain soon changed into hail, bouncing on the sidewalk and driving them back into the Land Office for shelter.

"No fooling," Boyd said in his dry voice, "this country is going to be a tough old turkey, and I'd sure like to hedge my bet."

Bird interrupted: "The weather gets better as the land is opened up," he assured them. "When we came in everybody said the summer was too short, you couldn't raise wheat. First summer we were here we threshed eighty per cent of the crop with snow on the stooks. It's never been like that since."

"There'll be another year next year," Boyd said, with delphic ambiguity.

Even so, the crop had been threshed, Bird reminded them, although it was back-breaking work lifting the sodden sheaves, and some of the grain had sprouted; none of it made a better grade than "tough", which knocked twenty cents off the bushel at the elevator and more for drying at the Lakehead.

"What d'you get from them robbers?" Boyd inquired.

"Forty cents for eighty-cent wheat," Bird replied. "That's the reason for the Saskatchewan Grain Growers Association." Boyd whistled his scepticism, but the others paid no heed. Boyd belonged to that category of professional pessimist who uses his pessimism to screen his tender hopes from withering in the blast of reality. My father welcomed his company as an important component of the community which he foresaw taking root on a regional basis in Township 12, Range 9, west of the third meridian. He repeated the figures under his breath like an incantation: 2—12—9, west of the third.

As soon as they were back at Bird's farm they began to plan how to fulfil homestead requirements by finding and cultivating the land on which they had filed. It seemed best to cling together, since they were already friends. There were eight of them, plus two wives and four children. They could pool resources, such as they were, and share such implements as they would need to begin operations. They cut these to a minimum. A wagon (running gear and box), together with a pair of horses to pull it, was an essential for each individual. As summer, with haying-time, was coming on, each man planned to build a hayrack as soon as possible; for winter hauling of grain to town, a bobsleigh was needed; and of course, ploughs — a single plough or sulky, with a breaking and a stubble bottom, taking different types of ploughshare. Four horses would provide fast traction for harrows and seeder, four oxen, slow but determined and virtually tireless, would be best for breaking.

Most of these implements had to be individually owned. The Sintaluta group decided to pool their seeder and binder, which were the most expensive items. This turned out to be a poor plan, however, for the man at the foot of the list could not sow at the critical time when optimum conditions of land and weather prevailed, nor could he harvest the crop at peak. So the pool was dropped after the first year on the land, and each farmer equipped himself as well as his funds, the bank, and the implement companies would allow.

At the bare-bones level, this still called for a capital investment of some $4,800, allowing $300 for lumber, tar-paper, and nails for a shack. There would have been little chance of the hired man's saving this in cash out of his $30 a month, all found. Fortunately the West in those days existed on "time". Everything was bought "on time", hardly any transactions involved cash. This enabled the farmer to get to his land, but he had to mortgage it for the machinery to work it. If his crop failed, his land was likely to be seized for default of payments. Farmers dispossessed for no fault of their own took their revenge in the dust-bowl drought years, deliberately loading up implement firms and insurance and loan companies with land they would never get a return on but on which they were obliged to pay taxes or lose it for a pittance in a tax-sale to some embittered farmer.

My father brought his own plough, running-gear, and discs, and with them their traction — two horses, semi-Clydesdales, and six oxen (Tom and Bill, Buck and Bright, Blackie and Jerry). The group loaded freight cars and shipped them west to Herbert, where the trail southwards avoided the big slough south of Morse, their original destination. The trail from Morse was better once the slough had been by-passed, but Morse was forty-two miles away from 2—12—9, six miles farther than Herbert, the next stop west on the mainline C.P.R.

Arriving at Herbert, my father off-loaded his wagon — the Bain, built by the Hamilton Wagon Company, with a two-tier box-and-spring seat, sturdy running-gear which would stand up to years of hard service and neglect of everything but axle-grease. He spent a day going around the dry goods and hardware stores, assembling supplies for the summer — a comprehensive list to avoid needless trips forty-two miles back to town for an item overlooked: a barrel of lime (for which he had ambitious but unrealized building plans), 100 lb. of flour, 50 lb. of sugar, half a dozen tubes of yeast-cakes, 5 lb. of Red Rose tea, 5 lb. of Blue Ribbon coffee, half a dozen cans of condensed milk, ditto salmon, a blue enamel hand-bowl for washing, washing-up, or pastry-making, baking soda, two pitchforks, one scoop-shovel to handle grain, one post-hole spade, one hand-hammer, one mallet, fifty fence-posts cut from willows at Sintaluta, two rolls of barbed wire, two water-pails, one milk-pail with sieve spout, one keg of 2½-inch nails, 10 lb. of 4-inch spikes, 10 lb. of staples, and a brace and bit; then he moved into house and stable furnishings: one axe, one hatchet, two files, one rasp, two fifty-foot lengths of rope, one logging chain, one tethering chain, two pair of hobbles, two halters, one box of copper rivets for mending harness, six pots, including a double-boiler (the Birds' staple diet had been porridge, cooked over-night, for which a double-boiler is essential). For the kitchen he chose a flax-burner. It would burn threshed flax-straw and keep him from freezing to death. He needed twelve feet of stove-pipe with one damper-segment and one metal chimney-pot, with flashing; also, one wooden water-barrel, one can of kerosene, one storm-lantern, and two table lamps. He decided against a table as too costly; he would build his own. Canned goods crates would do for chairs, which also were unexpectedly costly. Envisaging the kitchen, he bought a carton of Eddy's kitchen matches, a tin of his favourite Macdonald's cut-plug pipe tobacco, a sack of Old Chum, and a tin of Prince Albert. Thus provided against running out of tobacco with no re-supply within forty-two miles, my father bethought himself of food again: a bag of table salt, 20 lb. of coarse salt for preserving meat, and one block of rock salt for cattle to lick; then pepper, spices, vinegar, nutmeg, cinnamon, cloves, and oil of cloves (against tooth-ache). For the house and barn: two rolls of tar-paper, enough shiplap, droplap, common board, and re-saw, along with two-by-fours and two-by-sixes, to build a one-storey shack fourteen by twenty-four feet, longer than usual to accommodate us kids and completed by four square windows, one door and hasp, four hinges (two of them for a winter storm-door which my father would make himself; two for the store-bought door). The tally was completed by two horse blankets and two coarse grey blankets, a side of salt bacon, a sack of oatmeal, and a broom.

Next morning dawned clear, with a brisk westerly breeze rippling the sloughs. After a quick breakfast of porridge and bacon the company set out. Alf Annis led, by unpolled but common consent. He was the big man among them, with a dozen cows, implements, and enough lumber for a four-room house and a big barn in which he had invested the proceeds from the sale of his Sintaluta farm.

What brought him homesteading again? The lure of virgin soil in exchange for his exhausted acres, the challenge of a new scene, and leadership in the community. Annis and my father were joined by Frank Williamson and his brother Charlie, hot gospellers from the East. Frank stuttered badly except when praying, when his diction cleared like magic. What brought him to the prairies? There were souls to be saved from hell-fire, here as in Toronto or Gravenhurst, and a chance to serve the Lord and speak with the tongues of men and of angels. If more incentive were needed there was the chance of wealth in the golden grain of the boundless prairies, and escape from the petty, trifling round of peccadilloes and gossip in a small town down east. But the east was forever hard at their heels, tracking them down like William Blake's hounds of heaven, driving them ever farther west to a new heaven and a new earth, where their sins would be washed in the blood of the Lamb and the wicked man consumed in the everlasting fire.

Annis had been strong for the Herbert trail, as six miles shorter, but the choice was unhappy; the trail was ungraded, full of field-stones and badger-holes, no more than cuts across the prairie, fading to a greener line through the dry, dun grasses. After a few miles, Annis headed south-east to pick up the Morse trail. This had been partly graded, and the worst boulders had been removed and the holes filled. They made good time. By noon they had reached the Halfway House, on the north bank of Wiwa Creek. There they stopped for a meal and a rest. The creek was a problem. In summer it would be little more than a trickle and a few water-holes at the bottom of a coulee. But this was spring and the creek was in spate. Nobody knew how deep it was. Three feet would be fordable, but four feet would flood the wagon-box and ruin the supplies. Annis put the whip to his horse and pioneered across. The water was not too deep; the bottom was hard. My father put his horses to it at a gallop. The wagon bumped and churned through. The horses scrambled up the steep bank on the other side, and then, tired and breathless, refused to go farther. My father decided to let them rest there for the night. Twenty-two miles with a load over soft trails and a ford to scramble through was heavy going.

This was Old Country consideration for horses, which the Westerners lacked. The land was hard on them and they were hard on their horses. These were mostly broncos, half-wild creatures, quick to strike with their forelegs or kick with hind legs; unshod, half-broken, and easily frightened, they were dangerously inclined to run away, dragging hitch and driver behind them.

My father tethered his horses to the back wheels of the wagon, gave them an oat bundle each, and accepted Annis's offer of a lift in his buggy back across the ford. He was glad of a good meal at the Halfway House and shelter for the night. No point in roughing it needlessly; time enough for that when there was no option. He did not get much sleep, however. It was hot up in the attic; the windows could not be opened for fear of letting in mosquitoes. On top of all that, my father was keyed up for the first view of his land — the west half of 2—12—9. That would be journey's end, independence beginning. Down below Frank Williamson was seeking the Lord in prayer; my father cursed him quietly and fell asleep.

It rained in the night, so the trail was heavier going next morning. After four hours, Annis shouted aloud and swung from the buggy. His horse had tripped and stumbled over a deep, wide hole, one of four, with an iron stake in the middle. This marked the north-east corner of a section of land. Annis read off the Roman figures filed on the marker: XXIV, XIII, VIII. "Section 24, Township 13, Range 8" he chanted. "Another twelve miles south and five west gets us to my place. Let's get going." For another three hours they headed southwest across the prairie, making their own trail, skirting hills and sloughs, until they came in sight of a sheet of water, half a mile long by a quarter of a mile wide. "That's the big slough on eleven," said

Frank Boyd, recognizing the area he had scouted earlier. The horses caught the spirit of the moment and broke into a trot. Three miles farther on they halted on a level plot thick with short grass, buffalo willow, and low sagebrush, silvery-grey in the rays of the sinking sun. Terns and gulls screamed around them as they set up a sleeping shelter by the wagon and dug a wide hole for a fireplace, secure against a grass fire. They made the sleeping shelter by hanging horse blankets from a wagon, anchoring the lower end with stones: there were plenty in the turf around. One of them was curiously worked; a groove had been cut around the middle, both ends had been ground flat, and a thumb-hold on either side gouged out, probably by heating the stone and then allowing water to drip on it. Holding this neolithic artifact in his hand, my father marvelled at the patience which had worked this smooth groove into granite; it brought a message from his predecessor in this land — neolithic man. It said: Long shalt thou labour to live, but in the end thy labour shall be lost and a stranger shall take it and make it his own; thou shalt grow lean and the stranger grow fat on thy labour.

Between these fancies, the mosquitoes, and the chill night air, my father passed a restless night and was glad to roll out of his blanket early. The fire had died out; he was too anxious to find his own land to wait for breakfast. Stuffing a heel of bread into his pocket, he hitched up his team and pulled out. Roughly a quarter-mile south, he figured, there should be another survey marker. With this in mind he set out to find his land. An hour later he pulled up in the lee of a low hill among a skein of small grassy sloughs, from which wild duck took off in alarm at his approach. The water was brown and full of mosquito wrigglers and duck down. He strained them out through his milk-pail sieve, then tethered the horses to the wagon wheel and dug a new fireplace. This was a major task. The glacial deposit had settled in the course of thousands of years into near rock. Only the crowbar could pierce the virgin turf and get down to the underlying hardpan.

My father turned over just enough sod to be able to make a fire without fear of its spreading among the dry grass tops. Then he collected a few handfuls of last year's horse-dung, bleached and dry, for a quick, hot blaze. But by the time the kettle was boiling, he was too tired to bother with coffee, still less with porridge. Tea was easier to handle, so he threw some leaves into his japanned teapot and settled down to a quiet meal of tea and bread. Then he set out to find the survey holes which would mark off the boundary of his land. However, four holes sunk flush with the prairie, and a small metal post less than a foot high are not conspicuous landmarks on the boundless prairie, where the sight can range over twenty miles without meeting obstruction.

My father wandered about for most of the morning, stumbling over gopher hills and into badger digs, but never finding the marker holes. Finally, he worked on a grid plan, criss-crossing every twenty yards, until with the sun due south he stumbled into one of the four holes, and with a grunt of triumph pulled out the survey post. II.XII.IX., he read. This was it! This was the north-east corner of Section 2, Township 12, Range 9. There were 640 acres in this section, and of these the western 320 were his homestead and pre-emption. To reach them, however, he still had to pace off 880 yards due west. Keeping the sun high on his left he set off, and on the 880th stride he set up his own marker, a small cairn of field stones which would define the boundary of his land.

Chapter Seven

His land! My father looked around. To the north the land fell away in a gentle slope to the grassy verges of the Big Slough. Beyond it, a slow rise took the khaki-coloured grasslands to the horizon, marked by a low range of hills over which he had driven yesterday. West-wards there was a flat, possibly wet, but showing no signs of the dangerous white alkali which destroyed fertility. As far as he could see, there was neither tree nor bush — nothing to clear away before you start to plough, my father reflected. He was already plotting out his farm. A little cluster of low hills suggested a site for house and barn, if only because it was good for nothing else.

First, however, it would be necessary to find water. Slough water could not do for household use, and wells were tricky. There was no spring, nor any obvious depression which might indicate an under-ground water-course. However, at the foot of one of the small hills there was a heavy growth of buffalo-willow and plenty of water-weed, a low plant of the genus glycerrhizia, or wild licorice, whose roots were supposed to go down to water within fifteen feet. There were in addition a couple of ant-hills, which was also a good sign. Like the badgers, ants were supposed to go down to water not too far below the surface. My father built another small cairn to mark his trial well-site, and then realized that he was very hungry, and that his wagon and the food were half a mile away. Even as he headed back north-east, however, he noted the little ponds scattered among the hills, and determined to make this his pasture — good forage and water, and with luck, a well.

He headed for the stone cairn he had built at the corner of his half-section and then struck east, figuring he would find his wagon easily enough. He hoped so, for the mosquitoes arose from the grass like smoke, and while he slapped at them the enormity of his task began to overwhelm him. He tried to marshal his work in order of importance: prairie to be broken, crop seeded, well dug, barn built, cellar dug, house built, pasture fenced.

As he walked he collected horse-dung for his cook-fire. Weathered "prairie coal" makes a quick, hot fire, soon ablaze, soon dead; on it he put a pot of water for the inevitable porridge, and grilled a couple of rashers of bacon on the tines of a pitchfork. Between layers of toast these tasted good, but the porridge was lifeless — he had forgotten to put salt in it. However, the water in the double-boiler was good for tea once the duck-feathers and mosquito larvae were strained out. Porridge and bread were dull and my father noted: Should have bought some jam — or corn syrup would perhaps be better; it would go on porridge as well as bread. He began to realize that porridge would be his staple diet for some time. He had no disposition to linger over the meal, even had the mosquitoes permitted.

As soon as the porridge was consumed, he hitched up and drove back to the well-site. Taking a handful of laths, he strode west from the boundary cairn, driving in a lath every fifty yards. These would be markers for his plough; without them he would have little chance of ploughing a straight furrow to the west end of his land; dog's leg furrows made a man a laughing-stock and the land unfriendly. Anxious to run a straight furrow at the start, my father chose the single-share sulky rather than the gang-plough, as easier to handle for the first trip. He hitched up four of the oxen, Buck and Bright, Blackie and Jerry. Oxen were preferable to horses for the heavy task of breaking the prairie. They were slow, but when they felt an obstacle they stopped, where horses would jump into the collar and strain until something gave, either the harness, the evener to which they were hitched, or the plough. This could be expensive to repair and put the rig out of action until it was done.

At the top of the little rise where he had placed the marker, my father let the blade down. It scraped the gravel for a few feet, then bit in, furrowing the three-inch sod bound together with the roots and remains of grasses, flowering plants — roses, yellow bean and prairie crocus. This sod had kept the surface intact for ten thousand years of wind and rain, frost and sun and snow, since the retreating ice-sheet abandoned its hundreds of feet of debris shorn from rocks of the northern shield to form the happy hunting ground of a succession of nomad wanderers until the farmers came, intent on destroying that millennial ground-cover to produce a year or two of intensive crops until the exhausted fabric began to unravel and fall into ruins before the incessant beating of the wind.

There was no hint of all this in the brisk north-west breeze which rippled the Big Slough and drove the mosquitoes away from the straining oxen. There was no ominous flight of birds, no thunder on the left to suggest caution in disturbing the stable life-pattern of the short-grass prairie. The plough bit into the turf and turned it over in a long dark ribbon. At the foot of the hill the share struck a boulder buried in the turf. The eveners creaked, the oxen stopped in their tracks and allowed their chains to go slack. My father struggled to keep his seat and tripped the share out of the ground. The obstacle was an ice-borne intruder of grey granite which had lain there from time immemorial, almost invisible, with only a rounded tip protruding among the grasses. Fortunately for him the oxen had halted when they felt the extra weight. It would not be wise to risk another encounter between plough and boulder. He took the crowbar from the wagon and walked along the line of laths, watching carefully for other half-hidden impediments. He was learning the first prairie lesson, picking stone. All along the line he had marked for ploughing he unearthed small boulders, less than a foot across, weighing ten to twenty pounds each and showing great variety: limestone, pink, grey, and blue granite, an occasional piece of slate, and even old basic brown trap rock. He left them in a line, to be moved away on a stone-boat — whenever he found time to build one. That was another priority beating remorselessly on him — a stone-boat: two runners under a two-by-six platform, and a two-horse hitch.

He began to be aware of the ruthless pressure of time that bears down on the shoulders of every farmer and particularly of every new farmer. There is never enough time on the prairie. Ploughing cannot start until the frost is out of the ground, for the prairies freeze a foot or more deep during the long winter. Once the land is ploughed, seed must be thrown in as fast as possible at what the farmer guesses or senses is the optimum soil condition. Planted too early the seedlings can be damaged by late frost, frequent in May. Planted too late they risk frost damage before the grain has matured in August. Then the crop must be cut and stooked, again in a wild rush to secure optimum conditions, and threshed as soon as possible to get a good price before the new crop deluges the market and sends the price sliding downwards. In between seeding and binding, hay must be cut, cured, and stored against winter; summer-fallow must be worked, granaries and bins built, harness and machinery repaired, seed cleaned for next year, fences built and repaired, and all the thousand and six daily chores performed — cows milked, stables cleaned out, eggs collected, chickens feathered, peas picked and shelled, gardens weeded, leaks in the roof mended, wells cleaned out, potatoes dug and stored, hogs butchered, sausage ground, bacon cured, horses shod, shares sharpened, cream skimmed and churned, outhouse moved to a new pit and last season's Eaton's mail-order catalogue hung on the wall.

The farmer, and particularly the ploughman, is the poetical symbol of fruitful toil, celebrated in two thousand years of bucolic verse. The ploughman has been almost as romanticized as the good shepherd. It is time to look at the facts. There is not much poetry in ploughing. For the first trip the ploughman's mind is occupied in trying to keep the furrow straight and even. He notes for future reference the dry or sodden patches, the half-buried boulders which should be removed; he notes and avoids the killdeer's nest while the mother tries to draw his attention away by feigning a broken wing. After the first hour, the monotonous tearing of the turf numbs his senses. Nests and boulders appear under the share before they can be avoided. If the ploughman walks behind his implement, he is soon too weary to do more than set one foot in front of the other and too tired to think. If he rides the plough, the more common practice on the prairies, it is still no bed of roses. After the first trip or two (the trip is out and back, usually half a mile each way on the standard half-section farm) physical discomfort appears. The incessant joggling of the seat pulls at the posterior muscles. Ploughman's piles are a common occupational hazard. So much for the poetry of the plough: mind numb, tail sore, all the ploughman wants at the end of his day is a meal and a night's sleep. There were no such boons for my father at the end of his first half-day's breaking — two acres turned over.

In some ways the oxen looked after themselves better than their drivers did. Towards noon, after a hard morning's breaking, their patience began to wear thin. They were thirsty after hours in the hot sun, drooling long ropy saliva. There was a beautiful rippling slough just beyond the end of the furrow, but instead of slaking their thirst they were required to turn around for another trip. At noon the oxen revolted. With one accord they refused to turn at the end of the trip; they headed straight for that beautiful, shining water. My father set the plough deeper; the oxen put their weight into the collars and plunged on, cutting a six-inch furrow straight into the slough. There the team stopped, dipped their muzzles thankfully into the water, and drank their fill; then they moved quietly out, ready for another trip. The deep furrow persisted for years, a testimony to bovine determination to be their own master. My father cherished this memorial of his pioneer days, and refused to allow it to be obliterated. He had much in common with the oxen, he felt. At the time he was amused and thankful that the oxen had slaked their thirst and then moved on, instead of lying down, as horses were apt to do when they felt put upon.

My father was glad enough to make the oxen an excuse to quit. At the end of the next trip, he unhitched, gave them some hay and a bundle of straw, and left them to their ruminations until it was time to start the afternoon's breaking. He might have been wise to take a leaf from the oxen's book, but he submitted instead to the ruthless pressure of his calendar.

At the end of his day's ploughing, as the sun neared the horizon, he gouged holes with the crowbar into the tough prairie; then he hammered in the willow stakes he had brought from Sintaluta for fence posts. It was essential to be able to turn the oxen into pasture in the evening. After two hours of this, and little enough to show for it, he was too tired to do anything but spoon up the cold remains of the morning's porridge, and wash it down with slough-water, regardless of the wigglers and the feathers. He had no time or strength for refinements such as tea or a fire for himself — just something filling to eat; for the oxen hay and straw. Then he would roll up in his blankets under the wagon — a shelter against the dew. It is not hard to rise at sun-up from such a bed.

Fence posts in, barbed wire had to be strung. Barbed wire is dia-
bolical. It cuts and tears, trips and slips, tangles in knots, and breaks
with a savage backlash. My father unrolled a length of fifty yards,
wound one end to a solid corner post, and tied the other end to the
wagon. Then he drove ahead until the wire was taut, but not so
strained as to break. Then, as quickly as if he were securing some
wild beast, he stapled it to the posts, always careful to keep his head
turned away, lest the wire snap and lacerate him. It is like trying to
tie up a tiger with bare hands.

One strand would have to do for the time being; enough to dis-
courage wanderers. There were no tempting fields of oats or alfalfa
on the other side, against which three strands would have been needed to retain cattle. Horses are more timid, but if they do break
through they are apt to panic and cut themselves badly.

Priorities had to be revised as experience demanded. No matter
that he rose at daybreak, there were never enough hours in the day
for any but the most pressing tasks. He moved up to top priority the
stringing of a fence around the pasture where the horses and oxen
could be turned to graze with some assurance that they would be
there when wanted for the day's work. The little sloughs gave them
water, but these would not last forever. They would dry up before
the end of summer; those that escaped would freeze solid in winter.
A well was essential. No house should be built until nearby water was
assured. But the fearful labour and the uncertainty deterred him.
There were no post-hole borers, no well-drilling equipment on that
frontier. The homesteader had to dig his well with a crowbar and a
spade.

After putting it off for three days my father took the fateful
decision to start on the well, there where the buffalo-willow, water-
weed, badger holes, and ant-hill augured for success. Using the crowbar and spade alternately, he removed the turf from a circle six feet
in diameter. This was a generous width, but he knew that, once he
got down to his own level, he would need a wide hole in order to have
room to throw the earth up over the lip. But it meant that for each
foot he sank the hole, he would have to move 28.26 cubic feet of
earth. He could not expect to strike water short of twelve feet down
— lucky if he did then — which meant moving very nearly 340 cubic
feet of soil. The tough glacial clay, studded with stones like plums in
a pound cake, challenged his strength and endurance. It was too
much after a day's ploughing, so he limited himself to one hour every

evening, reserving his major effort for Saturday and Sunday. As a Lord's Day occupation it was not in the same class with St. Modwen's or reading W. G. Grace on cricket.

As he excavated deeper, the stones began to thin out, and the earth became more closely packed. At four feet it occurred to him like a thunderbolt that he was digging himself in with no way of getting out. But using his spade as a stepladder, and grasping desperately at the buffalo-willow growing near the lip, he pulled himself out and collapsed on the grass, sweating in panic at having so nearly buried himself.

To prevent any repetition, he built a ladder of two-by-fours with cross slats for rungs, and let this down into the pit. It was comforting, but it took up so much space that he found it difficult to toss the earth up over the lip. At length he was forced to the wearisome and time-consuming alternative of hauling up a bucketful of earth, then descending the ladder to fill it up again. It was back-breaking toil.

At ten feet he was encouraged by the appearance of sand, moist sand, which might indicate that he was reaching an aquifer. Another foot, and the crowbar sank easily into the sandy stratum. When he pulled it out, water welled up in the hole. That was it! He had found water! He hastily scooped a hole and watched, fascinated, as the trickle of sand and water oozed in from the south, very cold, as if it had just melted from eternal snows. "You and I, Water," he said, "came a long way to meet here. You look after me," he went on, addressing the water as if it were a living sentient thing, "and I'll look after you, give you a good roof over your head, and a strong cribbing so there will be no cave-in on top of you." You have to dig a well, he said to himself, and find your own water, to know why men used to worship at wells.

He filled a bucket with the muddy sand and dragged it to the top. In half an hour the sediment had settled, leaving half a bucket of clear water. He tried it. It was so cold it made his mouth ache; but it was sweet water, not saline, not alkaline, a little earthy still, but good for man and beast. He took a long draught of his water – his water! His mind went back to his youth, and a cold spring bubbling out at the foot of the Malvern Hills from which he had once drunk on a walking tour. He would call this Malvern Link, after that cold spring found on a sunny day so long ago. He consecrated it then and there, pouring a little onto the ground, like a tithe. He looked down into the pit and rejoiced at the gleam of water at the bottom.

Building a crib and well-head was almost as demanding a one-man task as digging the well itself. But it was essential and immediate, both to prevent the sides from caving in and to guard against cattle falling into the hole, as well as to permit water to be drawn up, which cannot be done without standing out over the lip. Like most operations on the raw prairie, crib-making was more difficult in the performance than in the conception. My father threw down four two-by-fours and some common boarding, of varied widths, one inch thick. He followed them down on the ladder. Then, up to the knees in perishing cold water and quicksand, he nailed the boards to the lower studs. The last six feet he put together above ground and lowered by rope to be fitted on to the bottom half. The meeting was none too exact, but it held. Then he boarded over the top of the cribbing, fitted a lid with a hand-grip, and hung bucket and rope over a dowel post. Building a winch was beyond him. He would be content to lower a bucket by hand and swing it expertly so that its lip scooped into the water with little or no disturbance of the sand and silt at the bottom, to be drawn up, brimming, hand over hand. By this method an expert with the bucket could bring up the mice, voles, or even gophers which had fallen into the well, to die either of shock, drowning, or chill.

I subsequently became skilful at this feat, and could capture, without stirring up the mud, any of the minor fauna which had found release there. When this came to my mother's attention, she renewed her pressure for a pump. The well came just within the working depth of a simple suction valve. The rejoicing when it was installed died away as soon as it was discovered that instead of entire mice coming up in the bucket, the pump brought up bits and pieces of mice which had got jammed in the valves and disintegrated. On one occasion I caught a small grass snake which had fallen into the water. He was a difficult catch, as he did not keep still long enough to get the bucket squarely under him. His water-speed slowed as the cold took possession, and he was a very subdued snake when I fished him out of the bucket and restored him to the warm prairie grass. Despite the disadvantage of morselled mice, the pump had these advantages: it brought up water in quantity without stirring up the sand and mud, and it eliminated the danger of my falling into the well, which was not negligible in winter when the cap and lid were sheathed in ice, and the rope itself was frozen so stiff it was like using a pole.

My father might not have dared to flout the odds on getting water had he known how heavy they were against him. We learned afterwards that Jones, who had come from water-rich Vermont to take up the adjoining section 3, dug five dry holes before getting water, only to find that his successful well was squarely on the road allowance and had to be filled in. For years he had to exist on a barrel a day drawn from the creek four miles away and none too good at that. By and large, however, with some unlucky exceptions, this was a good district for water. A stratum of sand and gravel underlay the surface cover at about twelve feet. It was not, however, fed entirely by surface water, for it survived years of drought. Geologists have since theorized that this aquifer was the bed of a prehistoric river, fed by the retreating icecap. Below it lay a band of heavy blue clay, twenty feet thick. Below this again was abundant water, but always so alkaline as to be undrinkable, scouring both cattle and men.

His own well completed, my father knocked together a trough against the day the sloughs dried up. He had difficulty making it watertight. In theory, if two-by-sixes are laid side by side, the contiguous edges bruised by a hammer will swell and effect a watertight joint. In practice this does not happen. Father's trough leaked like a sieve, and held water hardly long enough to give oxen their fill. He patched up the joint with tar-paper and lath so that it was reasonably watertight. Once winter came, the moisture in the joint froze and effectively sealed it for long enough to satisfy the oxen.

It was always a marvel to me how much water an ox would drink. In the dead of winter, with icicles hanging from the trough, the water about to congeal, an ox would take a mouthful, warm it for a moment over his tongue before downing it, then put his muzzle into the trough and slop up more and more and more. I counted them on a cold winter morning drinking eight buckets each. Hauling forty buckets to satisfy five of the brutes at twenty below zero was agonizing. Unlike horses they stubbornly refused to nibble snow, no matter how thirsty they were; they would die of dehydration first. For watering these brutes, the pump was a great boon. These, however, were solutions for the distant future.

Chapter Eight

The well completed, the most urgent problem was that work on the house and barn should begin. About a hundred yards south a steep hillock seemed an ideal location. The hill was too abrupt to be ploughed, so no land would be lost to cultivation by building a house and garden there. It would be dry and well-drained; there were no indications of underlying water, so there was no danger of a damp cellar. After considering these points, my father outlined a cellar area twelve by twenty-four feet just off the summit of the hill. He determined to dig this out as time permitted, giving it an hour or two every evening after the day's breaking was done.

The hateful pressure of time began to build up again. He would have to take days off to get seed, more days off for a load of lumber. He still had less than thirty acres under plough. He wanted to seed fifty acres before mid May, the latest he could sow for a crop that summer. There was nothing for it but to hitch up the horses and head north to Morse, forty-two miles away. The trip took two days as the trail was soft and heavy. He went first to the bank to obtain a crop-advance loan, so by the time he had bought a load of seed flax it was past noon and there would be no work time left when he got home on the fourth day.

The elevator man claimed that he had cleaned the seed flax. Examining a handful my father found black grains of what looked like pigweed. But to wait for the seed to be re-screened would have cost another day, so he took what was offered and put it all in — flax, pigweed, and stinkweed, which infested the flat for years with its sharp-smelling growth. The stinkweed, also known as French-weed, was particularly difficult to eradicate, as its seeds were small enough to go through the screens but about the same weight as flax and thus hard to eliminate by winnowing. Elevator men found them an excellent excuse for knocking a grade off wheat, on the grounds that millers objected to the smell, which, they said, carried over into the flour. Having some experience of milling himself, my father was willing to grant this. His willingness or unwillingness made no difference. He had to get the crop in.

To ease the pressure he worked out an exchange of services with Annis. Since he had to go to town again for lumber, he asked Annis to seed his flax, using the pool seeder; in return he would seed fifty acres of Annis's new breaking as soon as he got back. The stinkweed, with luck, could be cultivated out when they changed over to wheat.

This arrangement lightened my father's heart as he set off for Morse with the wagon stripped down to its running-gear, which is better adapted than the wagon-box to transporting lumber. With such a light load the horses made better time, but it was desperately fatiguing for the driver, sitting hour after hour on a sack thrown across the reach — the shaft that connects the front and rear axles. He lightened the monotony and his cramped position occasionally by walking for a mile or two.

Lumber is not an easy seat to ride for forty-two miles of prairie trail, any more than is a running-gear. It is tricky to load and has a particular malevolence in working loose. A keg of nails and two rolls of tar-paper had also to be wedged into place. My father was bone-tired by the time he got back to the homestead.

Returning with the lumber, my father found his fifty acres seeded — rather too heavily, he thought, but still it was in the ground. He dumped part of the lumber off for Annis, who wanted to run up some shelter before the June rains came. The rest of it he unloaded on the little hill where he proposed to build his own house.

On the way to Morse he passed an occasional sod shack, built from the long turves held together by roots of grass, wild roses, yellow bean, and other prairie plants which waited out the long winter underground. While he was at Sintaluta he had looked into the possibility of a sod shack.

It meant immediate shelter; it was reputedly warm in winter, and inexpensive to build and maintain; but vermin and farm animals found it a congenial environment; moreover, a sod shack did not conform to the Homestead Act's requirement of a house worth $300 to be built and occupied on the land before title could be obtained.

Perhaps the decisive factor in my father's rejection of a sod shack was its unpleasant suggestion of the peasant, living on potatoes and hatred *au gratin*, which was not the role in which my father saw himself, nor one of which W. G. Grace would have approved.

I was glad of his decision when I rejoined him; adjustment to the confines of a wooden shack was difficult enough, without the additional burden of sod, earth floor, and fleas. But the romantic urge to build was strong enough to set me to erecting a sod house for my dog, from turf turned over for the garden. I shared the kennel and fleas with Tim, the inevitable farm collie, happily enough, but it gave me a new respect for the spaciousness of the fourteen by twenty-four house my father had built.

When he turned to the task of digging the cellar, he found it was not as awkward as digging a well, but moving nearly 2000 cubic feet of glacial till by hand was a titan's task. Later on he would excavate extensions with a horse-shovel, but for the present all he had was the narrow post-hole spade. He worked long and hard, anxious to get the cellar dug and covered before the rains came, lest he be cursed with a damp, muddy cellar with crumbling walls. Years afterwards I marvelled at the long grooves made by the spade in the compact sides of the cellar, and honoured the dogged resolution to which they testified. It was seven feet deep, with a block of earth left at one side for a settle, beside which a ladder climbed to a trapdoor in the floor. In after years I found the settle a convenient stand on which to carry on photographic operations, using soup plates for the developer, washer, and fixer, and operating with a one-candle-power dark lantern made from two empty salmon cans, some wire, and a strip of red tissue paper. I still have the products of those early sessions in the cellar. At the time they caused high excitement. They still evoke the smell of a compound of chemicals, rotting potatoes, and an over-ripe prairie chicken hung from the rafters.

The fill excavated from the cellar was to be piled against the house to hold it down. But by the time the cellar was dug, my father realized that he could go no further by himself. Two-by-six timbers, even softwood, are heavy to handle. He laid them along the rim of the cellar for a sill, but the problem of attaching the two-by-four studs and raising them to perpendicular defeated him. The wind was rising and a thunderstorm brewing. In panic haste he went over to Annis's, and found him anxious to get his own roof on before the storm swelled the flooring and sprang the joists. Recalling that Annis had seeded the flax before putting his own in, my father reciprocated by working on his neighbour's house for two days. The storm swept around to the south, as storms were to do so often later when needed for the crops.

With the roof on his own house, Annis hitched a team of broncos to the buggy and drove my father over to his place at a dead gallop. In a nail-and-hammer race, they secured the studs at two-foot intervals, toe-nailed them to the sills — there was no time for morticing — and bolted on the lintel with four-inch spikes. They hauled the sides up, secured them, and began slapping on the wallboard. The first layer was shiplap, a one-inch board with quarter-inch step or bead along the edge, which was supposed to give a more watertight joint. The wood, however, was green and wet. The lumber companies wanted to take their profits fast. The boards had already begun to warp, which made for difficulties with the join at the outset, and created more when the wood dried out and warped further. A layer of tar-paper went over the shiplap, and droplap for the outside, as less likely to shrink and leave gaps and slits through which rain could seep and snow filter.

Tar-paper was the prairie's answer to insulation, waterproofing, and caulking as hay-wire was the answer to stress. Tar-paper's ease of application tempted builders to use it as an outer cover; this was ruinous, for, whether secured by tin caps or laths, tar-paper fell victim to the incessant prairie winds which ripped it to tatters. As a sandwich between layers of wood it was useful and durable, and my father used it in both the walls and the roof. He did not use it in the floor, although he put in two layers of wood, common board lengthwise, and shiplap cross-wise, to control draughts. They were only partly successful.

The roof was a grave problem. My father decided against a peak-roof with shingles in favour of a rounded car-roof — like that on a boxcar. Shingles demanded a greater area of roof and they were tricky to apply. In case of fire they blew away and spread the flames. My father dreaded fire, which was a real prairie threat. It was not easy to secure the correct curve for a car-roof. The two-by-eight rafters had to be raised by a two-inch chock to the requisite height above the transverse beam in order to give the necessary curve to the roof. Even for two men, two-by-eights presented a problem of sheer weight and unwieldiness, but once positioned and secured, they were a solid frame for the top layers of shiplap, tar-paper and re-saw. Re-saw is a half-inch board with little to recommend it but ductility and ease of handling. The rising wind neutralized that factor, however. It tore the re-saw out of Annis's hands; it bowled the tar-paper off the roof and rolled it down the hillside, unravelling it until it was little more than a twisted, torn strip, which had to be painstakingly rolled up again, patched, and parcelled out as it was applied to the roof and secured quickly by a strip of re-saw. Under these conditions it was hard to tell just where the rafter was. Time and again my father felt the nail drive in with a sharp plop against no resistance, which meant that he had missed the rafter. At first he tried drawing the nail out, but Annis pointed out that the hole remained and rain would surely find it. So, after that, whenever a nail missed its rafter, it stayed where it was. At the other points, sure enough the roof leaked. When it rained the house was decorated with pails, milk-tins, bowls, and jugs which resounded with the soft plink-plonk-plosh of drops; but they were messengers of a good crop, and after the first season nothing sounded more musical to our ears. The nails that missed the rafter contributed in another way. In winter they conducted the frost and were covered with ice, which thawed and dripped as the house warmed.

As soon as the roof was finished and the tin chimney-pot and its flashing in place, Annis hurried off to complete his own house, leaving my father to contemplate windows and doors. They were a nuisance, but necessary. A square frame holding a piece of glass could be fixed between two studs, if refinements like hinges or pulley slides were not desired. They may have been desired, but they were beyond the power of the home carpenter, who contented himself with holding the windows in place by a wedge, which could easily be removed if anyone wanted fresh air. For extra light a long window was fashioned with two frames, one above the other. This arrangement gave the house an odd appearance, as if it was winking at the passer-by. The system of installing the windows was primitive, but it served, and with some help from felt strips they were reasonably draught-free in wintertime.

Doors were another matter. Doors are a nuisance. Doors sag. They appear to be so simple to make, just cross-bars nailed over some planks and attached to hinges. But something must be added to prevent sag — either an N-brace or a Z-brace. By this time the door is too heavy for the hinge to which it must be bolted, and the hinge too heavy for the door-post, which needs auxiliary anchorage to the rest of the house. Another dilemma: should the door open inwards or outwards? If inwards, a great blast of cold air and snow sweeps into the house in winter. If outwards, the door must be hinged to the north door-post on the west side of the house; otherwise the wind will get at it, and tear it out of the strongest grasp, possibly wrenching it off the hinges in a splendid triumph of wind over man. Bearing in mind all these things, my father built a simple door, with a simple latch. Even so, the door sagged, the wind rattled it and tried conclusions with anyone trying to open it.

Wind is the curse of the prairies; elsewhere it masquerades occasionally as a gentle breeze, coaxing springtime buds into flower, but on the prairies it displays its true character as a malevolent demon, smashing down standing crops after a rain; drying out the land before the rain has time to soak in; tearing at the soil, and knocking the very seed out of its bed; snatching at any loose board until its incessant rattle banishes sleep; playing on draught preventers like a reed, with a demoniac cacophony; sifting fertile soil into vast drifts; sweeping dirt through and into every crevice as well as into eyes, ears, nose, and mouth; snatching reins from the driver's hands and tearing at them and the horses' mouths; an evil malevolent demon! Curse wind!

As the house progressed, another revision of priorities was forced upon my father. What to do about a lavatory? Annis had advised a bucket and a board. But to my father this seemed like a desecration of the temple he was just completing. There is something sacred about a house of your own building. You know all its strengths and weaknesses. You know every nail which missed the stud and every spike which bit deep into the scantling and would not shake loose in an earthquake. You know how well the two-by-sixes of the cellar steps are nailed to the beams supporting the floor, and you remember what a hell of an awkward job it was to drive in those four-inch spikes with no room to swing the hammer. You remember, also, the tiresome detail of getting the steps evenly spaced and level. Nothing is more dangerous than an uneven step in the darkness; so, knock the beading off the six-inch shiplap before fitting it to the ledge, to preclude accidents from slipping or angling of the step. Then secure a hinged trapdoor with a ring in it, cut from the floor immediately above the cellar steps: all solid and heavy, but carefully constructed — the nail-heads counter-sunk, lest they catch the feet, the points hammered down flat, to protect the head of anyone coming up from the cellar with his hands full of potatoes or a basket of eggs; no jutting nails or hooks, angles or corbels into which one could stumble in the dark if the candle flickers out. That is the house, built by your own hands, with less precision perhaps than a good carpenter would provide, with joints aligned more by guess than by mitre-board or spirit level, but no less firm and strong on that account.

The home-built house is a shrine, the temple of its builder's integrity, a shadow from the heat and a haven from the storm. Emphatically, no sanitary bucket should profane this sanctuary. The options were reduced to the great outdoors or an outhouse.

In Britain there is a prejudice against relieving yourself in the great outdoors. This insular taboo has even found its niche in English common law, where a distinction is made between indecent exposure and obedience to the demands of nature, when a nice regard for the amenities is observed by seeking the screen, however illusory, of a wagon wheel. On the European continent, however, in those parts where Latin hedonism has not yet been routed by *confort anglais* and *le water*, it is customary to enhance the simple physical pleasure of defecation by the spiritual and aesthetic satisfaction offered by contemplation of mountains, woodlands, or the seashore. Wordsworth might have been transported by this evidence of the appreciation of natural beauties had he not been inhibited by insular prudery. If he had visited the Sorrento Peninsula and picked his way carefully over the steps leading down the lovely mountainside to the sea he could not have failed to be impressed by the abundant evidence of this combination of physical and spiritual catharsis.

The prairie is less attractive. In winter the cold makes outdoor relief an overrated pastime for all but youthful chionographers, etching their initials in the snow with urine. In summer mosquitoes interrupt contemplation. There is also the problem of cleanliness. Rejecting the manual improvisation adopted by the Arab world, the Westerner, before relieving himself on the prairie, looks around for a soft handful of vegetation. Grass is not favoured, owing to the risk of introducing a hay-needle; the ideal material is the soft grey clump — loosely called sage, but botanically Artemisia — wormwood. Wormwood is a great little tissue that will get into places ordinary tissues never could, skinny, mini-places where anything else is too much, wide-open places where anything less is ho-hum. A non-abrasive handful should be within reach. The terrain must be carefully surveyed, free of cactus as well as hay-needles (fortunately, the two rarely grow together); and it should offer a firm, level toe-hold to brace against the everlasting wind. The sky should be scanned for indications of approaching storms. Gusty winds, rain, and hail are deterrents.

Rehearsing all these factors, my father decided against the outdoors. Since he had already vetoed the indoor bucket, this left no alternative but the outhouse. But this would mean shovelling out another pit. My father was sick to death of fighting glacial till and had no heart for another round. However reluctantly, he compromised on the stable; it had to be cleaned out anyway. Yes, the stable would do, but first it had to be built; so the stable headed the list for attention.

The first stable was a temporary, makeshift affair, a shed roofed with page-wire on which my father planned to blow flax-straw from his first threshing. Heavy rain would seep in, but the animals would have protection from the winter winds and snow. A drop-leaf immediately over the manger would permit hay and oat-bundles to be forked in from the ricks outside. It would do. Also it insured that the draught animals would be there when needed, fed and rested. There would be pegs to hang the harness on, an important aid to speedy hitching up, one more tactical gain in the everlasting fight for time.

Chapter Nine

Few city-dwellers realize how closely a husbandman — to use the expressive antique term — must husband — manage thriftily — his time. The year goes by in a kaleidoscope of seeding, summer-fallow (to keep down the weeds for next year's seed-bed), reaping, threshing, and moving the grain to town. These must be carried out precisely, but cannot be scheduled too closely, since they depend on the weather. With all the advances in the reporting and interpretation of weather data, there is still no reliable seasonal forecast that enables the farmer to decide in springtime whether it will be a dry season, in which case he might sow oats on the verges of his big slough, or so wet that the crop will be drowned. One reason for this is that city-dwellers really don't care what happens to the farmers. Over-represented in the legislatures, city-dwellers begrudge funds for meteorological research. In my father's day there was a theory that weather cycles might follow a sunspot pattern. Scientists scoffed, and waited fifty years before beginning a computerized study of a possible relationship between sunspots and weather.

The farmer must plan and work by guess and by God, the least rewarding combination conceivable. He must back up his guess by relentless observance of a time-table which commonly calls for twelve hours a day in the field: six o'clock in the morning until noon; an hour off for food and to feed the horses; then one o'clock to seven, by which time the dew has settled heavily enough to interfere with many operations. To be in the field ready to start work by six o'clock, the farmer must be up by four-thirty at the latest. He has to round up the horses, if they have been left out overnight; feed and harness them; milk the cows; carry a bucket of water up to the house; light a fire; make himself a cup of tea or coffee and stir up the porridge; fry an egg; throw a couple of pieces of bread on the stove to toast; either separate the milk or put it down in the cellar for the cream to rise; then get the team out, water them — horses will take two or three buckets each in the morning — and walk them to the implement, which may be half a mile away. Hitching up can take ten minutes if the horses are restive. Getting started at six is as harassing a race as Dagwood Bumstead catching the 8.15 commuter special, but unless the wheels begin to turn early there is no hope of putting in a twelve-hour day, and without that there is no chance whatever of maintaining the seasonal schedule on which the livelihood of the farm depends.

These considerations were implied in my father's decision to put together a stable and use it, temporarily, as a convenience. He may not have spelled it out in detail, but he was always aware of the heavy pressure of the seasons, as of old the pressure of credit and rent collectors; so that he seemed to have exchanged one master for another, King Log for King Stork. The demands of time and money created a variety of difficult choices, on which selections had to be made without adequate data.

For instance, what should be done about heating in winter? There was no open fireplace, since that would have involved bricks and brick-laying. The choice there lay between an inexpensive flax-burner, which would consume fuel produced on the farm, and a wood or coal stove. My father opted against a costly kitchen stove with oven and water-heater for an inexpensive flax-burner and a two-burner oil-stove. He was not enough of a cook to have made full use of a kitchen range, even had there been time; moreover, it would have been expensive in fuel, since either wood or coal would have had to be imported from British Columbia, and freight was costly; he could not have spent his days in summer collecting "prairie coal" and still work the farm, and none was available in winter.

A flax-burner was the logical choice. This was an iron barrel with a removable lid and a chimney pipe to draw off the smoke. It stood on brackets. The procedure was to ram it full of flax-straw, put a match to it through a hole in the lid, and wait. The barrel soon glowed red-hot. A drawback was that the charge did not last long; however, the lid could not be removed to refill until it was cold enough to handle, by which time the room was cold too. The burner then had to be rolled outside into the snow, the ashes carefully dumped, and more straw rammed into the barrel, without too much snow going along with it. The burner was then rolled inside, set up on its brackets again, and re-lit. It was a miserable expedient, but it saved dollars and removed some waste. It was believed that fumes leaking from the burner impregnated overalls and sheepskin coats, giving the farmer who burned flax a characteristic smoky aroma. I never noticed it, but then the flax-burner had been removed by my time, and the aroma, if any, had dissipated. When I arrived, the remaining flax-straw was still piled high against the walls of the house, where my father had placed it as an insulator. I never regretted that I had not been able to recapture the romantic aroma of pioneering from a flax-burner. Winter on the prairies was rugged enough without added tests of endurance, and we had more than enough of flax-seed in the house, without having to wrestle with the straw.

Rather than build a new granary, my father had boarded up one-quarter of the house to use as a bin and had threshed his first crop directly into this, putting the delivery pipe of the thresher in through the window to pour the rich, slippery brown seeds into the bin. He threw a mattress on top of the flax, and there he, and subsequently my brother and I, slept, with flax in our hair, our ears, and our clothing. The bin seeped, and flax got into everything — into the flour, into the tea, into shoes and socks, and into the breakfast cereals. Along with the flax went a certain amount of weed seeds; but no matter: mustard could be hot as fire, but it was harmless; so, too, were pig-weed, stinkweed, and charlock. Flax, fortunately, was not subject to ergot, which might have been a perilous condiment. Flax was too ubiquitous a guest for comfort, however.

Flax was easy to thresh into the bin, but it was a sweat to get back into the wagon when the time came to take it to town. The 1911 crop lacked even the redeeming feature of fine quality, for, along with the black grains of pig-weed, there were little white flakes of seed which had not matured. There had been an early frost that year, which hit my father's first crop of flax before the seeds had set. The pod did not rattle, it was tough to thresh, and one seed out of ten was white, which meant extra dockage and a lower grade. That was the consequence of getting the seed in too late, as a result of the crowding priorities of his first few months on the homestead.

That first crop was discouraging. Frost in late July or early August was supposed to be a rarity. The field of flax with its delicate blue flowers had looked like a strip of heaven. Each night the petals fell, each morning a new series opened until the buds had all shown themselves to the sun and the wind, and the embryos in their small round pods had received their stimulus of pollen. Frost a week earlier or a week later would have done little damage; but it came at the very moment to ensure maximum destruction, as if the malevolent demon which had the prairies in his power was enjoying a malicious practical joke. While disappointed, my father was not taken altogether by surprise. The critical period occurred just at the full of the moon, which every farmer knows to be a time when frost is likely.

Scientists scoff at this folklore wisdom, just as they scoffed at the idea of any association between weather and sunspots, or between the northern lights and blizzards, or (until they discovered the alternation of generations in fungus diseases) between stem-rust of wheat and barberry bushes. As soon as they discovered the strange phenomenon of alternation of generations, in which the offspring seem to be utterly different from the parent, there was a great flurry to root out barberry bushes from the neighbourhood of wheat fields, and much time and energy was wasted on this scientific chore until it was discovered that rust developed in the complete absence of barberry, if other conditions were favourable. The scientists then second-guessed and came up with the notion that black rust of wheat could be disseminated by red rust spores, wind-blown from Texas. Nothing could be done about that, since Texas could not be eradicated like a barberry bush, which more than one western farmer in those days thought was a pity. Just as well nothing could be done about it, perhaps, for it is by no means sure that Texas is the villain, and this again illustrates the unfortunate tendency of many scientists, particularly in the realm of farming, to forget that their revered "scientific truths" are no more than the latest guess, good only until overthrown by new facts or a more plausible guess. Others are not so scrupulous, and popular credulity gives the designation "scientific" undue weight over the wisdom distilled by generations of farm prag- matists. The prairies were ill-served by bureaucratic scientists and not-disinterested railroaders who reversed the rule-of-thumb verdict of Palliser that the treeless plains of the "Palliser Triangle", which he first mapped, were unsuitable for grain-growing. They were, said Palliser, an extension of the "Great American Desert". To give the bureaucrats their due, the pressures were heavy, from the landless who wanted free land, the railroads who wanted immigrants and their business, the politicians who wanted their votes, and the Amer- icans who were hoping to grab the prairies of Assiniboia and Sask- atchewan as they had grabbed Oregon sixty years earlier.

In their own behalf the bureaucrats could point to the annual rainfall figures, which on a ten-year average showed ample moisture for grains in the south-west.

My father knew nothing of the pressures which led to the opening of the south-west to homesteading. When he inquired about rainfall figures, he was assured that the statistics recorded ample precipita- tion. What neither he nor the bureaucrats realized was that what counted was not how much fell, but when it fell. Four inches of rain in June would mean an abundant crop; four inches in September could ruin it. Much rain in early spring would ensure a supply of moisture in the subsoil, but might so delay seeding as to risk the crop's being hit at a critical point by early frost.

At this point the scientists once more came into the picture by promising new strains of wheat which would mature early enough to miss all but abnormally early frosts. Ninety-day wheat — ripening three months after seeding — would be the new prairie wonder, and "Marquis" was the standard-bearer of the hosts who marched so gallantly to push the frontiers of food north and west, but who would pay the pioneers' tribute of hardship and casualties before the rudiments of self-preservation had been learned.

The plant-breeders fulfilled their promise. They produced that beautiful Marquis wheat with its sturdy stem, a high-yield, high- protein early-ripening wheat which for a time seemed to justify the opening of the Palliser Triangle to settlement. But Marquis proved susceptible to rust, and after the magnificent crop of 1915, the yield of 1916 was heavily cut by this parasitic fungus. In an unbelievably short time Dr. Thompson and his plant-breeders of the University of

Saskatchewan produced a new strain more resistant to rust; but the fungus developed variants faster than the breeders could cope with them, and successive generations of rust-resistant varieties appeared and disappeared, until a fresh opponent came on the scene, the saw-fly, a specialized insect which laid an egg on the growing wheat stem. Its larva bored down to within an inch or so of the ground, when it ate through its host, which fell to earth. The ingenious breeders developed a wheat with a nearly solid stem which defied the saw-fly larva's effort to turn it into a summer home.

Another parasitic fungus, smut, was easier to deal with: the seed wheat was simply sprinkled with a solution of blue-stone — copper sulphate — before going into the seeder. That took care of smut, but it added to production costs the blue-stone and the labour, although the price of a farmer's own work is rarely given an adequate cost-accounting. It was, however, heavy work, shovelling wheat in a close granary, and then splashing on the solution and throwing the heavy, soaked grain into the wagon again for a further transfer to the seeder. Although it was sweaty work, it had to be done, for a very small infestation of "stinking smut" made a load of wheat unacceptable to the miller since it would taint a full batch of flour, or so the elevator buyers insisted. The ease with which smut could be controlled removed the incentive to scientists to produce a smut-resistant grain, although, in their creation of strains to suit prairie conditions, the scientists had provided a heartening example of co-operation, not only on a provincial level with bureaucrats, but on the international plane between American, Canadian, and European scientists. They drew on Russian Kubanka wheat for quick-ripening characteristics suitable alike for the Russian steppes or the Western prairies, and they incorporated other qualities of protein content and good milling characteristics, as required. The first seed batch of the great Marquis wheat was shipped to the United States, where it helped farmers in the Dakotas and Montana as greatly as it benefited the Canadian prairies. After that, Canadian and American scientists freely exchanged both problems and solutions. A series of new grain strains crossed the border unimpeded, in a demonstration of international good-will and co-operation that passed unnoticed in an era when international quarrels promoted by wire-copy speculation and front-page haemorrhages dominated the headlines.

Problems of cereal production had not become pressing as my

father prepared to harvest his first crop. The frost had come early, but it was followed as usual by weeks of sunny, delightful Indian summer. It was wonderful threshing weather, so my father built a hayrack and added his team to the threshing-gang which collected around E. P. Walker's outfit. Old man Walker provided the separator and power unit — a Rumley Oil-Pull fired by kerosene, built at Racine, Wisconsin. Temperamental and hard to start on cold mornings, it gave his son, Chester, a rough time. He never quite learned to dominate its idiosyncracies, and the rig lost innumerable hours and much grain in unscheduled shut-downs while Chester played with the controls.

Chester was a good fiddler and called a square-dance very well; he was in great demand at pie socials and box suppers, but he was not a born engineer. His notion of enriching the mixture for the Rumley was to put his hand over the air intake. The drone of the rig slowing down was agonizing to his threshing-gang, many of whom were anxious for the rig to get to their place before the weather broke. They eased their worries by a ballad composed in the bunkhouse and sung to the tune of "Casey Jones":

> *Come all ye farmers, come all that can,*
> *If you want to hear the story of a thresherman.*
> *E. P. Walker was the thresher's name —*
> *On a 30-60, boys, he lost his claim.*
> *Chester called Walker at half-past four,*
> *"Come on, old man, let us thresh some more."*
> *The old man cried, "Where shall it be?"*
> *"Oh, let us pull east, and thresh Minifie."*

Chorus:

> *E. P. Walker mounted to the separator,*
> *E. P. Walker, with his oil-can in his hand,*
> *E. P. Walker mounted to the separator,*
> *Took his farewell trip to the threshers' land.*

> *Walker pulled to Jones to thresh his wheat.*
> *Before he got started it was time to eat;*
> *So after dinner they went out to run*
> *But Jerry said to Walker, "She's on the bum."*

Wilford Scott took off his team,
Said it was the worst outfit he'd ever seen.
Wilford said the threshing he would miss
As long as E. P. Walker was on the threshers' list.

He yelled for grain and said it was a shame
But you couldn't thresh flax in the gol-darn rain,
He told the boys to put on their coats
For he was going out to thresh some oats.
The farmers said that he'd go broke.
Walker said, "That's no darn joke."
He rubbed his arm, said it still was sore,
As a brand-new sieve went rattling out the blower.

When Leon Jones started to thresh
We said sure as fate something would smash.
While they were there it started to rain,
They tried to thresh flax, but they tried it in vain.
Turner's wheat was still on the ground,
He feared very much Walker'd never get around,
A. W. Annis said he wouldn't take a chance,
So he went to Regina and bought an Advance.

Walker's misadventures with the Oil-Pull Rumley did much to popularize the Case steamer, which old man Cooper, four or five miles to the north, had bought. It could at a pinch be fuelled with straw, so Cooper had a straw-burning firebox installed, thinking it would be more economical to operate than burning coal at fifteen dollars a ton. This was not as economical as it seemed, however, as a man with a hayrack had to be hired to keep up a steady supply of straw while another spent his day hauling water. This, too, was a problem since fresh water had to be found, for heavily mineralized water would have clogged the boiler tubes. That meant loading up in a slough, which was easier for an empty tank to get into than for a full tank to get out of. Sometimes the tractor had to be taken from the rig to rescue its water tank. But when it was operating the old Case steamer was a reliable power source, and when it was time to move, it performed wonders, towing the heavy separator, plus a bunk-car, plus the kitchen, with the water-tank and hayrack hitched on behind. When the threshing was done, the tractor could be put into service for fall ploughing or breaking. It made nothing of dragging a gang plough of eight or ten shares, which covered a big area, turning over an acre with each trip back and forth.

If the Case thresher had a disadvantage, from the hired man's point of view, it was that it broke down too infrequently, giving the man with the hayrack no time for rest all day. This was particularly trying when threshing flax. Flax is heavy to handle. It is not bound in sheaves, like wheat or oats, but dumped in bunches by a special flax attachment on the binder. The bunches are easy enough to toss onto the hayrack, but they mat together so tightly that a forkful can be pulled loose only with some effort. This makes feeding the devouring separator a man-killing job. After twelve hours of pushing flax into the separator, a thresherman turns up at the bunk-car as soon after six as he can get his team fed, watered, unharnessed, and bedded down for the night. He hungers for incredible quantities of food. The farmer must supply this. If the food is not plentiful and toothsome, the oddest things can happen — a pitchfork slips out of a man's hand and rattles through the separator, taking sieves and fans with it as it moves through. A big stone, easy to pick up with a bunch of flax, will do just as well. The Thresherman's Ballad dealt with this phenomenon:

> *E. P. Walker said the strain was tense —*
> *Then Jerry dropped in the big monkey-wrench!*
> *Jerry said, "It's gone out the blower" —*
> *Walker said, "Don't drop any more."*
> *The carriers slipped and broke a little trip.*
> *As it went through the cylinder, rip, rip, rip!*
> *She tore and she ground — Walker yelled, "Shut her down!"*
> *But the little engineer couldn't be found.*

Feeding a threshing gang of ten or fifteen men kept the cook and her helper on the ropes. I remember Mrs. Pearson, wife of a neighbour, and her daughter, Mary, looking at me as if they could not believe their eyes as I polished off one great plateful of meat and potatoes and handed it back for seconds. They cut a huge slice of pie for me. I learned afterwards that she and Mary did it deliberately, to see if I would come back for more. I did. Then I hitched up and went out for another six hours. In retrospect, I wonder how even young, healthy bodies could stand this treatment for long. My father, who was still a bit soft, had blisters right across the palm of his hand. So, in my day, did I. He told me of an extra woe which did not afflict me: the bones and muscles of his hand ached so badly he could not get to sleep even when the last inevitable bunkhouse raconteur had closed down.

There is another hazard for the thresherman. The water at each farm varies slightly in mineral content: not much, but just enough to throw the body off balance and produce a weakening looseness, which adds to the miseries of a sleepless night, even where adequate toilet facilities are available, an unlikely occurrence when casual labour is employed. Squatting at night in a field of stubble qualifies for Dante's Purgatorio.

Little wonder that under such conditions an occasional stone popped into the separator, or that in the evening before rolling into their bunks the threshers talked revolution, and passed on the word about the I.W.W. in Walla Walla, Washington, an organization that was giving Chambers of Commerce everywhere in the States a worse case of the runs than alkaline water could produce. These bunkhouse revolutionaries had no leader, and no tradition of burning down buildings, or the R.N.W.M.P. might have had something really significant on their hands long before the bloody farce they mounted at Winnipeg in 1919. Most of the crew, however, while countenancing occasional delays, had no desire to disrupt the gang until their own grain had been threshed, a desirable goal which receded measurably every time Chester — the "little engineer" — had a losing discussion with the Rumley.

The Thresherman's Ballad provided the emotional release demanded by their sense of being put upon: overworked, underpaid, poorly housed, and exploited by the wealthy farmers whose ranks they hoped to join one day. They were not in fact as badly off as Mrs. Pearson and her daughter, who toiled in the cook-house from the beginning of harvest until Christmas for ten dollars a week, and spent most of their days peeling the small potatoes which the farmers provided rather than part with their good-sized tubers.

The round of threshing, seemingly interminable, finally came to an end. The crew scattered, to prepare their farms for the winter. My father spent the time spreading flax-straw evenly on the page-wire atop the stable, and piling it high against the walls of the house for warmth.

An alarming, even dangerous interruption was created by a prairie fire, originating with a steam threshing outfit five miles north. Evil tongues of flame licked the lowering sky, spreading along the horizon with alarming speed. My father did not hesitate. He hitched up his team to the wagon, filled a barrel with water from his new well, tossed an armful of old sacks into the wagon-box, and headed north as fast as the horses could trot. He found a dozen wagons and buggies clustered beside a slough near the fire. Wetting a couple of sacks he joined the group slapping at the flames, holding them in check while Cooper ploughed two containing furrows before starting a backfire to deny further fuel to the main blaze. By nightfall it was under control. The steamer which had started the fire pulled a gang plough through the embers.

The fire-fighters, exhausted, smoke-begrimed, with whiskers and eyebrows singed when a tongue of flame had swung up in a vicious counter-attack, hitched up their teams and headed for home. No reward was asked or offered. To have done either would have been an unforgivable insult. This was a neighbour's emergency, to which the response was automatic and instant. Good neighbourliness coincided more obviously than in some other cases with good common sense. Helping another was so patently helping oneself that nobody felt any special glow of pride in duty well done, other than the satisfaction of knowing that a common danger had been averted.

To preclude further incidents, if possible, the thresherman fitted a wire-mesh spark-screen over this engine, and my father bought a little silver perforated cap for his pipe, lest a spark inadvertently set a new blaze. It was after dark when he reached his shack, but he could not rest until he had hitched up the plough and turned over ten furrows in a figure eight around the house and the barn. His dread of fire was sharpened by the afternoon's effort. The elaborate fire-guard was designed to prevent a fire originating in either house or barn from engulfing both. This ploughed, he went back, tired though he was, to Annis's. Of all the Sintaluta group, Annis's offered the pleasantest society for my father, as well as an opportunity to justify his keep, by milking and feeding Annis's numerous cows. He kept only casual contact with other members. During the growing season there was no time in the farm day for social distractions.

Chapter Ten

The frost came early and hard in 1911. So did the snow, after a brilliant Indian summer. By December a foot of snow had fallen. Unlike snow in England it did not fall in heavy soft flakes but in hard granules, which drifted with the wind into dunes firm enough to support a horse. It sifted into and over and through the pile of flax-straw which my father had threshed close to the house, and it made refilling the flax-burner a herculean labour. After two months of alternately sweating and freezing in the house, and freezing his nose every time he had to recharge the flax-burner, my father said, "The hell with it!" He hitched his team to the bobsleigh and drove over to Annis's, a mile to the north-east, taking with him a bushel of potatoes and a frozen side of pork, which Jones had butchered earlier in the fall, my father helping.

He had a standing invitation to stay with the Annises any time the loneliness and the flax-burner got to be too much for him. He resisted as long as he could. The homestead regulations called for three years' residence on the land in order to obtain title to it, and my father was reluctant to risk his homestead's being denounced. He knew that informers made a habit of reporting what looked to be abandoned farms on the chance of picking up a desirable homestead themselves. My father also had a deep-seated unwillingness to be beholden to anyone, even so good a neighbour as Alf Annis. This reluctance strengthened a sort of inverted snobbery which went back to his Shropshire days and the determination of the yeoman farmer not to be too friendly with the squire, lest he be thought to curry favour.

Annis was far from being the classical squire, but in that neighbourhood he presented a figure of affluence which was not the less impressive for resting chiefly on credit. He had brought twenty head of cattle in with him from Sintaluta. As soon as he arrived, he and Robinson, who had learned to handle stone down east, started work on a stone stable. This was a prestigious building, the ground-floor walls of fieldstone, surmounted by a hip-roofed barn which would hold all the winter feed needed by the stock housed below. Annis was not satisfied with this; he determined to lay a hardwood floor in the loft so that it could be a community centre where real barn dances could be held. He wanted my father to stay with him over the Christmas season, and asked if he would help move two loads of flax to Morse and bring back hardwood flooring and shingles.

Performing this service took care of the risk of being beholden to Annis; the temptation to taste a little comfort and company was strong, and my father figured that the homestead regulations would be complied with in the spirit if not in the letter if he were absent in order to move the crop to town. Finally, he rather enjoyed driving a bobsleigh. It moved fast when snow conditions were right, and it called for skill and tactical planning to avoid bare patches or drifts which might upset the load. It was not just a question of endurance, which was all driving a wagon demanded.

Annis came over to help my father put his wagon-box on the bobs. One man at a pinch could do it alone, but it was a tricky job. One end had to be lifted on to the forward runners. Then the back was raised and swung around until it fitted snugly on to the rear runners. Then the second tier of the wagon had to be fitted into its sockets, and the tailgate made secure. It was all a man alone could lift, and there was always the danger that swinging the box around would strain the back; and God help the farmer who "pulled his back", as they used to say before "slipped disc" became the fashionable term. He could not ride a plough or lift a forkful of hay with a "pulled back", and there was no recourse but a hired man, if he could find one. As a palliative many sufferers wore a broad belt of Turkey-red flannel, which gave some support to the back and more, no doubt, to the mind, but it did not permit heavy work, and all farm activity is heavy work.

My father dreaded something like that happening, and did his best to avoid moving the wagon-box alone. But farm operations could not wait upon the availability of a neighbour. Some things, consequently, had to be done alone or left undone.

The wagon-box adjusted, the two men went back to Annis's and loaded up two wagon-boxes with flax, each using only hand scoops. A bushel of flax weighs fifty-six pounds. Loading up each wagon therefore meant moving more than a ton of flax from the floor of the granary four feet up to the height of the box. Annis had a strong back, but he was glad of my father's help and insisted on paying my father's expenses for the trip. These were a significant item in the cost of grain.

The first day's driving brought them twenty-two miles to the Halfway House on Wiwa Creek. Getting a load down the steep banks and up the other side demanded skill of the order of a Roman charioteer. My father went first, putting the horses at a gallop, then waited on the crest until Annis's team came sweating and gasping to the top of the north bank, safe but exhausted, for they were much lighter than my father's team — little more than broncos. They stayed the night at the Halfway House, since the wind was picking up and moving the snow. Supper was fifty cents each. Their bed was one dollar each, with breakfast thrown in. Each team of horses overnight cost sixty cents.

They started up early and reached Morse before sundown. The elevator man had kept his approach covered with snow, so there was no difficulty getting the bobsleighs onto the weighing platform. They put up the horses at the livery barn; again sixty cents a team. The two of them bunked in the loft among the hay after giving the liveryman positive assurances that there would be no smoking. The night's lodging was included in the price for the team. They had supper at the Chink's, 40 cents, and breakfasted there next morning for 50 cents. Then back to the Halfway House. Annis would have driven right through, but my father was reluctant to overtax his horses; the heavy draught animals could not make the same time as broncs on the trail. That meant 50 cents for supper, $1.00 for bed and breakfast; 60 cents for the team. Total cost of moving two loads or 100 bushels of flax to town and return trip: for my father and for Annis, $5.70 each, plus four days' time. The two loads brought $280.

My father took the occasion to buy flooring for Annis, a saw, and two kegs of nails. Annis had big ideas, and could command enough credit to implement them. Not content with having the finest barn in the neighbourhood, he also wanted the biggest house. So Johnny Borth came over from his place on section 4, two miles west, to help. Johnny was a good carpenter who had built himself a very stylish house with many curlicues of carpenter's Gothic. The gable could just be seen over Jones's hills from our place. Mrs. Borth went with the house; she affected a high-necked black lace blouse, pince-nez, and a small gold watch pinned on the left above her bosom. She came over with Johnny to offer a few feminine suggestions about the lay-out of the house and to do some cooking for the builders. It was helpful at the time, but ultimately unhappy, for a romance developed and a few years later Annis eloped with her, and I lost track of them.

However, there was no thunder on the left at that time. The house ran up quickly, and Annis determined that it should also have that ultimate down-east luxury, plaster on the walls. It was bold, reckless even. There was no convenient plaster board in those days. Neither man knew anything about plaster or plastering, and after a day of futile daubing they gave up. The walls were all lath and one room had plaster, but the rest remained bare lath, a monument to the prairie conviction that if you wanted to do a thing badly enough, you could do it, and learn in the doing.

Obviously you could not learn plastering while you worked, and from watching Annis and Robinson complete the stone-work of the ground floor of the barn, my father realized sadly that he could not learn stone-masonry on the job, either. Nor, he discovered, were sand and lime all that was needed to make good mortar. Without a sack of cement his barrel of lime would be wasted. Earlier he had dug the foundation of his barn and laid the first few blocks of rough-hewn fieldstone, mostly pink and blue granite, before he reluctantly acknowledged that the rest would have to wait. Annis and Robinson were too pressed themselves to do much. Once threshing was finished they had come over and laid the first course; but it was then apparent that more cement would be needed, and that there was no good clean sand available in the neighbourhood. The first course remained for years a sad witness to the inadequacy of faith for trimming stone-work. Faith may move mountains, though this has yet to be shown, but it does not build stone barns. In after years I used to point this out to wandering circuit preachers when they stopped off for supper. They replied with the ready patter of a snake-oil vendor but they raised no barn.

When the house was finished, Annis decided on a warming dance. Among the treasures he had brought from Sintaluta was an organ, one of those foot-pedal types which keep the organist sweating to supply air. There was no need to call it into service for the dance, however, for Chester Walker promised to serve both as orchestra and "caller". He had a fiddle and a good repertory of square-dance routines. Mrs. Annis, rubicund and plump, presided over the kitchen and turned out masses of pies — apple pie, pumpkin pie with whipped cream and meringue, raisin pie, mince-pie. Little George and Myrtle were set to work in the stable to turn the handle of the ice-cream freezer, banked with ice and salt.

Annis had an abundance of cream and butter for the dance. Two quarts of fresh cream with eggs and a dash of vanilla flavouring produced half a gallon of ice-cream. The weary freezer operators dipped their fingers into it and licked the paddles clean. Annis had gone to the creek to get ice from Frank Burton, who had sawn blocks out of the frozen creek the winter before, and stored them in oat-straw in an icehouse hollowed out of the north side of a hill, and roofed over for insulation. When my father saw how effectively the ice was preserved over the summer, he determined that next year he would dig out an icehouse and pack in supplies as soon as freeze-up came. Ice would help solve the problem of preserving food without having to drench it in salt; it was a difficult problem on the prairie before the advent of the refrigerator. This was an almost miraculous relief, anticipated to some extent by the icebox, which consumed quantities of ice but kept butter, cream, eggs, milk, and meat fresh for a few days. Prior to the icebox it had been the custom to let perishables down into the cold waters of the well in a bucket. After a hard winter had put a sheath of ice over the surface the water temperature remained near freezing until well into the summer. This storage technique was adapted with minimal changes from the old springhouse of the earliest settlers on the eastern seaboard. Its effectiveness was limited. In thunderous weather it was impossible to keep milk for twenty-four hours without souring, or at least near enough to turning for it to curdle when used in cooking.

It was snowing lightly when Chester Walker turned up with his fiddle. Snow crystals whirled down like little Catherine-wheels, their six spokes connected by a fragile rim which rested intact for a few seconds on sheepskin jackets. Mrs. Borth drove in with Johnny to inspect the new house. In black lace blouse and gold watch and pince-nez she watched primly as Chester struck up "Turkey in the Straw". Faintly disapproving, she appeared to seek the contrast with Mrs. Annis, beaming, laughing, and dancing, light on her feet as most stout people are.

"Take your partner and don't be afraid," Chester chanted, "Turn to the left and a half-promenade." The square dance got under way. My father was used to the quadrille and the Lancers as they were performed sedately at the Coton farm-house in Shropshire. These were not too far removed from the square dances, which were designed to enable strange neighbours to get acquainted. He noticed that they were fulfilling their function as far as Annis and Mrs. Borth were concerned, so he jumped in and swung Mrs. Annis and Louisa around until he was breathless.

At seventeen Louisa was a strapping young woman, already displaying her mother's tendency towards buxomness, but none the less active for that. She delighted in the pedal-organ, and was able to roll out the few chords needed to get through simple hymns from the Moody and Sankey collection. She tried to relieve Chester at the orchestra, but an organ is not made for dancing, no matter how forcefully you pump it, and Chester was soon back with "Turkey in the Straw", the universal favourite.

People came from all over, on horseback, in cutters (the winter buggy), and in bobsleighs with hay on the floor to keep off the cold. A throng of Burtons came in from "the creek" — Notokeu Creek, four miles to the south, where a vigorous stock was developing a family community of its own, with a schoolhouse and a post-office, a church and a cemetery named after them. Dancers came in from the Turkey Track ranch where the Fosters were trying to fight off the influx of settlers who would fence in and break up their open range. The Goodings came in from the post-office in range 8 to the east; they had passed word of the dance to all who came to their shack for mail. Babies were laid to sleep on a buffalo-robe in a row; it was a wonder that they were ever sorted out, and my father some-times wondered aloud if they ever had been. They made no object-ion, but slept quietly all through the stamping of the square dance and the shouting of "Turkey in the Straw", and the renewed shout-ing when the pony of rye which the boys from Moundville had brought with them began to take hold.

At last Chester tired and laid down his bow, and Louisa gave up pedalling and brought around the blue enamelled pot of coffee and a tray of pies and a cold turkey that the Burtons had brought. By the time that had been disposed of, the wind arose; the snow was begin-ning to move, and the party broke up. It was day-light. No successful party ever ended before dawn, but the snow brought this one to an end. Driving fifteen miles to a dance was one thing, but driving through a blizzard was another matter.

When the last rig had pulled out my father went down to the barn in the grey light of dawn to check that all was well. With the amount of rye brought in by the Moundville boys you could not be too careful; he was always haunted by dread of fire — people could be real careless with their cigarette ends after a snort or two. He looked around the capacious stalls: nothing wrong. Nothing? There was *nothing there*! Nothing! His team had gone. Sleek Mike and old Meg, the part-Clydesdales he had tied up in the warm centre stall, had vanished. Unable to believe what he saw, or did not see, he called Annis, but the wind blew his voice into the snowdrift silting up on the east side of the barn. He ran to the house for comfort. It would be a cruel, ruinous loss. He could not farm without his team.

Together he and Annis examined the stall. The harness was there on the peg where my father had hung it. The horse-blankets were there, slung over the dividing wall of the stall. The head-ropes and halters had disappeared. That meant they were not loosed by mis-take or by some stupid drunk, Annis pointed out, or the snaps would have been undone; he thought the horses had nibbled the head-ropes loose, undone the knot with their teeth, and headed out without being noticed in the confusion of hitching up. My father did not like the imputation that he had not tied up his horses securely, but he agreed with this explanation. Annis pointed out that this was per-haps fortunate. If they had worked their halters loose, it would have been much more difficult to catch them. Once they were located it should not be too tricky to grab the rope trailing from their halters.

Where do we look? my father wondered. Annis thought they would drift before the wind which was blowing from the north-west; this meant they would be somewhere near the creek — this side of it, because prairie horses do not like pushing through bushes, and the creek banks were steep and covered with scrub willow, briars, and aspen. Prairie horses are afraid of this scrub which they are not used to; coyotes might be lurking in the thickets.

Annis insisted on hitching up his fast team to the cutter and driving down in search of my father's horses. My father was reluctant to trespass on his time and generosity; but the alternative of trudging five miles in search of the horses and then having to catch them if he did find them had little appeal. So he threw half a sack of oats into the cutter and jumped in behind Annis. They wrapped a buffalo robe closely about their legs. Even so, the cold bit in. They were travelling with the wind, but it swirled the snow around their heads, eddying it against their faces, where it thawed and froze again, fringing their eyebrows and my father's moustache with icicles. They were almost on top of the two horses before they saw them, grey through the drifting snow. Then began the most exasperating part of the chase. The horses played a tantalizing game. They waited until my father was almost in reaching distance of their halter-ropes, then jerked their heads and flounced away into the snow. Finally old Mike allowed himself to be cozened into putting his nose into the feed bag. Father hitched him to the cutter, and soon afterwards Meg allowed herself to be caught and tied alongside her team-mate. Then they all set off back into the wind and the snow, gritty as a sand-blast.

When they got back, chilled to the bone, feet, noses, and ears frozen, Mrs. Annis had a hot meal ready for them: Irish stew with plenty of their own potatoes, pumpkin pie with a top-knot of whipped cream, and the blue enamelled pot full of coffee. Both men sat with their feet in a basin of cold water, to take the frost out of their toes; then they treated their hands and rubbed snow on their ears and noses. As soon as they had eaten, my father set to work fitting snaps onto new ropes for the horses. He did not want another such chase, with a good chance of losing his team. Louisa helped pass the time by banging out "Shall We Gather at the River?" on the organ. It seemed apt enough: "But no horses!" my father insisted. "Nor oxen.

Nor snow." A Happy Hunting Ground full of horses and buffalo might be fine for Indians, but a white man's idea of heaven turned towards a reliable tractor and no wind or snow; a Ford and fair weather.

My father could be very companionable with people he liked. He got on well with the Annises and they pressed him to spend the winter with them rather than go back to batching it with the flax-burner. This was an attractive prospect, but the oxen had to be watered daily, so he went back and resumed the routine for the rest of the winter. It would not be too long before his family joined him, and he could stick it out for another three or four months. His account of the search for the horses, when it reached me near Lich-field, made the prairie sound so dreadful that my mother began to doubt the wisdom of going to live in such a god-forsaken place.

Chapter Eleven

My mother's concept of life in Canada had been keyed to a ranch in some area vaguely thought of as "the west"; had it been more clearly defined it would probably have been the foothills of Alberta or the Cariboo region of British Columbia. My own fancy had focussed on the Cariboo, possibly because we knew that my father had passed part of a winter in a lumber camp somewhere in British Columbia (he could never remember where, except that it was on the west side of some mountain range, where the snow was six feet deep). I was frightened at the time at the thought of his being out in that fero- cious wilderness, since I had read in my natural history book terrify- ing stories of cougars, lynxes, and other dangerous cats infesting the woods of the western slope. Consequently I was relieved when my father returned safely to the prairies, and I was excited at the thought that we should be going out there ourselves. My enthusiasm was stimulated by the circumstance that in anticipation of my de- parture I had slacked off work at school.

As I have mentioned, the sailing of the liner *Lake Manitoba* had been delayed while extra lifeboats were installed because of the sinking of the *Titanic*. The problem arose of how to let my father know of this delay. Letters would be too slow. They took an average of three weeks to reach Gooding, via Morse, Sask., from Lichfield, Staffs, England. The cable companies said they had never heard of Gooding, and doubted whether such a place existed. So far as telegraph facilities were concerned they were right. Gooding Post Office was Pete Gooding's shack. He brought the mail out from Morse by buggy, and whoever thought there might be some came calling to see. We could not know all this, of course, but it was obvious that there would be a strong chance that my father might not be there to meet us if we turned up ten days late. The C.P.R. took little or no interest in our problem. We had reserved a cabin and paid our fare, so it behooved us to be at the pier at Liverpool on the revised sailing date or miss our passage. They too knew nothing of Gooding and cared less. No such town was listed in any C.P.R. time-table. Morse, however, was there, and the train would stop if we told the conductor in time. If not, we could get off at Herbert, which was only ten miles to the west. These uncertainties increased my mother's reluctance to step off into the unknown, but my brother and I kept up the pressure, and ultimately the day came when we both tumbled into the Liverpool boat-train at Lichfield Trent Valley, wearing the dark grey cloth overcoats with black velvet collars lovingly provided by Uncle Ted. We each sported our school cap and laced black ankle shoes. My brother was three years younger and had not yet graduated to the long trousers which I enjoyed. Otherwise we looked like penny-ha'penny, the same design in different sizes. We were both immune to sea or train sickness, and by the time the west-bound transcontinental reached Morse, we both felt like seasoned globetrotters.

This was the background of my brief reply to my father's tentative approach to common ground: "No, I took gym." I have never ceased to regret the English tradition of reticence which virtually forbade communication between parent and child. It made a fetish of that stupidest of conventions, "the strong silent man". My father made several attempts to meet me on my own or common ground, always to be met with a curt withdrawal into monosyllabic reticence; I was a grown man before I overcame this. So we marched in silence along the wooden sidewalk of Morse, while my mother and little brother Dick followed. A man brought up the rear with a hand-truck piled high with a black wicker trunk, a rectangular armoured trunk, two portmanteaus, and a roll containing a steamer blanket, a plaid blanket, a red eider-down, an umbrella, two walking-sticks, an air-rifle, a cricket-bat belonging to my father, and a bow and arrows. That was our equipment for settling the prairie. The air-gun and bow and arrows were of course for defence against whatever might threaten.

My pride and joy was the bow, a junior weight presented by my Uncle Tom Vaughton, who ran a successful manufacturing jeweller's business in Birmingham, and was always good for a half-sovereign tip to a deserving nephew on occasions like Christmas and Birthday. That little gold coin was a godsend; it could be passed from fingers to palm unobserved by any but the recipient, and had none of the ostentation of the ten-bob note, neatly folded but trying to pass itself off as a quid, a charity for all to behold. The air-rifle had been a useful source of income. The farmers near Lichfield paid 1½ d. a head for sparrows, the English house sparrows which raised such hob with seedling peas and blocked gutters with their nests. I got to be a crack shot with my single-pellet gun; one day I collected eight gory heads in a small tobacco bag and took them down to Hellaby's farm. I had in mind a fountain pen for which I yearned; great was my disappointment when Mr. Hellaby told me that the bounty had been discontinued. Taking pity on my crest-fallen appearance he dug down and fished up "a couple of tanners" as he called them. I pocketed the money thankfully, and blew it at once on the pen; from that time on my fingers were never free of ink stains, until I lost the thing scrambling through a copse in search of a hazel branch from which to fashion a bow.

This, then, was the little group which descended on the Elkhorn Hotel early in May, 1912, asking optimistically for a room and bath. The proprietor assured us that he had a room and he had a bath; the two were separated by the length of a corridor, but they were on the same floor, the second floor, which he pointed out was the best, nice and private, but not as hot in the afternoon sun as the top floor, which got real hot, he said, in summer. My father hastily interrupted to say that we should not be there all summer. but would leave in the morning if the trails were dry enough. If it rained in the night we would leave the following day for sure. The proprietor said that was all right, and he would charge off my father's work against the bill as long as we wanted to stay.

It then turned out that my father had been expecting us two weeks earlier, no word of the postponement of sailing having reached him. When he learned at the depot what had happened, he got a job looking after the heating plant, for the Elkhorn boasted hot-water heating as well as baths. The job kept father while he waited for our arrival, which was fortunate, for he could not have afforded the expense; it was bad enough to have lost all that time just when he should have been out on the land putting in the crop. Our non-appearance at this point was an unfortunate set-back to his prospects for a good crop after last year's frosted harvest.

The Elkhorn was a long three-storey frame building, painted white with the usual green trim. It was a couple of blocks from the depot, which was not far enough to give full relief from the clatter and clang of railroading. Our windows looked south over the yards and out across a large slough crowded with ducks, gulls, and terns. This water was melt from the winter snows, my father explained. The slough was so large that we would have to detour around it to the west, which would add another six miles to our trip. We looked longingly at the two ribbons of green which threaded south up the long tawny slope of the prairie on the far side of the slough; that was the Morse Trail, he said, and we would be following it to our homestead tomorrow as early as we could get started.

We went to bed early, but passed a restless night. We were not accustomed to the wailing sirens of the big C.P.R. engines, and their long-drawn-out notes kept us wakeful for hours. We were up early and ready to pull out by eight o'clock.

Chapter Twelve

Our vehicle was no covered wagon, with canvas top strung over hoops, as depicted in western movies. It was an ordinary farm wagon, painted green. It boasted a sturdy pink running-gear, which could be used for hauling lumber, and a tough wagon-box of hickory-wood, to which two additional tiers could be fitted to hold seventy-five bushels of flax. The basic box survived years of rough trails and exposure to wind, snow, sun, and rain until it was retired to serve another term as a coal-bin. For the trip home from Morse my father brought extra horse-blankets to protect the load in case of thunder-showers. A spring seat was fixed on the wagon-box and on it was perched my mother in her neat brown tweed dress and jacket, with a brown felt hat turned up at the side, secured by a grouse-foot pin with a silver mount. My brother and I arranged ourselves as best we could over the trunks and supplies my father had bought, but it was not a very comfortable ride. We averaged three miles an hour, so it was after three o'clock by the time we pulled into the Halfway House, weary and bruised from the alternations of walking, scrambling back on the wagon, and riding. From time to time we had varied the monotony of the wagon floor by climbing onto the seat, which at least had springs, but they absorbed few of the potholes, stones, and ruts of the prairie trail.

My father stood up to drive. I was fascinated by the shouted commands "Gee" and "Haw", which I had not heard before and which meant swinging to the right or left, and a more general command which I identified as "Uriah!", but which seemed to be a short form of "Where are you?", an incitement to push into the collar and get moving. Old Mike was a willing horse, always up to his side of the whippletree, but Meg was a narrow-chested, disillusioned barren female who let her willing partner do most of the work, since he seemed to like it. Occasionally she bit him to emphasize her point. My father evened this up for Mike by adjusting the whippletree slightly, so that he had the lighter load; but they were not an easy team to drive. That was one reason my father was ready to stop so early in the afternoon.

Another was the threatening sky. In the south-west a vast blue-black cloud had hidden the sun. From time to time this purple screen was rent by a jagged golden flash, followed by a theatrical roll of thunder. For years I had been terrified of thunderstorms. Before my father went to Canada, the first mutter of thunder was enough to send me pattering downstairs in my nightgown to curl up in the wicker chair while my father dealt with his supper of bread and cheese and a bottle of Worthington's India Pale Ale. All the assurances that thunder could not harm me and that bed was the safest refuge from lightning left my terror intact. I was even chilled when I read about a growl of thunder in some book. But this first evening on the prairie I found to my astonishment that I was no longer afraid; indeed, the display was so magnificent that I watched eagerly for the next flash to rip through the purple drape and measured the time for the thunderclap to reach me, to calculate the distance and the storm's speed. My father, doubtless remembering my earlier fears, warmly approved this development, but urged me to come inside. This storm was no English Midlands fireworks, he said, but a wild struggle between earth and sky, which should be avoided whenever possible. He took time to rope two horse-blankets over the wagon, and check its wheels, before coming inside to supper. He secured the horses carefully, for they were made restive by the oncoming storm. Watching through the west window of the attic, I was amazed to see the grasses lying flat against the earth. Then the wind struck the house like an Atlantic roller. It shook and trembled, but held fast. "Hope our house stood up to it," my father said, adding that he had purposely limited it to one storey, to give less advantage to the wind. He fretted, too, about the stable and Annis's barn, if that storm had gone through our district. My first night on the prairies was filled with these forebodings.

The attic was hot and airless. As soon as the storm was over, I pulled out a window, and the room filled with cool air, fragrant with strange perfumes of wolf-willow from the banks of the creek and of the yellow prairie bean, just rampaging into flower in every buffalo-wallow. The yellow bean to some extent eased my disappointment at not seeing the banks of purple prairie crocus which my father had described as in full bloom on his way in. By this time the blossoms had been succeeded by grey, hairy tufts of seeds. Sleep was no easier even when the room cooled off, for a swarm of mosquitoes took advantage of the open window and the air resonated with their reedy notes.

We were up early in the morning, relieved to find that little damage had been done by the storm either to the groceries or to the trunks. The horse-blankets had deflected most of the water. On this optimistic note we set out. The rain had swollen the creek, but the consensus was that the water would not be above the axle. With that assurance my father put Mike and Meg to a trot and we splashed and bumped through. The bottom appeared to be all boulders, and I feared for the axles; but they held, and momentum carried us through and up the far bank in a terrifying rush. After four hours we stopped for sandwiches and a thermos of tea my mother had brought. Thirty-six miles south of Morse, my father warned that he was going to leave the road, such as it was, and head south-west across the prairie for the next six miles. We soon picked up a faint trail which wandered about, dodging hills and skirting sloughs, but maintaining a generally south-westerly direction. Those were the longest six miles I ever travelled. I walked most of them.

My English boots were not ideal for a long hike and I was limping by the time a peaked roof peeped over the next rise. My father warned me that this was not our house. He pulled up to let me climb aboard. As we skirted the rise we saw a two-storey house, white with green trim, and a big red barn topping a stone stable. In between the two, a dozen cows milled about, followed by a stout woman with a box in one hand and a pail in the other, who was trying to milk whichever cow stood still long enough.

"That's Mrs. Annis," my father explained. "And that black poll-Angus she's milking is our cow. Hey, there, bossie!" he shouted as we drove up. Acknowledging the greeting our cow switched her tail in Mrs. Annis's face and kicked the bucket over.

"She's a mean, miserable cow," Mrs. Annis said to my father, "and she held her milk back. Anyway it's on the ground now, and I guess there goes your cream for supper. Better let me give you some." Then, as she realized who we were, Mrs. Annis roared a welcome and asked my mother how she liked the West.

"Not very much," my mother said truthfully; it had been a poor introduction.

"After you've milked twenty cows twice a day, you'll love it!" Mrs. Annis replied. Then, repenting her flippancy, she handed half a bucket of milk up to my father and urged us all to stay for supper. We declined. We were all desperately anxious to end this interminable journey; I wanted to see our home and get everything unloaded and unpacked. I was tired of wandering about like an Arab. So my father put a halter over the cow, tied her to the wagon, and started up. She was stubborn and unwilling to follow, so I was deputed to follow her on foot and stimulate her with a switch. She responded grudgingly, and the last half-mile was a martyrdom for us both — self-inflicted in her case.

As I inquired for the hundredth time, "When shall we get there, Daddy?" we topped a small rise. "There she is," said my father with a note of pride in his voice. "Built her myself, every nail and board." He said it reverently.

On a knoll a quarter of a mile away stood a small unpainted brown shed. It was exciting, but at the same time disappointing after Annis's splendid establishment. A little to the left on another knoll was a smaller shed, the stable, snuggling against two ricks of hay. We skirted the pasture, fenced in with two strands of barbed wire. As we drew even with the well we noticed smoke coming from the tin chimney pot of the first shed. We were all puzzled, but the answer was not long delayed. As we pulled up the knoll and halted, a man flung open the door and dashed out, roaring at us.

"Thought you were never coming," he said. "What happened to you?" Those were his words but they were spoken in such a strange accent that I could not understand them. I asked my father and he told me brusquely, "Pipe down." Then he presented the strange man: "Jim Pearson from over there to the north-west, on Ten." Pearson wore the standard western uniform, overalls with a battered weather-beaten hat that shadowed his sun-scorched face and tawny moustache. As he spoke he twisted his neck as if to prevent the words tumbling out helter-skelter, his Adam's apple jumping up and down like a chopper. I still could not make out what he was saying, for he spoke in a broad Yorkshire accent, in which all the vowels were diphthongs. They made even familiar words hard to identify, and he used many unfamilar terms in which the Yorkshire speech is rich. The words may have been strange, but the friendly enthusiasm was unmistakable. He told us that he had come over every day for the past week in order to have a fire going and a hot meal for our arrival.

He helped my mother and Dick down and took them in. In my eagerness to get inside I grabbed the blanket-roll. It was caught under the ploughshares my father had taken to town to be sharpened and when I forced it free I broke off the head of my precious bow. Disaster! Brought so far, so carefully, only to be ruined just when it could be used. I put as brave a face as possible on it, but it was not an auspicious arrival, and I threw the rest of the blanket-roll on to the ground. The air-rifle I guarded carefully. Mr. Pearson introduced me to local wildlife: "Gophers," he said, making it sound like goa-phers! "You go after them for one cent a tail." There was one, he disclosed, living in a hole under the house, right by the limestone slab which served as a doorstep. He produced a length of string and a shoe-lace from his overall pocket, and with vast twitchings of his moustache and gyrations of his Adam's apple, showed me how to make a noose and set it at the mouth of the gopher's hole. It was my introduction to western hunting. I sat patiently, but no gopher appeared.

Inside, the room was dark, filled with the aroma of eggs frying in butter. There was a shiny, glittering cooking stove with a couple of saucepans, a kettle, and a frying pan; a very tall table of unpainted pine, two yellow kitchen chairs, and an empty orange-crate. Nailed to a two-by-four was a calendar for the year before from the Northwest Life Insurance Company, featuring a flight of ducks taking off from a slough. The floor was rough boards with wide cracks, innocent of paint or varnish, but showing marks of mud and manure through a dark stain. Pearson and my father hauled the two port-manteaus inside.

There was no bag, basket, or container in the shack for my father's dirty clothes, all of which had simply been thrown in a corner — all, that is, but some woollen underwear, which I found hanging on fenceposts. My father explained later that last fall, after a trip to town, he discovered that he was lousy. To ensure that the house-of-his-own-building did not become infested with vermin, he stripped to the buff, hung his underwear on fenceposts for the winter, had a quick dip in the slough, and pulled on a clean set. By springtime the frost had taken care of lice and nits; none of our visitors brought any visitors with them. Other homesteaders were not so lucky, but we were spared the misery of lice or bedbugs, for which in those days virtually the only insecticide was to burn the place down. Home-steaders three or four miles west of us nearly went crazy trying to get rid of bedbugs. We avoided visiting them as soon as the word got about, but if they had turned up needing shelter in a blizzard, we could not have turned them away, though we might have empha-sized the attractions of barn accommodations. Fortunately our hospitality was never put to this test; the only parasite we had to beware of was an occasional tick which Tim picked up, I suppose, from the cattle.

As soon as we got into the house, my mother started to move dirty clothing out of corners into four sacks, but the room still looked dim and dreary.

Pearson took the team up to the stable, brought back more eggs in his hat, and trundled the two trunks inside. That did not leave much room for dancing, he observed. One-quarter of the space was board-ed off as a bin for flax. My brother and I hustled about and collected a boxful of neat, dry horse-droppings, weathered silvery grey over the winter; with these we fed the fire, where sausages and eggs were frying. We sat down to eat. My father and mother had the chairs. Dick and I had the orange-crate. We had some trouble reaching our plates, for Father had built the table to his own measure and he was over six feet tall. So the table stood four feet high; it was uneven, and creaked and squeaked, but it stood and supported the white iron-stone crockery well enough.

Pearson poured some steaming coffee, and cut slabs of home-made bread, which he threw on to the hot stove to toast. In the middle of the meal the gopher came out to see what went on; he obligingly posed on the doorstep while he worked on an ear of grass growing just outside. Pearson drew my father's attention to charred boards where the stovepipe met the tin chimney pot. They guessed that the flax-burner must have overheated the stovepipe in one of its furious glows last winter. My father shuddered at the possibility that his shack might have gone up in flames one cold winter's night when the flax-burner was taking the wind. That evening we tacked up some tin tobacco-lids as an insulation for the boards; whether they served this purpose I often wondered, but at any rate, the roof never charred further, and we watched it with anxious eyes.

Our first prairie meal was completed with a can of peaches, which I considered a great luxury. Pearson added a gay note by reminiscences of his days with the Metropolitan Police Force in London. After some years with the Force he had gone to Australia; not finding it to his liking he had moved to Ontario, then to the prairies to secure a homestead and be his own boss, or so he thought. In all these wanderings he had never lost either the Yorkshire warm heart or the accent. I was embarrassed by my inability to understand what he was saying to me even after the second or third repetition; each repeat seemed to thicken the accent, as his rebellious Adam's apple struggled with the spate of words. He gave up in the end, rose abruptly, announced "Ah'll moock out t'bearn!" and roared off.

My brother and I nicknamed him "Old Pear-bugs", but were set straight by my father, who warned us that Jim Pearson's pride was as touchy as his heart was warm, and that he was much too good a neighbour to be mocked by silly boyish irreverence. Further, Pearson's mucking out the barn would save us a heavy chore, so we might well be considerate. His kindly determination to see to it that there was a fire and food waiting for us at the end of a long journey in a strange land touched my mother particularly. Since he did not know when we would arrive and there was no way of letting him know, he had simply turned up every day for a week, and stayed around until dark.

The first night at home was awesome. We had expected to be oppressed by silence. Instead the night air vibrated with an orchestra of thousands of frogs, their notes swelling and falling in a rhythmic diapason that enveloped earth and sky. The pasture by the house had half a dozen little sloughs, each with its quota of frogs. It was like trying to sleep in the middle of grand opera. Above the frogs' chorus was a more sinister aria, the ululating wail of coyotes enjoying the remains of a dead horse. My brother and I shivered and snuggled closer together under the blankets on a mattress thrown on top of the flax bin. We soon learned to sleep quietly, or risk immersion in the sea of flax.

Chapter Thirteen

Dick and I were awakened bright and early by my father raking the ashes out of the grate. This was an illogical impulse because horse-dung leaves practically no ash. But his first action every morning was to rattle the bars of the grate, humming as he did a little Victorian song:

> *Come little birdie, come to me;*
> *You shall be happy, gay, and free.*

There were two more lines, but my father never got around to singing them. They were the theme song for the day. I don't know what nostalgic memories it conjured up for my father, but Shropshire echoes lingered long in his spirit, and his song made me think lovingly of Lichfield.

Nostalgia soon gave place to the practical question: where was the W. C.? There was none. So what did we do about that? It seemed we went down to the stable. This put another aspect on Pearson's haste the day before to muck out the barn. My mother took a poor view of this and said firmly that it wouldn't do. Something would have to be done about it, and soon. At once. Even that wasn't soon enough for me so I trotted off to the stable. Here I found that defecation *à la nature* is not everybody's act, so to speak, particularly if indulged in in the neighbourhood of two restive horses and four anxious oxen. After this experience conventional pictures of the Nativity stable always carried an extra and intimate message for me. I did my best and trotted back with my combinations full of straw and chaff, to find my father pounding at the prairie with the post-hole spade. He was only about a foot down. It was high noon before he completed the hole. Then he set about building the "cathedral". He had trouble with the seat. Unless you have special instruments it is not easy to cut a hole with a form-fitting profile. My father cut his seat square, with two boards, and planed them down smooth. It did well enough. We heaved the cathedral vertical and secured it to a stake with hay-wire, and by mid-afternoon it was in operation. My father fortunately was already on the T. Eaton Company's mailing list, so a catalogue was available to hang on a nail handily. When Simpson's also weighed in we had encyclopaedic information on home and farm furnishings always to hand, the foundation of a liberal education.

Everything seemed to be working out well. The sun shone, the meadow lark sang on a fence post, and the flax, seeded by Annis while my father was in Morse waiting for us, was already breaking through the sod in long beaded green lines. The house, its plain boards streaked with rust from the nails, looked a little drab, to be sure, but inside, the sunshine pouring through the little window was reflected in a hundred aurioles from the lavish chrome-work of the stove.

"Isn't this lovely!" I exclaimed, and meant it. I was surprised and disturbed when my mother burst into tears, and sobbed, "No, it isn't. It's terrible." I laid an awkward hand on her shoulder, assured her that everything would be all right, and then went out to find my father; but he and my brother had gone over to Jones's to get a couple of pigs. They would not be back for some time, so I went in the house to try to find out why my mother and I took contrary views of the situation. One of the difficulties was that there was little in the way of household ware, and nowhere to put what little there was. Half a dozen dirty white ironstone plates were stacked in a corner, along with some cups and saucers of the same durable material. A corn-flakes box held the cutlery, such as it was. There were neither dish-mops nor towels.

There were no indoor plants to cheer things up. I brought in a clump of yellow bean to stick in a jam-jar. These filled the room with colour and perfume. My mother was encouraged to write to Aunt Clara Vaughton requesting that a dish-mop, a slip of geranium, and a root of aspidistra be wrapped up in copies of the Birmingham *Post* and mailed as soon as possible. It would be at least six weeks before they arrived, since only train and ship transport were available, but the initiative was something done to relieve the bleakness, and by the time my father and brother returned mother felt more cheerful.

Leon, the eldest Jones boy, drove them back in a buggy with a handsome black gelding. In the back a pair of shoats in a sack squealed and tussled to escape. Leon, it appeared, would not be averse to selling the horse, which he said was an unusually fast pacer, sound of wind and limb and worth every cent of fifty dollars. This excited my mother, who liked riding and saw a chance to escape the house-prison, get some healthy exercise, and see the countryside. My father, who had just paid ten dollars for the porkers, felt that the price was too high. Leon was willing to bargain, and after a week or so of chaffering and hesitation my father to our great joy bought John for twenty-five dollars.

Even before the deal was concluded my mother had written to her brothers, ordering a saddle to be sent out by Christmas. Until it arrived she vowed she would ride bareback. This was a rash boast. John had a bony spine, and clung to his training as a pacer, which meant he moved rather like a camel, near-legs and off-legs co-ordinated fore and aft. This was hard to adjust to even with a saddle; he complicated matters further by switching to normal stride in mid-course, which was unsettling. Aware of these facts, Leon said we could borrow a light western saddle until Mother's arrived from England. This secured the deal and Mother then turned her attention to a buggy.

By the end of the afternoon my father had committed himself to a McLaughlin buggy, which would come to nearly $100, for Christmas. He turned to other problems, such as building a hog-pen — or pigsty, as my mother insisted on calling it. This is no easy matter by whatever name it is called. We drove in fence posts, nailed boards to them, and turned the two squealing porkers into their new quarters. By tea-time they were galloping happily about the prairie. With coyotes in the neighbourhood they would not have enjoyed liberty long after dark, so we organized a battue. The four of us chased those little brutes until we were breathless. They, unfortunately, were in fine wind and easily outpaced us. My brother fancied himself as a cowboy and by some happy chance managed to loop a clothes-line around the head and shoulders of the black-and-pink pig. We dragged him to the pen, flung him in, and fed him some oats and stale milk. He made such appreciative gurgling noises that his brother, an off-white, ill-natured, scrawny rickling, consented to be caught too and penned in. We added a two-by-six to the pen, strung some more barbed wire around it, and topped it with page-wire and flax-straw to make very comfortable quarters if they cared to keep them. They did not.

Most of that summer was consumed in a battle of wits between prisoners and wardens. The pink-and-black pig, whom we named Timothy, was a gentle, chatty, contented soul, but his off-white brother was a rebel, prototype of all rebels against the Establishment: dirty, unkempt, ungrateful, and forever trying to bilk his brother of a fair share of the swill. He was a resourceful jail-breaker, ceaselessly rooting with his long snout to discover weakness. A point of vantage was ruthlessly exploited, with an insensate disregard for his current situation or his future, and a destructive bent for anarchy which marked him as a spiritual forebear of a generation of hippie rebels. Had the porkers been content to puddle in the sloughs and pasture and retire to their pen at night where they would have been reasonably safe from coyotes we could have ignored their pranks. But the garden, carved with infinite labour out of the tough sod of the fireguard, was irresistible. They went down rows of new lettuces and radishes in a minute. This was bad enough, depriving us of all our prized anti-scorbutics, but then they started on my own particular patch of garden, where after long germination two tiny columbines were clinging grimly to life. The sight drove me to fury. Grabbing the air rifle, I rushed at them screaming, and peppered them with shot. They galloped off, squealing indignantly, but apparently none the worse. The sequel to this occurred the following summer when we were preparing sandwiches for a picnic to the Turkey Track coulees to pick berries. Cutting into the late Timothy's ham we dislodged a pellet, much to the amusement of our neighbours, the Scotts, who claimed that the same thing had happened to them, and charged that this was proof that we had molested their hogs when they were paying a friendly visit. It was quite possibly true, but did nothing to improve relations. The Scotts lived over on section 1, poor hilly land a mile to the east, and both their horses and their pigs considered our property and fields their own. My father kept for a long time in his files an unfriendly letter from the Rev. P. A. Scott, recommending a more amicable solution to such neighbourhood problems.

From the Joneses, along with the pigs, came a typical country dog — basic collie (locally pronounced coalie, but we clung to the English pronunciation). We named him Scottie. He started life as Scott, since Jones believed that one of Scott's dogs had sired him, but that was too dignified a name for such a scatterbrain. He lacked all aristocratic collie points, and looked and acted like a country yokel. Scottie's background colour was white and he sported a chestnut patch on one flank. He had brown ears and muzzle and an off-white, dirty tail. He never failed to rush out barking whenever anyone drove or rode up to the house; when fondled he yelped and often snapped, owing to the pain occasioned when his hay-needle boils or familiar ticks were touched. Aside from these flaws he was long-suffering and amiable, and turned into a great gopher-dog.

My brother and I soon found that there were not enough hours in the day to wait for a scared gopher to stick his head up through the noose at the mouth of his home to see what was going on. We developed a faster technique — pouring water down the hole until the wretched gopher poked his head out, when Scottie grabbed him; if he made a dash for freedom the result was the same unless he had a spare hole handy into which he could dive before Scottie got him. We could usually count on catching ten or twelve a day. We stripped off their tails with a quick jerk, and packed them into an Old Chum tobacco sack of father's, which we carried on our persons until my mother objected. Every time we went to town we took our collection of tails in to the municipal office and received the bounty of one cent a tail. It was a useful and reliable source of income, far more remunerative than the sparrow bounty we had subsisted on in England. Also, since there was nothing to spend the money on, we soon established a substantial savings account at the Union Bank.

Besides taking part in the gopher battue, Scottie moonlighted as a draught animal. I built a simple harness for him out of old reins, pieced together with copper rivets. He objected at first, but ultimately gave in when for a heavy four-wheeled "express-wagon" we substituted a light two-wheeled "dog-cart" which my mother and I built between us. It was not too successful, however, as the wheels squealed like a Red River cart — and for the same reason, that there was neither grease nor roller-bearings between wheels and axle. We had simply scored a hole through a board with a red-hot poker, and rounded it off as well as we could. However, by the time Scottie was properly broken in, we had given up the dog-cart and turned the wheels into lids for the churn. Scottie's real triumph came with winter when he was hitched to a hand-made sled. He galloped over the snow with this at great speed, until it occurred to him that life would be easier if he rode and we pulled. Thereafter he never missed a ride on sled, cutter, or stone-boat, and we were willing enough to tow him about, just for the paradox.

But he had bad habits. His favourite diversion was chasing chickens and occasionally catching and eating one. We had to break him of this depravity by the extreme method of tying a dead chicken, or what remained of it, around his neck. After a few days chicken became distasteful. But one sinful joy was no sooner renounced than he discovered another — a dangerous taste for bad company. About a quarter of a mile away, over the hill where the cactus grew, was the carcase of a horse. We never knew who had towed it there, for by the time we found it the coyotes had been at work and most identification marks had disappeared. The coyotes made a wild cacophony every evening which fascinated while it frightened us. One bright moonlight night soon after my father had given me a .22 rifle, Dick and I, greatly daring, headed over the cactus hill until we saw, and shuddered to see, shadowy forms dancing around the carcase, making little darts at it and then backing away. I chilled with horror when one of them loped in our direction. I aimed the rifle, but in that light I could not see the sights. My brother hissed in my ear "Stop! Don't shoot! It's Scottie!" Sure enough, the "coyote" developed the brown patch, muzzle, and floppy ears of our dog, who came up with a hang-dog look justified by the blood on his collar. He did not even stay to protect us but skulked off home, leaving us to follow with many a frightened backward glance lest the shadowy draws be peopled with deeper shadows. Scottie must have had a bad fright, for he loped home and never again appeared with blood on his collar. It was generally believed that coyotes killed dogs who joined them at their feasts. I once saw one turn on Scottie, who was following him in daylight, but he made no attack. The legend may have been just one more anti-wolf myth, although my father told us of two children who had been killed on their way to school near Sintaluta when coyotes jumped at them as they were passing a copse. There were no copses in our neighbourhood, and that first summer there was no school, either, so we did not worry much about coyotes, although their wailing at nights was eerie. I never saw them around the barn or the hen-pen or the pigsty.

To my great surprise, I soon found unlimited holidays boring and began to yearn for the old routine of studies. Even *Ora Maritima* looked good at this distance. I had so gladly discarded that dreary Latin reader only a few weeks before; by this time I would have welcomed it.

It was not that we lacked reading matter; we had, in fact, an extraordinary supply of books, considering their weight and bulk and our scanty resources in baggage. By midsummer our stock was doubled by the happy arrival of a vast crate or packing-case containing most of our household linen, drapes, and curtains. Along with this there arrived two boxes the size of military footlockers, though this term was then unknown; we called them ottomans. Topped with green plush, which at home had been used in front of doors to cut draughts, they made cosy seats for reading beside the stove, and I spent many comfortable hours there working through the books they had contained.

Once the ottomans and the crate were unpacked the shack began to take on the feel of home. The crate stood against the partition which boarded off the flax-bin and my parents' bedroom. Mother covered it with a red and yellow drape, and arranged on it my father's rosewood writing desk, a compact treasure with little compartments for pen, ink, paper, and envelopes. It was adorned with a little monogrammed silver seal. Atop this desk was placed a smaller one of my mother's, also in rosewood but of lighter hue. Then there were two brass candlesticks, two silver photo-frames, a light-yellow tortoise-shell tea-caddy; a dark ditto; a pewter inkstand in the shape of a water-lily; and a tall silver cup, presented to my grandfather for the best fat sheep shown at Bridgenorth Fair some time in the early 1880s. This was a souvenir from the old farm-house at Coton, Shropshire, where my father was born. There was a picture of his mother, in ringlets and a beaded black satin dress, and cabinet photos of himself and my mother in their early twenties — touching, beautiful, light-hearted young things with little presentiment of the stony life-path their feet were to tread.

We always referred to this assembly on the vestmented packing-case as the "Altar", and so in a way it was — dedicated to the small Lares and Penates of our household. It also served as a closet for sheets, blankets, and eider-downs. It swept upwards in a pyramid, of which the terminal step was my mother's small writing-desk. On top of that stood a cherished souvenir of her youth, a brass-and-glass travelling clock in a purple velvet case. Built solidly in Birmingham by solid Midland workmen, it was a simple, reliable clock. There were no chimes, bells, or irradiated hands; only a white face without even a maker's name, and only the simplest design of Roman numerals. One key wound it, another set it. The only concession to novelty was the glass case, through which the balance-wheel could be watched for endless hours of assurance that time was not standing still. This clock accompanied my mother on all her travels, from the time she attended finishing school in Germany.

Little by little the shack became a house and the house a home. The arrival of the packing-case gave it an air of permanence which my mother and I furthered by painting the house white with green trim. We built a rough wooden eavestrough or gutter, carrying rain to a water-butt, which we also painted white with green hoops. I found painting a tiring chore. The dry wood drank up paint at a fearful rate. The endless summer afternoons wore out my painting arm and I was thankful when my father decided against painting the addition to the stable he built to house mother's horse.

I was so sick of painting that I welcomed as a merciful release a menacing blue-black thundercloud which loomed out of the south the next afternoon. The direction of the storm was unusual — they almost always boiled up out of the west, passed overhead, and formed in the east an indigo backdrop to double and triple rainbows of an intensity never seen in England's smoky Midlands. The direction from which the storm advanced combined with its terrifying aspect alarmed me. The long black cloud seemed barely to mount the ridge of the Cactus Hill; a sinister spiral slid from it like the tentacle of an octopus. Grasping at the chance to knock off painting, I dashed inside and slammed the door just as the storm struck. I peered timidly out of the window as the lumber piled outside, left over from the stable, whirled away like straws. It never entered my head to dive into the cellar. Nor did it occur to me that the house would not ride out the storm. The studs creaked, the roof and floor trembled, but nothing gave. My father had built well, and his forethought in piling fill from the cellar around the base of the house paid off. In less than a minute the crisis was over. There was a brief drenching rain mixed with hailstones which drummed against the tin chimney, and that was all: two brilliant stabs of lightning and instantaneous crashing thunder, then silence.

As soon as we dared we went outside to assess the damage. The air was wonderfully fresh and cool after the burning heat of the afternoon. It was heavy with the pungent fragrance of wolf-willow; but we had no time for aesthetic appreciation. The hayrack, newly built, had disappeared; the addition to the stable, completed the day before, had been overturned, very neatly, and there in the stall was black John, still roped to the manger. We rushed up to find him trembling and sweating with fear but uninjured. We rubbed him down, and gave him an oat-bundle and a bucket of water, and his trembling stopped. The vast purple castle of cloud had moved north-east; but against this backdrop there was neither rainbow nor lightning. We recognized that this was something unusual, but we did not know how lucky we had been until we learned, some days later, that the hurricane had devastated half of Regina that same afternoon, cutting a swath a mile long through the capital of the province, killing more than two hundred people and doing vast damage. We lost the hayrack and the lumber left over from the stable addition, and that was all. The stable could be salvaged and we found sticks of lumber a mile away. The outhouse had simply been blown down; it was soon restored, over a new pit, well anchored again and not noticeably the worse for wear. There were cracks, but we set to work to paper them over with comic drawings from a flood of "summer annuals" which had just come in. During the long hours I spent there I became well acquainted with the British humorists whose works cut the draught and diverted the occupants of our privy.

With what lumber could be salvaged I was commissioned to build bookcases. I built two, one for the main room and one to be nailed to the wall over my bed. They were not masterpieces of joinery, but they held books and they held together. The one over my bed developed a list, but it was fastened to the studs with many 2½-inch nails, so I never feared to sleep beneath it. Our library consisted of:

Cassell's Illustrated History of England in 12 Volumes. This was a disaster by someone who could not write illustrated by someone who could not draw. It was offered by Cassell to anyone who advertised in one of his magazines, to get it off his hands. He unloaded on my father. However, I staggered through all twelve volumes the first winter out west. I wish it had been Macaulay or Greene, but it was better than nothing.

Shakespeare: in a red-bound, gilt-edged edition, inscribed "To Marion from Dick, 1898". Odd present for a young man to give his sweetheart, but touching in its recognition that the better things of life were for them. I read *Henry IV, Henry V, Henry VIII,* and *The Merry Wives of Windsor* for the sake of Falstaff. I found the others too tedious even for long winter evenings; I still find the so-called comedies boring and the tragedies unconvincing. I prefer Marlowe.

Tennyson: also red-bound and gilt-edged; pleasant reading, my favourites being, of course, "The Charge of the Light Brigade" and "The Lotos-Eaters", followed by "Locksley Hall", to which my mother directed me.

Moore: particularly "Lallah Rookh" and "The Dismal Swamp".

Burns: particularly "Tam O'Shanter".

Longfellow: obviously "Hiawatha"; lacked patriotic fervour, and too partial to rebellion.

Scott: "Marmion" and "Lady of the Lake".

That took care of the poets. There was no Byron. He was too wicked, I guess. The novels were a mixed bag. Dickens was represented by *The Pickwick Papers,* my all-time favourite, read aloud by my mother whenever anyone was poorly. Also *David Copperfield, A*

Tale of Two Cities, and *Oliver Twist.* Thackeray with *Vanity Fair, The Virginians,* and *Pendennis.* Scott: *Ivanhoe* and *The Talisman,* both Christmas presents from loving aunts.

Then there were some odd numbers by Marie Corelli, a popular Victorian Fannie Hurst; she starred with *The Sorrows of Satan.* Then Ouida, another such; low points were Charles Garvice in a sixpenny edition and Hall Caine — both purveyors of simplistic trash. My favourite was a paperback edition of W. B. Maxwell, *Vivian,* which I read three or four times. There was better fare: Belt's *Naturalist in Nicaragua;* Church's *Stories from Homer,* with illustrations after Flaxman. This was a Latin prize won by my father at Bridgenorth Grammar School. I did not find it attractive, although generally I was fond of the classics. I was fascinated by our single French book, Fénelon's *Télémaque,* but it turned out to be another dreary adaptation from the Greek. There was also Darwin's *Origin of Species,* which enjoyed a dubious fame as a dangerous book. Despite this I found it unreadable. Rider Haggard was there with *Montezuma's Daughter,* which at least led me to Prescott and Bernal Diaz's account. From *King Solomon's Mines* I picked up the historical place-name Zimbabwe, now a word to conjure with. There were also *Ayesha* and *She,* simple trash, both of them. There were Nansen's *Farthest North,* and H. M. Stanley's *In Darkest Africa,* which was regarded as very unsuitable reading for a boy. Also Swift's *Gulliver* and Addison's *Essays,* holdovers from Lichfield.

As a collection this library had obvious defects, but it offered a reasonable survey of English literary achievement at its peak period. I became so fond of Tennyson that after I joined the Canadian Army I carried around with me a small pocket selection of his poems; odd lumber for a soldier, although I also jammed into my pack an India paper edition of *Pickwick* and a small *Omar Khayyam.*

The routine of prairie life allowed time for reading only for those who could seize it. When he was ploughing, my father got up at 4.30 a.m., laid the fire, and called my brother and me at five. Dick got up at once to round up the horses and harness them. Father fed them, milked the cow, and brought up to the house a bucket of water and a half-bucket of milk.

Our poll-Angus cow was not a very good milker, although what she gave was rich. She was a consummate fence-crawler, and as a result went through life adorned with a cluster of suspended sentences — a log slung around her neck by a chain, a wooden collar, such as Chinese prisoners used to wear, and an iron collar with a hook in the tip. This was not a good idea, for when she felt contact with the barbed wire, instead of backing off she lurched forward and took three or four fence posts with her, wrecking that section of the fence and scratching her udder on the barbed wire. I do not recall that we had any name for her but "That cow!" To cap all she produced nothing but bull-calves, never a heifer. She was touchy and stubborn, and in that mood would hold back her milk, whisk her tail into your eye, and kick the bucket over. We had a screen over the milk-bucket spout, and for good reason. It sifted out the stable sediment. We had no separator the first year, so when my father got back to the top of the hill with the milk, I took it down to the cellar and poured it into wide shallow pans, where it sat until the cream rose.

For breakfast there was porridge which had simmered on the stove all night until it was almost the consistency of jello; cream went with it well. There followed toast — a piece of Mother's bread flung on the hot stove to char — strawberry jam from a 4-lb. tin, and milk — coffee was not supposed to be good for growing boys. We finished up with boiled eggs — brown, for preference. I do not know whether there was any difference, but we thought the brown ones tasted richer than white eggs. The horses thought so too. The hens liked to lay in the manger, and we had to keep a sharp eye on the nest when the horses were stabled. Breakfast was over in time for my father to get the team out and hitched up by seven o'clock. There was a strong competitive spirit in the neighbourhood. Pearson could see when we were late to work, and sometimes commented, asking if there was any difficulty. We in turn could see him, and Robinson and Annis as well. As soon as my father had gone to work I settled down for a long read on the ottoman beside the fire.

Chapter Fourteen

My unexpected longing to go back to school, and probably my
mother's representations as well, prompted a quick response from
my father. He began corresponding with a Mr. Ball, who was then
Deputy Minister of the provincial Department of Education, looking
to the establishment of a school. Jones and Scott, neighbours with
children, were conscripted to form the school board, my father
being secretary-treasurer. He spent every Sunday afternoon on the
business of the school or of the local Grain Growers Association, of
which he was also secretary-treasurer, since he wrote in a legible
hand and had a writing desk in which he could file his correspondence, mainly letters to and replies from Mr. Ball.

Augustus H. Ball was a model civil servant, intelligent, courteous,
and exact. He was a product of one of the great English trade
schools, the Haberdashers', in London, where he had been born in
1873. Soon after leaving school he left England for Manitoba.
Like so many young emigrants, he yearned for the learned life he had
left. He turned to the classics and graduated B. A. from Manitoba
College in 1895. He began a distinguished teaching career by lectur-
ing in classics at Manitoba College and followed this up with teaching
posts at Fort Qu'Appelle, Maple Creek, Moose Jaw, Yorkton, and

Regina, where he was Acting Principal of the Normal School. He trained teachers for work in the remote prairie schools where they would have to struggle with seven classes in a single room all day, and with the Board of Trustees in the evening to convince them that twenty-five dollars a year for the school library was not throwing money down a badger-hole. In 1898 Mr. Ball organized the first Territorial Teachers Association, which he served as secretary.

Mr. Ball was thus ideally equipped for the post of Deputy Minister of Education, to which he was appointed in 1911. The provincial government of that day was too loosely organized to operate on the Peter Principle of hiring indifferent personnel and allowing them to rise to their level of incompetence. It was a blatantly efficient operation which put qualified and experienced people in posts where their talents could be used, in defiance of bureaucratic principles and regulations, and kept them there despite a proven ability to perform within or without the rules. As a result of this mismanagement Saskatchewan matriculation and degrees are universally recognized and no Saskatchewan graduate or drop-out has ever been sentenced to preside over a North American university. Let us therefore burn a small votive light for Augustus H. Ball, who lit such a candle on the prairies as shall never be put out.

My father co-operated by sacrificing his Sunday afternoon naps to exchanging letters with Mr. Ball. As secretary-treasurer of the newly formed School District No. 717, my father submitted a page of plain note-paper with a pencilled list of suggested names; it is preserved in the Saskatchewan Archives:

1. Walkerville (E. P. Walker owned the local threshing rig)
2. Mulvernlink (My father's spelling was frequently phonetic. He meant Malvern Link)
3. Meadowside
4. Hilldale
5. Gordon
6. Shakespeare
7. Stanley
8. Selkirk

In addition to the eight names on the list, two more were submitted of which all trace has vanished: Jonesville (Walter T. Jones was chairman of the Board of Trustees) and Annisdale (Alf Annis was the Man of Property in School District 717 and had four children of school age).

The list came back with the notation OK. in red crayon against Mulvernlink, which Mr. Ball transcribed correctly as Malvern Link, by which name this school district is still known. I often wondered what memories of his youth brought this name to my father's mind, or what chord it aroused in Mr. Ball. It turned my mind to medieval studies as soon as I discovered that Langland's Piers Plowman had his vision "on a May morning on Malverne hulles". The beautiful Malvern Hills were not far from my father's home in Shropshire, so there may have been a nostalgic reminiscence involved, and it is more than likely that Mr. Ball read *Piers Plowman*.

I am everlastingly grateful to Augustus H. Ball for choosing Malvern Link; physically, however, it was inappropriate, for there were neither streams nor links nor woods. Politically, the choice had a touch of genius. Five hundred years had brought little change in and no solution of the ploughman's problems, since the day Langland dreamed of

A fair feld, ful of folk, . . . the mene and the pore, . . .
Somme putte hem to the plogh, playde ful selde,
In settynge and in sowynge swonken (worked) ful harde,
And wonne that this wastors with glotony destrueth.

Mr. Ball's selection of Malvern Link as the school district's name gave my father lasting pleasure, compensating for the tedium of long, hot afternoons spent at his writing desk. Mr. Ball wrote that before an issue of debentures could be authorized to pay for building the school, a full list of proposed expenditures should be submitted, together with details of the planned buildings and their cost, as well as a description of the school district. On June 29, 1912, my father replied identifying the 8,960 acres in the school district, and naming the twenty-two "persons" and sixteen children living there.

Details of the school, given by my father, specified that it should be twenty-four by thirty feet with cement foundation, with all windows standing east and west on the south side. The stable should accommodate twelve horses, the school furniture would meet departmental regulations, and the trustees requested authorization to issue debentures for $1,800 for the following expenditures:

Lumber and cement	*about*	$900
Furniture		$270
Builders contract		$450

Haulage to be let by tender.

The department replied that this totalled only $1,620, and could my father supply them with a revised total. So, on September 17 my father revised expenditures upwards by $180:

Carried over	$1,620
Lumber for stable	$ 85
Coal stove	$ 40
Land (2 acres @ $10)	$ 20
Fence and gates	$ 35
	———
	$1,800

On October 16, 1912, the trustees were duly authorized to borrow $1,800.

"High time, too," my father commented, "for we've built the school, ordered the furniture, and hired the teacher, and everybody wants his money."

My father felt he had done his share for the afternoon towards founding Malvern Link School, so he settled back in his Morris chair, put the *Farmer's Advocate* over his stomach, and went to sleep.

I walked down daily to inspect progress on the school as soon as workmen began to pour concrete for the foundations. It went up fast on two acres in the extreme south-west of the School Section in the flat about half a mile away from our house. As soon as it was finished it was painted white with green trim; the barn, to hold twelve horses, was red with white trim. Two outdoor privies, also white with green, were stationed on either side of the barn. I marvelled at the complex desks which combined seat and writing surface in a single unit — an American monument of unreason, for every time a child in the front seat wiggled, he jiggled the desk behind. This infuriating invention introduced me early to the thoughtlessness of American academic planners and the readiness of Canadians to adopt the worst features of the complacent civilization to the south. Furniture consisted of a desk in fumed oak veneer with a mouse's nest in the top drawer and a swing-back chair for the teacher, a pedal organ, a map-case, a clock, a globe hanging from the ceiling on a clothes-line, a bookcase, a water-bucket, and a broom. In the middle of the room squatted a pot-bellied stove. It was the function of Tommy Jones, as school janitor, to lay a fire ready to be lit in the winter as soon as teacher got there. After school, Tom swept out the room, carried out the ashes, and laid the fire for next day; for these services he was paid seventy-five cents a week, when there was money in the school bank account. Once the schoolhouse was finished it served as social centre for dances, pie socials, and on Sunday for church services, at which my mother played the organ and ground out suitable tunes from the Church of England's hymns, A. & M. — none of that Moody and Sankey stuff for her — it reeked of "chapel", non-conformity, and, as like as not, disloyalty.

The American Mission provided a succession of worthy curates, who came out by buggy or on horseback. They were agreeable at tea-time, read the services flawlessly, and preached with restraint for no more than ten minutes. None of your Bible-thumping hellfire-and-brimstone hot-gospellers for Malvern Link; the Turkey Track school was the place for that, although we occasionally attended just to see at first hand how terrible it was. I was reminded of the Turkey Track hot-gospellers when years later I came across the medieval exponents of the fiery deterrent reserved for the pomps and vanities of this wicked world and all the sinful lusts of the flesh.

After the school was built a well-driller was hired who guaranteed water. Charging one dollar a foot for the first hundred feet, he drilled confidently through the blue clay, ignoring our warnings. Sure enough he found water just below, but so alkaline as to be undrinkable. It could not even be used for horses, which some of the children rode to school. Its only use as far as I know was for christenings, which were held in the schoolhouse once the area began to develop. The font was a tin bucket of water that I drew from the well. The minister blessed it and touched the infant's forehead with it, and I threw the rest out of the cloak-room window, having ascertained that Divine blessing had not improved the quality of the water, or reduced the alkali. Frank Boyd, who cultivated a reputation for audacity by shocking us with calculated irreverence, observed that it would have given Christ Almighty the trots!

Our faithful regretted the levity while acknowledging the realism. Some recalled that Moses had dealt with bitter waters for the benefit of the Children of Israel at Marah by throwing trees into the pool. The school board, however, thought the solution would be to demand another well from the drilling rig for the same price. This was refused on the grounds that water had been found, that the contract had not specified quality, and that if the Lord had sweetened up the water for Moses, He could do it for us too. The school board thought this smacked of heresy and decided to divert the funds for a new well to the purchase of a harmonium; Jones, whose experience with wells had embittered him, agreed. Scott, who had a degree in theology, joined my father in a unanimous decision, but cautioned against throwing sanctified water out of the cloak-room window as verging on sacrilege. The episode fostered in me a sceptical approach to unseen powers who seemed to dissociate omnipotence from responsibility or accountability. The kids could bring their water to school in lard-pails.

The school board had not thought it necessary to include among the school furnishings any portrait of the reigning monarch or his Canadian representative, but we did have a Canadian flag, and it was raised daily with a simple but effective ceremony. This was long before the controversy about whether or not there was such a thing as a Canadian flag. There was because we had one: it was the old Red Ensign with the Canadian shield on the field. In my loneliness and nostalgia for Lichfield I applied myself to the formerly scorned Boy Scout lore; I picked up the art of bundling up a flag so that it could be released at the mast-head by a twitch of the lanyard. I put this skill to effective use the first day of school when, as the eldest of the eleven kids on the roster, I did the trick, raised the flag, and broke it out successfully while we sang "The Maple Leaf Forever", which we then took to be the national anthem; it was more sprightly and easier to sing than "O Canada", and we liked the tribute to "Wolfe, the dauntless hero". There were no little dissenting frogs, which was perhaps as well, for they would have had a thin time. The little German and Hungarian kids from over Gooding way could not have cared less, but they knew they were expected to fit into the picture, and they did, very well.

That first academic year, however, was not an outstanding success. The board had engaged as teacher a young man from Queen's University, Kingston, who presented outstanding testimonials to his academic and personal qualifications. He had no teaching experience, however, and unfortunately had been touched by the infection of permissiveness which became epidemic about that time. Mr. Cummings made a gallant attempt to apply his principles; the result was pandemonium. We sat on the backs of our desks or roamed and ran about as we felt inspired; nobody could get any work done, and one had to be perpetually alert to defend pencil-box and scribblers against raiders. It was trying, hateful, and a waste of time; we longed for discipline and an ordered life instead of being perpetually on guard against surprise attacks.

If we made life hell for the teacher, we also made it hell for each other. Lunch-time was particularly disagreeable. Most of us brought our lunch in one lard-pail and drinking water in another. My lunch was usually a salmon sandwich and a piece of pie. In the free-enterprise world of the permissive school, strange things happened to the menu; barter or robbery played havoc with the balanced diet, and half of us ended up with two pieces of pie and a stick of gum. Fortunately this was before the age of bubble-gum; it was plain old Wrigley's Spearmint — the exhausted chew could be parked under the seat. I sometimes had a few pieces of dried apple or apricot, more rarely a dry prune, for dessert. We had no fresh fruit or vegetables.

Fresh meat was a rarity, for there were no storage facilities. We became avid for fresh food, sick of canned stuff. Eggs and an occasional hen helped somewhat, but poultry is not the same as red meat, though it was better than that everlasting canned salmon. We tried gophers, and found them indistinguishable from rabbit. I went after jack-rabbits, but they are not an easy mark for an air-gun pellet. By accident I shot a tern on the wing, which I was sorry for, the more so as we left it hanging too long in the cellar, under the impression that it was game, and the flies got to it first.

I was mortified to find that gophers were looked down upon by the Scotts and the Joneses, and eating them was considered comparable to eating rat. This disfavour extended even to jack-rabbits, which was so obviously unreasonable that I ignored the whole taboo and skinned and disembowelled every gopher I could shoot or snare. I learned a good deal about rodents in the process, which was helpful to me later on when I came to study zoology. In this I was encouraged by the young teacher from Queen's who promoted universities as disciplined havens where everything could be learned. *"Every*thing?" I inquired one day as we trudged back through the flax-field after school. "Yes, everything." "Even astronomy?" I was hipped on astronomy at the time. "Certainly astronomy." This set my sights on a university career, which appeared the more desirable from the unsophisticated association of the university with academic discipline, as I was later innocently to associate it with meditation and communication of thought.

A problem at the school was cleanliness. We started the day at home with a hasty dousing of the face, neck, and ears in a hand-bowl. There was another hand-bowl at school, but the alkaline water did not lather and was as unpleasant for washing as for drinking. Most of the boys carried on their persons tobacco-sacks full of gopher tails, prior to turning them in to the municipality for cash. When these heated up in the summer sunshine or before the stove in winter, the academic air became very rich. We Minifies were very snooty about this because we took a ritual bath every Saturday night. We had a collapsible rubberized bathtub which took ten gallons or so of water hauled up from the slough in the pasture and heated on the stove. My mother was first on the bath list, followed by my father, myself, and my brother Dick. We applied plenty of red carbolic soap and scrubbed with a loofah, so that we came out as pink and prickly as if we had just been through a Turkish bath. I am surprised that the Finnish sauna never took root on the prairies. Perhaps the extremes there would have been too taxing.

Chapter Fifteen

During school holidays I reverted to non-academic activities. After breakfast as soon as father had taken the team out to the summer-fallow I went down to give the stable a quick run-through, collect the eggs, and brush out the chicken-pen – a job I hated, for it was always full of fleas, and hens have few endearing qualities. The calf got his drink of skim milk and a kick in the end if he acted skittish; then I went back to the most hateful task of all – sorting the potatoes.

Father had stowed his potato crop in the cellar beside the settle and covered it with straw. But he had dug them too late – right after that early frost in 1911; also the winter temperature in the cellar had probably dropped well below freezing, given the difficulty of maintaining an even temperature with the flax-burner. At all events, the potatoes had been frost-bitten and when they thawed out they rotted into a stinky, slimy mess. My job was to single out the sound tubers and throw the others away. The unsound ones were identified by my finger and thumb sliding into them. I spent hour after hour, day after day, at this task; then I had to peel some of the sound potatoes for dinner, which we ate at about twelve-thirty. Father quit at noon, or as near thereto as he could guess, which was when the sun stood due south at the end of a trip. We used the same time-signal, so

119

it worked out well enough, rarely varying by more than ten minutes.

The land was worked from east to west, which was convenient because it offered a half-mile strip and avoided a cross-wind tugging at the reins. The wind usually blew from the west, and could be vastly tiring to both horses and driver unless it was at their backs or dead ahead.

With animal traction it took three weeks to seed a 100-acre field, for horses could not work more than a ten-hour day. That meant that only one-third of the crop was seeded during the week of optimum germinating conditions. One-third of the crop would be in too early, liable to damage from late spring frost, and from hot weather just when the wheat kernels were in the milk and most vulnerable; one-third would be seeded too late, risking damage from early fall frost just when the grain was in flower. New mechanical tractors can operate twenty-four hours a day with headlights and relays of drivers, seeding a 100-acre patch in one week or less, during optimum germinating conditions. The same is true of the harvest; it can be reaped during the brief optimate, thus ensuring that more of the larger, better-quality crop is secured. Really prolonged inclement weather has to occur to create crop damage such as occurred in 1968 when, with exemplary cussedness, the skies poured endless rain on the swathed crop until the grain sprouted in the ear.

However, back in 1912 these problems were all in the future. We assumed that if we could break up the virgin turf and keep the soil clear of weeds and rubble, the crop would take care of itself. There was also an easy assumption that the Canadian government, having released these lands for settlement, would take reasonable measures to guarantee that settlers should be able to dispose of their crops to advantage and their costs be kept as low as possible. Government did nothing of the sort. Its tariff policy ensured that operating costs would be unduly high; it left the farmer to the mercies of the elevator companies and the railroads; and, if the farmer could defeat all these hazards, it moved in to tax his profits, but left him to lump his losses.

And its experimental stations, with the best intentions in the world, gave some monumental bad advice. Notable among such blunders was an ill-fated effort to help farmers in the south-west raise a shelter-belt of trees.

In 1911 the Dominion Experimental Farm at Indian Head, which had been most successful with shelter-belts, sent any farmer who applied some two hundred seedling trees — Manitoba maple, ash, willow, pine, and spruce. My father made a special trip to town to collect them, lest they perish in transit. By that time our nearest town was Vanguard, only twelve miles away, a great improvement on Morse, forty-two miles off. He was back by evening. In great excitement we prepared to plant a forest. Our eagerness was enhanced by the failure to survive the winter of two beech trees, which my father had bought the year before from a travelling peddler for a Quebec nursery. We hurried to the fireguard. My father ploughed a furrow and we threw in the maple, ash, and willow and tamped the soil over their roots. For the conifers we took greater care, digging holes for each in the gravelly topsoil of the hilly side of the garden, under the mistaken impression that they liked it dry and hard.

We shadowed the trees with daily scrutiny, and to our intense joy the broad-leaved trees sprouted from the dry twigs. We had trees! However, the experimental farm's choice of species was based on rainfall and other climatic conditions obtaining in south-eastern Saskatchewan, which were less rigorous than those in the south-west. The ash proved too susceptible to the late spring frosts, which destroyed the tender new leaves. The Manitoba maple was subject to a stem-borer which destroyed its growing tips, and in any case it had a diffuse, shrubby growth which never concentrated naturally into a single trunk. The willow flourished and so did the caragana, which grew to a nine-foot shrub but was very subject to a voracious beetle indigenous to the south-western prairies where it normally fed on the abundant milk-vetch. The pine and spruce died. I returned to the prairie at the end of the First World War expecting to find the shack sheltered by a beautiful wind-break. There was one pine recumbent, about a foot high; a few half-dead spruce, straggly willows, and Manitoba maples; and a caragana hedge. After another long absence I returned in 1935 to find the pine twelve feet high and dying, the rest victims of drifting soil.

E. P. Walker may not have known much about a threshing machine, but he knew how to raise a shelter-belt. In 1917 he ploughed a strip and pushed in twigs of cottonwood. They flourished. Annis took cuttings to stick in the earthwork of his dam on section 10. They grew, so in 1919 I cut off two small branches and stuck them into the earthwork of a small dam we had built between the house and the barn. By 1935 they were substantial trees, the biggest for miles around. I felt then that had Indian Head been a bit more knowledgeable about trees in the first place we might have been spared much of the heartache of struggling with unsuitable seedlings towards certain defeat.

This was a small but significant instance of the failure of the establishment, or the bureaucrats, or whatever you wish to blame, to give the homesteader significant help in his battle with a hostile environment. There are extenuations. The bureaucrat, also, was experimenting; he was doing his best. But it was disappointing to me to find out, long afterwards, that the Russians had done a much better job of raising wind-breaks on their Siberian steppes, where they successfully grew long strips of poplar which broke the force of their winds. To even up the record, however, Russia appeared to be as incapable as the democracies of learning from the experience of rivals, for the great Virgin Lands Program, which was to make the Soviet Union independent of foreign food supplies, committed the same mistakes as the settlers of the prairies and suffered even worse consequences. The errors grew with the bureaucracies that made them; their leaders were firmly committed to the mistakes on which their glory rested.

I doubt if any political moral can be drawn from these tragedies; the only conclusion is that information is localized, and even when available is sparingly used by men and women who have been trained from childhood to surrender reason to faith, whether political or religious, in all matters of consequence.

On mornings when I was not busy in the dark room, I made the butter. The cream was skimmed off the shallow round milk-pans every afternoon and evening and dumped into a five-gallon crock, where it stayed for a few days until it turned sour. We did not use rennet — a thunderstorm did just as well. The crock was fitted with a round wooden lid, pierced to insert a broomstick. A cross-bar paddle was nailed to the end of the broomstick. Churning meant beating the paddle up and down with a steady rhythm, just hard enough to slap the cream without bruising it. If the cream was the right temperature the firm sound changed after about twelve minutes to a watery slap-slop, which meant that the cream was disintegrating into butter-milk in which small pin-heads of butter floated. If the cream was too warm, the butter came sooner but never attained the proper firmness; it remained an oily, oozy mass which no amount of working could bring to proper consistency. This was lazy-man's butter, and I was warned against it. At the other extreme, if the cream was a degree or two below temperature, you could paddle away until your arms fell off before any welcome change occurred in the sound. On churning mornings, I used to sit on the ottoman by the cook-stove, reading and paddling until the contents started sloshing about, and occasionally paring off with my finger the delightful deposits which formed around the hole in the lid; these were churner's perquisites, and tasted better than anything but honey on butter. I got through most of the Bible in that fashion. When the butter came at once it took only two chapters, but on a bad day, most of Leviticus was consumed before the butter came.

Churning by ear produced the best butter: you stopped when it sounded watery; then the butter was the size of pin-heads clinging lightly together. If you continued paddling past that point, the lumps were too large and the buttermilk could not be worked out without bruising the butter. Most factory butter tasted bruised, as if it had been churned too warm and too long and worked by insensitive machinery.

Once the point of separation had been reached, we gave an extra two or three slaps, for luck, then poured the mix into a sieve, which strained the butter from the buttermilk. We assembled the butter in a wooden bowl with wooden paddles, all freshly scalded, and worked it over to press out the moisture and do it up into a variety of forms — balls, rolls, and slabs — adding salt as the operation proceeded. Proper working was essential to the keeping property of butter; gentle paddles and not too much salt were important for the flavour. You would no more want bruised butter than bruised ham or bacon, which was a hazard of pig-sticking.

My mother, though a pious Anglican, was none too sure about the wisdom of indiscriminate Bible reading for a growing boy, and on the first slow churning I discovered why. However, I ploughed through the Old Testament, absorbing an astonishing amount of mayhem, fornication, riotous conduct, murder, and incest along with the butter pickings from the lid of the churn. I thought it would be better when I got to the New Testament, but that occasioned more questioning. With my new-found interest in astronomy I had no difficulty in visualizing the bright star in the East; a new star would fill the bill and would attract attention among the eastern nomads; but the phenomenon of the star going before the astrologers until it stopped above the place where the child lay was something else again. It was at once too precise and too vague.

I went over the problem in my mind while I was churning. This was a day when the cream had been too cold, so I paddled and paddled while I pondered perspective, height, apparent speed, ground speed, and apparent and true size of the strange apparition. Before the butter came I had decided to refer the question to my teacher; he had been promoting the university spirit of inquiry, insisting that nobody ought to believe the incredible, and that a question you could not answer was much more important than an answer you could not question. I could no more bring myself to believe that a Nova had halted over Bethlehem like a will-o'-the-wisp than that the sun (or rather the earth) had stood still for Joshua's benefit. Teacher approved my doubts without being able to resolve them, but took the opportunity to recommend that I go behind the English text to the Latin, and see what that offered. As it happened, being a scholarly young man, he had a copy of the Vulgate. Seeing my interest, he went into the difficulties of a translator, touching briefly on the work of St. Jerome and the achievement of the committee appointed by King James I to translate the Vulgate into English. I glanced into the Vulgate and was amazed to find that it was not much more difficult than good old *Ora Maritima*. My teacher explained that this was intentional too, that St. Jerome was putting Christianity's sacred writings into language which could be understood by everyone, not just the learned; the Vulgate was the ordinary man's language, the vulgar tongue. And he went on to suggest, with good Anglo-Saxon pride, that it might have been better if Jerome had been able to consult King James's committee too, instead of sloughing over hard words in the original Greek, or just transliterating them, substituting Latin letters for the Greek alphabet in words he did not understand.

This glimpse into the delights of higher learning aroused in me an avid curiosity and a desperate desire to know more and to find answers to the most difficult questions, answers of which one could be sure. I was very fortunate that first Christmas on the prairies. My mother's family rallied around in fine style; the Post Office did its job efficiently, and a series of bundles arrived in good time. One of these contained a book from my kindly and sensitive Uncle Tom Vaughton (the goldsmith who had contributed so many gleaming half-sovereigns on appropriate occasions). He pulled off his shelf and sent off to his faraway nephew on the wild prairies a book on astronomy, *Through the Telescope,* by the Reverend James Baikie. It dealt simply with the solar system as then understood, comets, star-clusters, and nebulae, copiously illustrated with excellent photographs made possible by the great new telescopes just coming into use. The Reverend Mr. Baikie must have been a typical English vicar, informed and ready to inform, brimming with the latest hypotheses and happy to expound the accepted answers to acceptable questions. He, too, I felt, like my teacher, knew the importance of having questions you could not answer rather than answers you could not question. He dealt with Laplace and Lagrange, the nebular hypothesis and its weaknesses, stellar parallax, and the unreliability of Cepheid variables as measures of distance. He guessed at the position of the solar system in the universe, and hinted at the possibility of much vaster universes. As a crutch for the ignorant who had to deal with the Greek-letter designations of stars, he included in his notes at the end of the book the Greek alphabet.

Discovery of Greek opened a new world for me. It was the gateway to knowledge, and knowledge meant power, or at least a reasonable living at something other than piling cow-dung and ammoniated straw on to a stone-boat every morning to work up an appetite for dinner. I learnt the letters in groups, rehearsing them as I watered the cattle; alpha, beta, gamma, delta, brought the bucket up to the half-way mark; after that I took shorter, faster reaches with epsilon, zeta, eta, theta, and the bucket was at the well-head, brimming and dripping. With iota I flipped out the inevitable dead mouse and offered it to the cats. After a brief inspection with sceptical whiskers, they rejected it. Kappa was for carrion and chilled carrion at that. They liked their dinner lively, responsive to a stimulus of paw and claw. So I poured the bucket into the trough to the music of lambda, mu, nu; xi, omicron, pi. With rho, sigma, I put the rope's end across the muzzle of whatever beast was trying to crowd out his neighbour. Then with tau, upsilon, phi, chi, psi, the rope slid through my mitts, the bucket hung poised above the surface, and at a masterly flick of the wrist it turned over and gulped another fill and another mouse; omega!

An extraordinary number of small prairie creatures went to their deaths in those chill waters: mice, voles, shrews, once a weasel which left a taint on the water for days, and, of course, gophers; but I do not recall ever recovering a mole, nor for that matter seeing any signs of them, which was not surprising, since the prairie turf could by no stretch be called a lawn, and what is a mole without a lawn? The worst problem came when one of the cats fell in. Fortunately this happened in dead of winter, after a firm skin of ice had formed over the surface, so the poor creature probably died on contact with the ice. Her removal posed problems; it was some days before we solved them. In the meantime the ice had to be kept from forming too thick a skin which would deprive us of water for the rest of the winter unless we took the heroic expedient of throwing rocks down onto it. Ultimately we repaired and extended the ladder, let it down the well gingerly, and I climbed down to the surface. Getting a dead cat into a bucket with one hand without falling into the water called for more sophisticated gymnastics than I was capable of. So I sloshed about in the water stirring up mud and quicksand until I secured the cat in the bucket along with a gallon of water, mud, and ice, while my brother groaned and complained as he drew it up, drenching me the while as water slopped over the rim of the bucket. I was thankful to get out alive, although thoroughly chilled. I set out for the house at a run, but by the time I reached the door my overalls were literally frozen stiff, as were my mitts, while my fingers and toes were all touched by frostbite. A group of cats sitting outside the door made a concerted dive for warmth and security and had to be escorted back to the stable. Their colleague lay stiff and stark beside the well for some days, a grim warning against adventure, until, I suppose, a coyote carried her off as a pleasant change from horse.

The cat population originated when we took shelter from a thunderstorm at Ted Lewis's shack on his homestead near Vanguard. Ted Lewis had a good farm, but his shack was faced with tar-paper and lath, which the wind was already beginning to work on. Inside it was the customary bachelor muddle of unpainted bare boards, unmade beds, unwashed dishes, and old porridge-pots and news-papers. Among this refuse played two of the prettiest kittens we had ever seen: one of them was pure tortoise-shell, with solid patches of black, white, and orange; the other displayed a pattern of stripes over this groundwork; both were bright and sparkling amid the confusion. As soon as the thunderstorm had passed over, we prepared to hit the trail again. Lewis wanted to get rid of the kittens, which he felt only added to the overwhelming burden of bachelor house-keeping. We did not need much persuading. I put them in a bag and threw them into the back of the buggy. My father succumbed to their charms as quickly as we had done, and immediately named them Bubble and Squeak, after an Old Country dish of fried cabbage and potatoes which he liked. They were too young to mind the change; they soon settled down to the routine of the barn, became friendly with the horses, and learned to be on hand at milking time to get an old tobacco can full of warm, foamy milk, into which they could plunge their muzzles, their tails straight up, their whiskers pointing forward, their whole existence concentrated on milk. In the mysterious way common to cats, they soon had kittens. I say mysterious, because they must have been too immature to be with young when they came to us, and there were no other cats within a mile; they must have strayed far to find a mate, for none came visiting.

Nevertheless, one fine morning when father went to milk, he found the stable crawling with kittens — ginger, tabby, and tortoise-shell. Bubble and Squeak were going out of their cat-minds salvaging their babies from too close association with the horses' hooves, carrying them like dead mice back to their birthplace beneath the manger. Marvellously, they survived, all eleven. Soon they learned to sit in a semicircle behind the cow while father milked, waiting for him to direct a stream of milk at them. The old cats developed into mighty hunters, supplying their young with mice and gophers as a supplement to a strict milk diet. There were no rats. Fortunately, rats had not yet reached the third prairie steppe, although they were working their way west from Rat Portage, Ontario, which the City Fathers had renamed Kenora rather than hire an exterminator. Dogs would co-operate with boys, but the cats' hunting was strictly indi-vidualist. They cared nothing for the partnership with us which so delighted Scottie. They operated on their wild lone, as Kipling re-marked of his cats. As the autumn chill crept over the stubble fields, the mice and shrews sought the friendly warmth and shelter of the stable, and the cats waxed fat. They also waxed gravid, as a result either of parthenogenesis or incest. We suspected the latter, and pointed a finger of reproach at the big ginger tom who cozened his way into the house when the snows came, leaving his mother and his sisters and his cousins and his aunts to sit outside until the tips of their ears froze, shrivelled, and ultimately dropped off. By springtime the social gap between the privileged and the deprived, the Establishment and the proletariat, between stable-cats and house-cats, was clearly defined by the feature of rounded or pointed ears. But the gap was not unbridgeable, as Ginger proved; for although his favoured access to fireside warmth earned him such unpopularity that he had his ears boxed by the proletariat every time he ventured outside, he was not excluded from feline intercourse, and we soon had nearly as many cats, in assorted colours, as gophers.

The old cats moved from the stable to the sod-built dog-kennel for their next litters. Presumably the move was motivated by the ever-present danger of the kittens' being stamped on; also, the stable was getting damp and smelly as moisture seeped through the flax-straw on page-wire which roofed it over. Some powerful drive must have been present, for the new nursery was farther from the hunting-ground. One of the old cats used to wander off every morning to the pre-emption, more than a quarter of a mile away, and heavily infested with gophers. She would sit patiently beside a hole, pounce swiftly the moment a gopher came up to see what went on, kill it fast with bites at the back of the skull, then begin the long march home, dragging her prey between her forelegs. She used to lay the victim down in front of the dog-house to give the kittens their first taste of blood.

One morning I watched Squeak staggering back with a big gopher slung low. I looked inside the dog-house and was horrified to find there the ginger tom, sitting in the middle of the litter like Saturn, quietly devouring his own brood. Poor old Squeak arrived at the same moment. In guilty panic the tom rushed out. She tore his ears as he passed; then she laid down the gopher and threw herself flat on the earth, too dead beat and too shocked to care about anything else. She just gave up. When she came to she took the survivors back to the stable. After that Ginger went in fear of his life; the females never missed a chance to slash at his ears and his eyes every time he left the house. He got to be a bit ragged, but he survived, fat and unctuous like any other successful predator.

The survivors grew up without any noticeable psychological scars resulting from their nativity feast. There was no inheritance of acquired characteristics, as generation after generation of outdoor round-eared cats littered normal kittens. They joined the battery of client cats which sat around waiting for fresh new milk from our fence-crawling cow. The population stabilized in the twenties, when the death-rate by misadventure caught up with the exuberant feline birth-rate. They got on well enough with the dog in a delicate relationship of mutual forbearance. Two of them used to accompany my father on his walks up to the pre-emption to study the crop and the weeds and to plan future use of the land. It was odd to see two of these pretty multi-coloured creatures tagging along behind him, never diverted from their course as a dog would have been by stray gophers, but occasionally yielding to old instinct when a grasshopper crossed their path. They chewed up grasshoppers as if they were shrimps.

My father enjoyed walking over his half-section. My mother got away for tranquil meditation by going for a ride on old John; but my father preferred to walk. He did not like horses, having to rely on them for power. Walking soothed him, reconciled him to the long hot hours of daily labour on the land; walking diminished the power of the wind to frustrate and torment. On any horse-drawn implement, the wind was always tugging and tearing at the reins, moving the dust in an enveloping cloud, beating it into ears, nostrils, and eyes, sometimes making harvesting impossible and always reducing haymaking, which should have been a rhythmic dance, to a losing struggle with sprays of grass. On foot, with his pipe drawing well, and the silver cap closed down to catch stray sparks, my father strode into the wind, bracing himself for the next unwelcome task on his list.

By the time the wind had a nip in it, the list was headed by butchering the pig, a chore which my father disliked. He had no taste for the slaughter-house, even if it were only a bench on the open prairie.

Chapter Sixteen

After eighteen months the everlasting struggle with the hogs reconciled my father to butchering them, a task for which he had no taste. To nerve his hand to drive the knife into the jugular, my father had named the mean white pig after the contemporary Minister of Finance, Sir Thomas White, who was beginning to make threatening noises about taxes.

Like many other immigrant homesteaders of the day, my father believed that he had been promised no direct taxation in Canada save for roads and schools. This belief was fortified by the reflection that the tariff, then described as "for revenue only", amply compensated in its indirect levy. It was further strengthened when manufacturers adopted the slogan "Protect infant industries" as justification for privileged tax treatment.

I discovered in the provincial archives the statements which accounted for my parents' conviction that Canada was a tax-free paradise; it was a living faith, strengthened by the feeling that if infant industries were to be protected, then surely the prairie farmer was an infant industry *par excellence,* and worthy to enjoy untaxed what was left to him after frost, drought, hail, grasshoppers, gophers, storm, rust, mice, smut, ergot, and the C.P.R. had taken their toll.

130

When the farmers were disillusioned they felt they had been deceived. I joined in their sentiments, and joyfully smacked Sir Thomas White, the pig, over the snout with the feeling that I was dealing righteously with publicans and sinners, as the New Testament put it.

To Timothy, the pink-and-black pig, I took a shine. Timothy was clean, reasonably well-behaved, a tax-payer at heart, who never got more than two feet in the trough, was grateful for favours received, and gurgled appreciatively whenever he was spoken to. There was no obvious relationship between him and "publicans and sinners". Timothy and the Finance Minister were born of the same sow but had little else in common.

Butchering could not be delayed too long lest the winter weather set in. It could not be done before it was cold enough to freeze the carcase for the winter. Late fall was ideal.

Preparations were intensive. My father built a bench about eighteen inches high, a solid job of two-by-sixes, with two-by-four legs. We set up a barrel with a tripod and a pulley and tackle above it. We had a container of water boiling on the stove. Preparations included a bucket for the offal, a couple of iron scrapers which had started life as garden hoes, and a lard-pail for the blood. It was to be my job to catch the blood and stir it well to prevent clotting, fetch scalding water, and scrape the bristles off the hide. This meant dunking the carcase in the barrel as soon as the pig was dead; if there was delay, the bristles did not come out, and a dinner of roast pork was like eating hairbrush.

Dick and I were charged with bringing the sacrifice to the altar. We took the clothes-line and a length of light rope which we fastened on to Timothy. We urged him protesting to the bench; he had no desire to expiate our sins on the altar of sacrifice. Mother held his foreleg, I grabbed his left hind leg and dug my elbow into his ribs as we laid him flat on the bench. Father wrapped the clothes-line a couple of times around his snout, and plunged the butcher-knife into what he thought would be his jugular. My father lacked the instinct for the jugular, or was imperfectly schooled in anatomy. At all events, poor Timothy squealed and struggled and bled, but not profusely. "Get around and catch the blood," my father ordered. I obeyed. It was a mistake. As soon as I let go his leg, Timothy gave a mighty heave, shook himself loose from my mother's and Dick's grip, and was off and away, trailing blood over the prairie. "Better shoot him," my father ordered. I grabbed the .22 and ran after him. About fifty yards farther on, he turned on his murderers. I took careful aim, hit him in the forehead, and dropped him. It took all four of us all our strength to carry him back to the bench. There was blood everywhere but in the lard-pail; pig and we were drenched with it. My father was so upset by the whole performance that he determined to end it, so he stuck the knife in deep. Timothy gave a great thrust, then went limp. Father had stuck him in the heart; he bled no more. We hurried him to the barrel, dunked him in, and scalded him. Then we frantically scraped at the bristles, slung him up by the hocks, and disembowelled him. So far, so good, but when we came to chop him up, it was plain that he was not bled white; there was still much blood in the carcase, too much to permit the hams and the flitch to be properly cured. There would be no bacon from Timothy; he would not even freeze up well. We would have to eat him up as soon as possible: roast pork, pork chops, sausages, spare-ribs, pork-pies, chitterlings, chine, trotters, jowl and brains, liver, kidneys, spleen, and a bladder full of lard. We went at him manfully, but a half-grown hog is a lot of pig, and we got very tired of eating bloody pork.

My father determined to put this experience to profit. He boned up on anatomy, and resolved to butcher Timothy's brother, the Finance Minister, the following week, and to make sure that he bled well, for good ham and bacon. A tax notice which arrived from Ottawa the following day nerved my father's hand. "I'll bleed *him*, for a change," my father said grimly. "It'll be a pleasure." The sacrificial pig would atone for the sins of Sir Thomas White. For this second encounter the Table of Equipment was identical, but the order of battle was revised. I was deputed to stun him with a shot from the .22 close beside the bench. My mother was assigned to catch the blood and keep it stirred. I was on no account to let go of his left hind leg; we did not want a repeat of the Timothy disaster. The Finance Minister must have been warned in a dream, for he rushed at me the moment I climbed into the pen, and I barely had time to scramble out to escape his tusks. Dick secured a noose around his neck, I slipped a cord above his hock, and we dragged and chivvied him towards the bench, taking care, however, not to bruise his hams.

The Finance Minister was a dirty, ill-favoured hog, scurfy, with sore cracks behind his ears; he had none of the innocent wiles and jollity of Timothy; he was a cold, pigpen politician, who could be counted on always to get both feet in the trough before Timothy got near it and then try to oust Timothy on the grounds that he, the Finance Minister, had got there first. I used to even things up by belting him over the snout with a pitchfork, but he still managed to hog most of the swill, without, however, getting much fatter. Timothy was the chubby one, who honoured his victuals, enjoyed a chat, and wanted to be good friends with everyone. He had gone to his fate with something approaching philosophic resignation, reserving his strength for the escape attempt. But the Finance Minister contested every step of the way, and made the prairie ring with his squeals as he caught the scent of blood still clinging to the barrel and saw my father standing, butcher-knife and steel in hands, while my mother readied a wooden spoon in a Swift's Silverleaf lard-pail. "Don't be all day," my father urged. "Bring him up, and go get the .22."

"Now be careful this time," my mother warned: she was always self-contained about the necessary business of slaughter for food, and she badly wanted some good black pudding, a taste for which she had picked up in Germany. "Be careful! Go for his jugular, not his heart." We got him to the bench, and father grabbed the clothesline and looped it around the Finance Minister's snout. I took careful aim and shot, at the very moment when the hog lunged. My father roared: "Christ! I'm shot!" The hog dropped; my father hopped. The bullet had knocked out the pig and ricocheted into my father's calf causing him to bleed freely. We hoisted the hog on to the bench; my father struck, this time accurately. "Here's the bucket, wait for me," my mother called anxiously as she scurried around to the head of the bench. A severed jugular waits for nobody. The blood gurgled into the pail as though from an ill-fitting faucet; she stirred vigorously. "Better tie you up," she told my father, "or you'll be whiter than the pig." She called Dick to take over the stirring as she guessed that the Minister would be too weak to make a breakaway, while she put a rough tourniquet around father's leg. It distressed her, she said, to see so much good blood going to waste, but she took poorly to suggestions from Dick that she had held the bucket to the wrong wound. However, the Finance Minister soon uttered a liquid grunt, heaved, and gave up the ghost. The moment he stopped bleeding we hoisted him into the tub, poured scalding water over him, and hauled him up again to be scraped; the bristles came off cleanly; all went well, the drawing and the quartering was accomplished without a hitch, and we soon had his hams and flitches down in the cellar ready for the saltpetre, displacing my photographic equipment on the settle. Mother stirred pearl barley into the pail of blood and we squeezed the mixture into the large intestine for blutwurst. I regret that black pudding is carried on so few menus; it is still one of my favourite dishes. Any time the current Minister of Finance has problems to discuss, let him drop around; be my guest! We'll go to the Chinese Village and have dragon's-blood sausage.

Dick and I got so much blood on our overalls that the problem of new britches could no longer be postponed. School would soon re-open, so mother boiled some flour-bags with lye to bleach out the trademark, unlimbered her hand-driven sewing machine, and soon had us decently clad. The material was tough and strong, but light for fall wear; the dye was retentive, and for months afterwards Dick and I went around advertising Robin Hood and Lake of the Woods flour on our backsides, while some humorist pretended to trace the legend "No. 1. hard", the designation of our premium wheat, on Dick's pants. All this was in preparation for the re-opening of school with a new teacher.

Dismayed by our reports on permissiveness, the school board had resolved not to renew the contract of the young man from Queen's. After some hesitation they engaged a young woman, chiefly on the strength of her reputation as a disciplinarian.

Susan Winnifred Reaman was a graduate of Orillia High School in Ontario; this was her first teaching post away from home. She was to board with Mrs. Boyd, whose son, Frank, owned the east half of section 2, next to us. Frank had been lumbering around Gravenhurst, Ontario; when the white-pine woods were exhausted, he was out of a job, so he decided to come with his mother and his sister, Lila, to the prairies where he could get land of his own and be his own master, or so he thought. He had forgotten, if he ever knew it, the old English proverb: "While grass groweth, horse starveth"; and he soon found that if he wanted to eat before harvest, he would have to find money. The best way to do that would be to board the teacher. The school board considered this an ideal arrangement; Mrs. Boyd and Lila would be company for her and would see that she was well fed and reasonably comfortable, as comfort went on the prairie. She could either have a bedroom to herself or bunk with Lila. If she wanted a bath, there was a clean slough near by, and standard outdoor plumbing, with Simpson's catalogue. She would have a mile to walk to school, but what of that? If it was snowing or blowing too hard in the winter, there would be no need for her to come because none of the kids would venture out. The standard test was: if you can't see the barn for snow, don't go to school. That winter, however, was mild and we missed only a couple of days.

The opening day with the new teacher we were out in force: Tom Jones, Mary Pearson, Bill and Olive Annis, Hartzell Scott, Katie and Joe Fliegel, Anna Kovac, Bert Robinson, my brother Dick, and myself; eleven of us, ranging in age from eight to twelve, and in grades from three to seven. We had had a year of freedom, doing what we liked, being our own masters; and we were sick of it. We wanted order and peace. We got it.

We were scuffling when Miss Reaman entered. She wore a brown hat and suit, sturdy shoes, and a firm expression. We dived for our seats. "Everyone will stand and answer present when I call the roll," she said. We did, and without shouting or screaming. Then we sat down and got the word that we might leave the room on request, but only briefly; it was not to be taken as permission to go snaring gophers. Also we would not bring bags of gopher tails to school with us, nor would we trade contents of lunch pails with each other. This was a great loss, for astute traders had been able to amass rich and varied lunches at the expense of the ingenuous; but it was a gain for balanced diet.

Another device which had distracted her predecessor was vetoed by Miss Reaman. She brought to school a stout four-volume encyclopaedia. Questions designed to bring all school work to a stop while the answers were expounded were referred to the enclyclopaedia or to the dictionary. We soon became expert in the use of reference sources, and informed ourselves in the process on a variety of contiguous topics.

One of the treasures Miss Reaman brought from Orillia was the Ontario High School botany textbook. I spent the winter studying it, and impatiently awaited spring when I could put my skill to the test in Spotton's *Canadian Wild Flowers.* I hovered over the first crocus which pushed through the prairie sod in our pasture on April

7, 1914. As soon as it was half-open I seized it for examination and identification as *Anemone patens*, variety *Nuttalliana*. I went on to an even greater triumph when I brought in a small white flower which grew in patches like little snowdrifts. Miss Reaman had tentatively identified it, but with a question-mark, as Waterleaf. I puzzled through the Key to the genera, and came up with *Phlox Hoodii*, Moss Phlox or Prairie Phlox. It was a tremendous event, enhanced by Miss Reaman's ready acknowledgement of her mistake, which she erased by appointing me school botanist, charged with identifying all flowers brought in by pupils. It was wonderful training, but the *Compositae* or Daisy Family presented grave difficulties. They demanded a dissecting microscope, which we did not possess, for solution. I made do with the bull's-eye lens of a flashlight. It served, but a simple loupe would have taken much of the guesswork out of my identifications. However, such luxuries were hard to come by on the prairies.

Another great contribution to learning made by Miss Reaman was her subscription to the *Scientific American*, which published excellent star charts — white figures on black background, constellations clearly outlined, and individual stars given their popular names as well as their Greek-letter identification. This was my joy, and I spent hours copying out these charts when I should have been filling up the mangers in readiness for my father's return from the fields, or cleaning out the cow-stall, a job which I usually put off until morning.

Chapter Seventeen

My preference for the pen rather than the pitchfork did not add to my popularity. It reached a new low after the pig-sticking mishap which had wounded my father. Soon after that he went to Gooding for the mail, which brought a notice from the Department of the Interior, Land Patents Branch, that his homestead title had been endangered by a denunciation which charged that he was not fulfilling the statutory obligations of the Homestead Act. This was a common practice indulged in at that time by peddlers, or others who happened to be passing through the district, on the off-chance of picking up a nice homestead for themselves. My father decided to go in to Vanguard and kill two birds with one stone: to get his leg fixed by the doctor and his homestead by the Dominion Lands Office representative.

After several misleading surveys which put speculators off the scent the C.P.R. elected to establish in 1913 a depot and village to be named Vanguard, in a marshy oat field, purchased cheaply from a farmer and retailed by the C.P.R. in expensive lots; doctors, liveryman, lawyers, and a post office soon moved in and the village was ready to operate with a population of about 1,100 by the fall of 1913.

My father's business with the doctor was soon over. Dr. Robertson's view was that most of these small injuries were better left alone unless it was a matter of pitchfork or rusty nail punctures, when there was danger of tetanus. He was not callous, but he had a philosophical scepticism about the absolute values of "science", and he watched with amusement the swings of the medical pendulum. A few years earlier the accepted remedy for a sore throat or a sore thumb had been a poultice, applied as hot as the patient could endure. The treatment was then reversed to a cold compress. Dr. Robertson suspected that in time it would return to thermo-therapy, possibly in a milder form. The thorns, slivers, splinters, and similar foreign bodies which lodged under the skin were left to fester until enough "matter" had gathered to eject them under slight pressure. Failing this, a herculean remedy was to apply a piece of the interior skin of a fresh eggshell; this would "draw" the foreign body and almost anything else in reach. Treatment of blisters was a matter of rustic dogma, as fiercely defended or opposed as if the welfare of the soul were at stake. Originally, orthodoxy held that a water blister should never be touched; but as these broke under pressure to expose a very sensitive hypodermis, a technique was developed of tunnelling into the blister from the side without breaking the surface skin. Through this channel the fluid drained out, and the blister collapsed, effectively protecting the hypodermis until it hardened. Blood-blisters were never to be touched, lest septicemia follow. Boils also had their vicissitudes. A few years before that time, prairie boys had endured boils, usually on the backside, as imposed by an allegedly benevolent deity to neutralize the delights of puberty. They were left strictly alone until they "came to a head", when pressure, often accidental, relieved them after a moment of anguish. After a brief but occasionally disastrous foray into prophylaxis, this practice was resumed. Dr. Robertson respected the convictions of his patients, who put their whole trust in him in return. This made for successful practice, but imposed such heavy demands on the doctor that his slight constitution broke under them and he succumbed during the "Spanish flu" epidemic at the end of the First World War. His name is perpetuated by the Vanguard Hospital, where his memory is still venerated as the ideal country doctor.

When my father first went to consult him, Dr. Robertson had a two-room shack on Main Street. The waiting room had two chairs, a desk, and a stove with a kettle boiling on it. The surgery boasted a table and a hand-basin on an upended fruit-crate. Father lay down on the table. Dr. Robertson washed his hands quickly in steaming water, pulled up the overall leg, and gently squeezed the wound. A BB pellet popped out. Dr. Robertson applied some iodine, taped on a wad of gauze, and gave my father the pellet as a souvenir. "No need to go to Swift Current. That will be one dollar," he said, as he pulled down the overall leg. Father paid and limped down the street to Smaill & Hogg's legal office, which carried a sign "Commissioner of Oaths".

"Goldie" Smaill and his partner carried on most of the legal business of the village. They drew up wills, made out warrants for the Mounties, held court as J. P. when necessary, and notarized documents. Mr. Smaill brushed a few crumbs off his table, readied a Dominion Land Office date stamp, and gave my father Form No. 11, a Statutory Declaration, to fill out.

The encounters with Timothy, the Finance Minister, and my .22 must have left my father upset and a little confused, for when required to set down his age, he wrote "36 (I think)". He noted that he had "obtained entry" to his homestead in May 1910, had begun actual residence in March 1911, and had since been in "continuous" residence there. His house was built, he testified, in April 1911. My father, impressed by the solemnity of a statement under oath, questioned whether he had been right in ignoring his absences from his homestead when he took grain to town, or waited two weeks in Morse for our arrival.

"Forget it," Smaill counselled. "The silly buggers who draw up these questionnaires don't want a lot of bother if you are a legitimate homesteader and I know you are. In any case, six months per annum is all the Act calls for. So we'll just say 'Continuous residence', and the hell with them. Now, do you solemnly swear . . ."

My father put his hand on the Bible, said "So help me God", forked over twenty-five cents, and that was it. No need to waste time and money going up to Swift Current. Smaill sent the document to the Assistant Deputy Commissioner there, who duly filed it away, raising no issue either about residence or about my father's uncertainty about his age. I attribute my father's perplexity to his upbringing by his twin maiden sisters, who had deeply rooted objections to revealing their ages either directly or by arithmetical deduction from my father's. I think he was off by at least a year when he testified before Smaill, but I never did firm up his age, and forty years later his death certificate listed him as "about 74". To the Statutory Declaration's inquiry as to any special circumstances which should be considered by the Department in dealing with his case, my father wanted to offer his opinion of the parentage and character of whoever had denounced him, but Smaill ruled this out. So he substituted in a firm Victorian hand: "I have laid out something like two thousand dollars in buildings, animals, implements, etc.

"I have also *given* [twice underlined] as Secretary-Treasr. quite a bit of my time in getting our new school District formed & school built.

"Also getting G. G. Association Branch formed. I have also broken 120 acres & croped [sic] 60 acres on my Pre-emption."

God was required to help my father in his description of the house, buildings, and other improvements justifying his claim to a patent for this homestead under the provisions of the "Dominion Lands Act". The details did not agree with the over-all figure set down by my father, but for the record, here is what he swore to:

House 14 x 24 wood	$400.00
Stable	$200.00
2 Granaries	$140.00
2 Wells	$ 60.00
Fencing 4 acres	$ 30.00 (Nearer ten acres, I would have said.)
Minerals or quarries?	None
Any other homestead entry	None
Mortgaged or transferred	No

As a result of this submission, Mr. A. Sharp, local Agent of Dominion Lands for Swift Current, recommended the foregoing application for Patent, believing that "the homestead requirements of the Dominion Lands Act have, in this case, been complied with." It bore the seal of the Dominion Lands Office, Swift Current, Sask., dated December 11, 1913. It took nearly a month to work its way through the bureaucracy, for Mr. F. F. Dixon, Assistant Deputy Commissioner in Ottawa, did not accept it as sufficent until Jan. 8, 1914. It is now filed in the Saskatchewan Archives.

In the listing my father gave, no account was taken of the work involved in digging wells, in building granaries, stable, and house, or in digging post-holes for the fence. The thirty dollars was for wire, staples, and posts. Just getting fence posts into that hard prairie post-glacial deposit was a herculean task. It called for a crowbar, that prairie tool-of-all-work, to plunge down into the hardpan and loosen a hole. Then a mallet operated from the wagon, to drive the post home. The wagon also pulled the wire taut until it could be stapled to the post. Corners were hell; no matter what we did, short of weighting them down with a heavy stone, they pulled out, and a quarter-mile of fence went down with them. In winter the wire sometimes snapped under shrinkage from the cold.

The item of sixty dollars for two wells included in my father's declaration must have been the cost of the wooden cribbing which kept the wells from caving in. The second well was sunk as a reserve in case the first well should run dry. It was a much less arduous task; my father had had all he wanted of solo digging, so he traded labour with Jim Pearson to sink a well for each of them. They had no trouble finding water on Pearson's place near the coulee. For our second site my father chose a slight depression midway between the shack and the stable. The standard portents of water-weed, ant-hills, and badger-holes were less emphatic, suggesting that there was a larger element of chance involved. The risk seemed worth taking, for if water was found it would be nearer and more convenient to the house. Pearson had heard of water-diviners, but put little faith in them, as he had no direct experience of or personal aptitude for the art. The site felt right, so that was good enough for him. With two men on the job a smaller diameter was possible, about four feet, against Father's six-foot solo dig. They made fast progress and struck wet sand at about eleven feet. Another foot brought the well in with enough head to provide three feet of water, and a heavy flow. It was good, drinkable water, but proved to be harder than the old well; it did not lather readily and left heavy deposits of "fur" in kettles. Owing to the heavy flow and smaller pool, I found it difficult to draw two buckets of clear water without sand or silt. My mother disliked the new well for this reason and for its poor lathering quality, so we continued to use the old well for the house, despite the long, uphill haul. We could never account for the difference in quality, since both aquifers lay in the same stratum less than two hundred yards apart. It argued against the hypothesis of an underground post-glacial river. Despite its stronger flow the new well was less resistant to prolonged drought and later went dry.

But this was long after the interview with Smaill and the Statutory Declaration which he notarized. As my father was leaving the office, Smaill called him back.

"There's another page to this bloody form," he said. "Might as well be filled out even if you've said it all before, or those fellows in Ottawa will send it back." Question 12. How much land has been broken and cropped on the said homestead in each year? Answer: 1911 broke 60 acres, cropped 60 acres (this would be the big patch of flax by the house, the first land my father broke); 1912 broke 10 acres, cropped 70 acres (there was no time to break more owing to waiting for our arrival in Morse). Question 13. What area of the said homestead can be brought under cultivation? Answer: 160 acres. Question 14. What area of said homestead is hay land and what area swamp? The questions here were redundant and inevitably drew conflicting replies.

"You can see this questionnaire was invented by those guys down east," Smaill said. "They think in terms of tamarack swamps or beaver meadows."

"Well," said my father, "there's plenty of hay in the sloughs, but what are sloughs for the purposes of Form No. 11?" "Forget it," Smaill counselled again. "They'll think up some absurd word in the course of time. Sloughs will be potholes, and coulees will be ravines, so other bureaucrats can understand the language, whether you do or not. Sign here." Father signed and strolled down to the post-office, hoping Coleman would have the mail sorted by then. On the way he stopped by Best's drug store to pick up some more Velox for my photography. The wooden sidewalk swayed under his walk. A meadow lark sang on a fence post. The sky was populous with woolly clouds like sheep in a pasture. My father had an absurd impulse to go back to Smaill's and add that item to Form No. 11. Instead he bought a pound of chocolates from Best. They would cheer up my mother, who had been worried by the denunciation.

Then he dropped in at the Hendersons', who had just finished their hardware store, the first brick building Vanguard boasted. It also had Vanguard's first brick outhouse, which customers were free to use. Father bought a saw, charged it, used the outhouse, and headed back to the livery barn to pick up his team. Feeling hungry after a long morning, he turned in to the Carlton Cafe, run by two Chinese who served up a solid two-course meal of meat and two vegetables, choice of pie or ice cream, and coffee, for forty cents. The team at the livery barn cost an extravagant sixty cents, for Father had forgotten to bring an oat bundle with him.

The mail brought Father a letter from Mr. Ball of the Department of Education in Regina, asking why the School Board of Malvern Link School District 717 had hired a new teacher instead of renewing the contract of their first man, and would he send in a list of books for the school library which the Department was being asked to pay for. My father resigned himself to the loss of another Sunday afternoon answering this request, but it was reasonable, and getting off such a report gave him a feeling of accomplishment. He decided to give the book list job to Miss Reaman; it would give her something to do over the weekend, and take her mind off the dullness of life on the prairies.

Automatically, he stepped into Smaill & Hogg's office. Smaill expressed surprise at seeing him again. My father was almost as surprised to find himself there. He cast about for an excuse for disturbing Smaill again; all he could think of was Ball's letter. "He wants some information, but he hasn't sent a questionnaire," my father said. "You don't happen to have a handy, all-purpose form, do you? It doesn't have to make any sense, and the questions don't need to mean anything, but nobody's going to look at what I say unless it's on a printed form."

"Take it easy, old boy," Smaill replied. "Don't let them get your nanny! Keep your hair on." My father twisted his moustache, but said nothing. "Trouble with you fellows," Smaill continued, "you all come out here thinking you'll be your own master, or your own man, or whatever you like to call it. Well, it just ain't so. So better forget it. The C.P.R.'s your master here, and the weather's your master, and the wind, and the hoppers, and the rest. There'll always be something or someone. To start with, these fellows up in Ottawa who let you settle out here are your masters; and if they weren't, someone else would be, like the implement firms and the high tariff men. And pretty soon you'll find the Grain Growers Association you're working so hard for will be your master, and then you'll really have something to worry about, because they'll tell you what you may grow and what you may sell, and you better not have too much to say about it, or you'll be radicals, and they'll call out the Mounties to take care of you. They'll be worse than the Kayser, that these Dutchmen and the Mennonites came here to get out from under.'' Smaill warmed to his favourite topic: "You fellows were spoiled in the Old Country, and you brought a lot of silly ideas out here with you. Yet you don't like our own idea, that 'Jack's as good as his master'. That's good for your hired man, for they're hard to come by, because any hired man who's any good wants to be his own master and have his own land; and that's the biggest of all loads of bull. You think because you have your own land, you're your own master; well, let me tell you, you're a slave of your land, that's what you are. If you go away for a day some swine comes along and lays a cancellation against you, and the cows aren't stripped properly by your hired man, so they go dry before they should, and they climb through the fence and into Pearson's oats and either burst themselves or do fifty dollars' worth of damage, or both, and the dog gets into the hen-pen and the sow eats her farrow, and the rain gets into the granary, and the bottom drops out of the price of wheat.''

"Stop it," my father shouted, appalled by this roll-call of calamities. "You haven't mentioned the house burning down.''

"Could be happening right this minute," Smaill retorted. "Better let me sell you some insurance. Ploughed a fire-guard yet?''

"Yes. Figure eight around house and barn.''

"Fine. I'll give you $500 protection on both. Like a nice head-stone, too?''

"Too many stones on my place already.''

"You'll need a nice headstone one of these days. Pick your own lettering. Finest marble, won't flake; guaranteed to last longer than you do. You can have it on time. Put the date in later.''

This practical approach to the realities of life and death so depressed my father that he stepped into Pelletier's pool-hall and picked up a pint of rye. It would cheer the three-hour drive home. My mother did not approve of this wayside cheer, so when he had finished the bottle my father used to throw the empty flask under the granary. Tracking a wounded gopher under this same granary one day, I discovered a treasury of old containers. I carefully retrieved them all with the garden rake and proudly displayed my discoveries to my mother. It was some little time before I connected this episode with the chill which came over my relations with my father about that time. I guess maybe I was not too bright, or was too innocent, which might be the same thing.

Driving north, my father crossed the railroad tracks which marked the limit of the village of Vanguard. The thrice-weekly mixed train which ambled down from Swift Current was snorting to itself, prior to undertaking the return trip. Ten grain cars were completing their loading at Smaill's elevator; half a dozen salesmen travelling in harness, hardware, and drugs were comparing notes while they waited for the passenger car which brought up the tail end of the Vanguard Mixed to pull up to the depot platform. It had been a long day for them, catching the Mixed at Swift Current at six in the morning, trundling down the roughly laid track to Wymark, Blumenhof, Neville, and Pambrun, shivering until the stove heated up, then being half-stifled during the shunting of freight and grain cars at each stop, until at last the train squealed out around the turn-around just before Vanguard, and backed in stately triumph to the depot about eleven o'clock.

"Five hours to move forty miles," they complained as they swung their sample bags down to the wooden platform. They hurried off, their bright yellow shoes with bulbous toes squeaking with every step. There was no time to waste if they wanted to get their business done and be back in Swift Current that evening. Nobody wanted to get caught for the night in Vanguard, although the Vanguard Hotel was better than most, with an inside lavatory highly regarded as the most modern appliance in the west. It ground up the material and deposited it in a deep shaft. Nobody knew what would happen when the shaft was full — another would be dug, presumably.

Walking about Vanguard was no hardship provided one stayed on the wooden sidewalks, but crossing the street was a major hazard after a rain. The streets were wide and unpaved. The blue gumbo on which the "town" was built — it had been a field of oats the year before — was notorious for its adhesive quality; it stuck to everything, pulled off rubbers — galoshes as people were beginning to call them — after a couple of steps. The sign manual of Vanguard was a solitary galosh stuck in the gumbo. In the one-block sector of Main Street where most of the stores clustered, a stretch of steel pipe on wooden stanchions served as a hitching rail. Many of the farmers parked and often fed their teams there. Those who came in from near by grudged the sixty cents the livery barn charged. Broncos enjoyed mixing a mouthful of green oat-bundle with a bite at the baggy end of a drummer's blue peg-top pants. Aware of this hazard, my father always edged along the inside of the sidewalk.

He felt in the pocket of his sheepskin coat, discovering with a guilty start a letter which my mother had given him with strict instructions not to forget to mail it. It was too late now to put it on the train. He hitched the team to the rail and hurried to the post-office. Half a dozen heavy-set farmers were stamping about, scrutinizing the notices pinned to the wall, or peering through the glass doors of their postal boxes. Coleman recognized my father's measured tread. He threw up the wicket: "There's another letter for you, Dick. From Australia. Your brother, likely — it's from J. Minifie in Melbourne."

"Yes, that's my brother, Jim," my father said.

"Nice stamp," Coleman returned. "Map of Australia and a kangaroo on it. Mind if I peel it off? George collects them."

"Better leave it," my father said. "My boys go for them too. It's a good hobby; teaches them a lot of history and geography."

"Gives them itchy feet," Coleman said. "Young George can't sit still. Wants to be off somewhere, he don't know where."

"Well, I guess we were like that in our day," my father said, "else we wouldn't be here today."

"These young people are different," Coleman contradicted. "I tell my boy, 'You don't know when you're well off. When I was your age we were pulling stumps back in Ontario; trying to clear a stump meadow broke your heart. They clung like back teeth. You don't know how lucky you are to have no trees,' I tell him. But they don't listen. They know better. 'Back there,' my boy tells me, 'back there you worked for the stumps,' my boy tells me, smart-aleck, 'now you work for another set of stumps, those fellows up in Ottawa.' "

"I guess he has something there," my father replied. "But what's he going to do about it?"

"He's crazy," Coleman replied. "Keeps talking revolution, and down with the Mounties! Crazy stuff like that. Throw out your masters, like some of them square-heads or Hunkies who want to throw out the Kayser."

"I hear that sort of talk on the threshing-gang," my father said, "and I don't like it."

"Where they get all that stuff?" Coleman asked.

"Down in the States. From the I. W. W. down in Walla Walla, Washington."

"I see some of their stuff in the mail," Coleman told him. "Here's your brother's letter. He coming out to see you?"

"No," my father told him, shortly. "Not yet anyway. After I've got established a bit, maybe he will. But things are still a bit rough. Things will be a lot easier once I'm my own master."

"That's what they all say," Coleman muttered. "They never learn. That's the way they talk down in Walla Walla."

To my father he suggested a look at the sale notices pinned to the wall. Ted Lewis was offering a "waggon and small team" for $200; my father made a mental note to look at this on the way home. Larsen wanted to sell ten cows for $350 and a separator and churn for a further $60. Father figured Larsen must be going out of dairying, and wondered why.

"He's getting to be a slave to them cows," Coleman said. "Can't go to the Current for a day without something happening to them, either scratching their udders on wire or dropping their calves or getting into his oats and like to burst; and if he hires anyone to look after them while he's away and help milk them while he's home, it takes all the profit out. He can get sixty bushels of oats to the acre off that heavy gumbo of his. At twenty-five cents a bushel that gives him fifteen dollars an acre. He wouldn't do that well with milk at ten cents a quart and butter at twenty-five cents a pound."

"How about the new creamery the co-op built at the Current?" my father asked. "It pays twenty-five cents per pound of butterfat in the cream and they collect it."

"It's a good deal if you ship it up to Swift," Coleman allowed. "But he'll still do better with that pedigree wheat he's raising. With hired help thirty dollars a month and board. The young fellows from down east didn't turn up this year."

"What's he want for the wheat?" my father asked. "I might get some."

"It's pinned up on the wall there. Why don't you read these notices? Registered Marquis seed wheat, seventy-six cents a bushel cash, eighty-six cents on time. That's a real bargain; it's bound to rise by spring, and you'd pay eighty-nine cents at the elevator for mixed seed. Pedigree seed ripens evenly and about ten days earlier, which gives it a chance to beat the frost."

There were a dozen other items, including a plough for $25, a disc for $40, and a couple of pigs for $25. My father was only interested in the wheat, which he wanted to get at this low price, treat with blue-stone for smut, and have all ready to seed as soon as spring weather permitted. It could spend the winter outside in the wagon without harm.

As he was leaving, Coleman passed him the final instalment of his mail, a fat envelope from Regina. My father regarded it with some surprise. It did not bear the familiar label of the Department of Education but originated with the Department of Agriculture. Coleman was curious about it, too, so my father opened it up, to find a voluminous questionnaire topped by a polite letter asking if my father would furnish the department with statistics on local farm operations, moisture and crop conditions, and his estimate of the yield. He thought he would check this request with Larsen.

He found Larsen enthusiastic about wheat; it was the coming crop, he said; the new strain only took ninety days to mature, the yield was heavy, and there would always be a demand since the world was full of hungry people and would soon be fuller. My father suggested that the time was not far away when Russia would be a strong competitor. Larsen scoffed at this idea. "Those Grand Dukes don't know how to use land," he insisted, "and they milk it dry; as long as there are Grand Dukes in Russia, we won't need to fear competition from them." My father doubted the relationship between Grand Dukes and low production, but he was not prepared to argue the point. He picked up fifty bushels of seed wheat and set off again for home.

A mile north of Vanguard he left the slippery road allowance, which had been indifferently graded with a deep ditch on either side that gobbled up anything that skidded on the grade. He drew in to Lewis's to look at the "waggon and small team" offered in the post-office. He found the team were light broncos which he did not think would stand up to heavy farm work. He liked the heavy semi-Clydesdale type like Mike and Meg, who could put a ton of bone and muscle into the collar when it was needed. Lewis asked after the two kittens which he had given us the year before, and was amused to learn how they had naturalized themselves. After a brief chat about crop yields, prices, and freight and elevator charges, my father pulled out, headed east again for another two miles until he passed Kuhlman's slough, already frozen over, then struck across the prairie north-east, following a winding trail which skirted sloughs, slanted up hills on a practical gradient, and cut off a mile of slippery graded road. He passed the Olsens' two shacks, where Ole and August were cultivating between rows of young trees, and on to the height of land, from which he could look north five miles to the low semicircle of hills on the three-quarter section belonging to the Hudson's Bay Company. Westwards he could see the elevators of Neville and Pambrun twenty miles away, and the trail of smoke and steam left by the Vanguard Mixed, as it chugged along to Swift Current carrying the drummers back to the excitements of the metropolis. There was no tree, nor even a bush, in sight. The prairie rolled like a dun-coloured ocean to the horizon; the scattered shacks seemed to bob about on this illimitable flood like derelict windjammers. He urged Bonny and Jewel, two mares he had recently purchased, to a burst of speed, feeling a pinch of hunger as he noted the plume of smoke coiling from the chimney of his shack, speaking of a kettle singing on the stove and a pot of tea steeping on the table.

He had picked up three rolls of heavy red paper — comfort felt, it was called — to finish off the inside walls, cut draughts, and make the room look a little more attractive. Sticking the "comfort felt" to the re-saw walls would be a priority task for next week. He remarked with some concern what he considered the scrabbly job done by the tractor-drawn gang plough in breaking the pre-emption. There were long patches where the plough had skipped before it re-entered the turf after being jumped out by a big stone which had somehow escaped attention. It made an untidy-looking field which offended my father's longing for neat furrows in long, straight lines, evenly carved and six inches thick. He had paid the people with the Case steamer and the eight-share gang plough four dollars an acre. He compared the result unfavourably with the neat, pleated tucks Jones had put in the prairie on his land which he had broken slowly, painstakingly, with a team of oxen and much profanity, an essential for success with oxen.

My father thought he had been poorly served by the Case team; but, in fact, the rough ploughing was a godsend, for it broke the force of the wind in summer, preventing it from sweeping away the topsoil, and acted as a snow-trap in winter, ensuring deep ground moisture as the snow thawed gently when the frost came out of the soil with the break-up. My father was fortunate in getting the work done at that time, for he was able to crop the land to flax twice, which broke up the sod, before putting in wheat.

Chapter Eighteen

The cow, being with calf, went dry early in the winter of 1913-14, so every morning I trudged half a mile east to Mrs. Boyd's to pick up our day's milk supply. The wind made the trip an ordeal. It usually blew from the west, whirling dusty snow in an eddy into my face, where it melted and froze. Long before I reached Boyd's I sensed the warning feeling as if flies were crawling up my nostrils, which meant my nose was freezing. I waited at Boyd's as little time as it took to thaw me out, and then set out on the homeward trip into the wind, which meant another nose-freeze. Both Dick and I wore Balaclava helmets, knitted by loving aunts, which covered the head and neck all but the face. They were not really as warm as standard cloth caps with turn-down fur ear-flaps, but my mother thought they looked much nicer. They did well enough save for a nip on the lobe of the ear, which was perpetually peeling as a result, but at least it did not drop off like the cats'. However, I was glad when the cow belatedly calved and came back into milk. Coming late it was a bull-calf, a natural phenomenon which I used later to predict with some accuracy the off-spring of our pregnant friends, establishing thereby a reputation as a minor prophet which stood up well enough provided it was not pushed too hard, and no mention made of the analogy on which the forecast was based.

We frequently heard that winter the characteristic sharp crack, like a pistol-shot, of boards splitting in the frost, either because they were green and wet when used or because the cold shrank the nails. On the ceiling-roof we could see the nails which had missed the joists coated white with frozen humidity. We feared they would thaw and drip, but the metal conducted the cold too well for that to happen. At night the temperature fell with the fire. By morning our breath was frozen on the sheets; if we had left water in the bucket it was frozen solid and the pail ruptured by the expanding ice. We lost two pails before we took that lesson to heart. If we left no water for morning, someone had to go down to the well to get a pailful before there could be any coffee for breakfast. This was a miserable chore. The wind was up before we were. It whipped water out of the bucket to freeze on my overalls. I got back to the house with the bucket half full, the rest of the water in ice on my legs; it thawed out in a puddle on the kitchen floor. It was a poor way to start the day.

The winter of 1913-14 was long and cold; as usual in such weather cycles, spring lasted only a day or two. Suddenly we were up to our knees in mud. We frantically loaded the seeder with wheat for the fifty acres close to the house. The ground had plenty of moisture, so germination was fast and even. It looked like a good crop year and we were cautioned not to beat too wide a path through the field on the way to school, but to keep it to the thinnest possible trail.

One Sunday in August when the wheat was heading out, Mother, Dick, and I walked over to the Pearsons' for tea and chatter. We found them deeply concerned over the possibility of war with Germany. It was August 2, but the Regina papers wrote as if it had already begun — anticipating the beginning of the war as they were later prematurely to report its ending.

We discussed the prospects as we wandered back home through the wheat, waist-high, green, and even — the promise of a good crop if the frost held off.

My mother, like the patriotic Englishwoman she was, felt that the Royal Navy would soon teach the Kaiser to sing "Britannia Rule the Waves". This comfortable assurance withered as the Navy sat at anchor behind torpedo nets. When it did venture out, the report we received from the English papers differed materially from the accounts brought to school by the Fliegel and Kovac children from German and Hungarian news sources, which put quite a different face on the Royal Navy's role. This led to friction and occasional unpleasantness at school with a hyper-patriotic enthusiasm on my part and a passionate desire to "do my bit". Most of my male cousins had volunteered for military service.

The *Family Herald and Weekly Star* contributed to my martial ardour by distributing a war-map of Europe. We hung it on the wall, piercing with coloured pins such unpronounceable strategic targets as Przemysl, Lvov, and Cracow.

A sharp attack of tonsillitis during the winter of 1914-15 dimmed my military ardour, while heavy snow, and the prospect of another good crop as a result, kept our thoughts at home.

Despite trouble with my throat, the winter of 1914-15 was much more agreeable than our first winters in the West, which had been disappointing in their failure to produce the snow we had expected and looked forward to. This third winter was better in that respect. How different this sharp powdery stuff was from the big, wet flakes we were used to in English winters; but we soon discovered the beauties of the six-spoke crystals which sifted in but broke up almost before they could be observed.

The wild drifting into hard snowbanks was also a novelty. Whoever heard of snow you could cut with a saw, and fashion into blocks like building-stone? Using this material, Dick and I learned the role of the keystone in the circular arch. Much of my difficulty with my throat may have been the result of spending hours crouched in our snow house, built from materials carved from the big drift between the shack and the outhouse.

This quarry made emergency travel to the outhouse hazardous. My mother called it a death-trap. The outhouse was bad enough, she said, with its freezing draughts which discouraged contemplation. We defanged the draughts by papering the inside of the outhouse with comic drawings ripped out of the English Christmas magazines with which loving aunts deluged us. Before winter was over, I knew by heart their lively patter. They encouraged contemplation of the vices, follies, and misfortunes of mankind which are as appropriate to the backhouse philosopher formulating his *weltschmerz* as to the historian viewing the decline and fall of empires.

The year 1915 was a fertile one in many ways. All through the winter of 1914-15 I had noticed my mother growing more unwieldy in body, but at the same time, more tranquil in mind. An unusual and welcome placidity infused our lives. By the second week of April 1915, it was obvious that my mother was nearing her time, and it was no surprise to me to be ordered to take the buggy post-haste to pick up Mrs. Hudson, the local midwife, a stout woman with an extensive and successful practice, who lived on her farm five miles away. On the way home she briefed me on my role, which would be to fill the wash-boiler with water from the slough, dig a hole on the fire-guard for the afterbirth, and then go over to Boyd's until Mrs. Hudson hitched a sheet to the clothes-line as a signal to return.

It was a pleasant day, sunny and fresh. The sloughs were full of water and clamorous with frogs. My father went up to the pre-emption to look at the crop. We both came back on Mrs. Hudson's signal, to find my mother looking very happy, with a red-faced baby in her arms. Mary Pearson, who had seen me go by with Mrs. Hudson in the buggy, had hurried over for what she correctly diagnosed as an exceptional occasion, and was slapping diapers around as if she had been doing this all her life.

She was then only sixteen, but she came to regard my little brother Eric as her private property, which was lucky for him, for my own attentions to his needs were sporadic and perhaps occasionally a trifle slapdash; but when he was a grown man he was embarrassed in town when Mary dashed across the street to embrace him, shouting "That's my baby". Mary was a girl of character. With her father she had walked out from Herbert, on the main line C.P.R., just west of Morse, three years earlier. They covered thirty-six miles in a single day, because he was anxious to get on his land and brooked no delay. Jim Pearson carried a bag of tools — hammer and nails, drill and screwdriver — slung over his shoulder. He was as glad as Mary to see Vandermark's shack as night fell; but there were still six miles to go so they had pressed on and reached his farm, triumphant but exhausted, both of them. Thenceforth not much happened in Malvern Link unbeknownst to Mary. She was undisputed leader of the school, despite her sex; she welcomed order and imposed discipline on boys and girls alike.

In 1915 our pre-emption bore thirty bushels to the acre. Stooking was a nightmare that lasted three weeks — interminable rows of heavy sheaves to be set up, while the binder clattered remorselessly around the field, adding to the rows faster than I could stook them. Happily I had Frank Boyd to help me; we worked with pitchforks, getting stooking down almost to a ballet rhythm: first a sheaf each, butt down, leaning together like a church window; two more, one to right one to left; another two, then one at each end; the last sheaf on top to shed the rain.

At four o'clock each afternoon my mother brought out a can of tea and some sandwiches. The baby, four months old, came with her for the outing; the dog came for the outing too, and the off chance of a stray gopher. When my father came abreast of us he halted the McCormick binder, and threw down the whip, to which he had tied a black rag to attract the flying ants away from himself; they prefer dark colours, which is a mercy, for they are miserable little creatures with a sting that can make life quite uncomfortable for their hosts. They drive horses crazy by crowding on their withers. My father sat beside us on a sheaf of wheat and held out his mug for tea, to cut the dust and chaff in his throat. The horses jangled their bits as the cowbirds cleared their withers of ants; crickets shrilled; the dog bounced about after gophers; the baby wet himself, so my mother laid him on his back between two rows of stubble and handed me the diaper. I threw it at the dog. Over all was the warm fragrance of ripe wheat; a killdeer piped in a nearby slough and we knew that this was the best wheat country in the world. I took an ear and ground it out in the palm of my hand. I blew the chaff away and counted thirty-five plump grains to the ear, which meant better than thirty bushels to the acre. The kernels were hard, too flinty to chew. My father felt in his pocket for another handful of ears, and talked about feeding the world — markets forever as long as people were hungry. It was a simple faith in supply and demand; but he was well aware of the bottle-necks in moving grain to markets. He did not dream at that time that Ottawa would later prefer to pay for non-production rather than find markets. He thought the answer to the problem was for the government to push through the railway to Port Nelson, on Hudson Bay. From that point wheat could move anywhere in the world. Frank Boyd had other views.

"Don't expect the gummint to do anything until this war is over and we have our own men up in Ottawa," Frank said in his dour way. "We should build our own railroad, and our own elevators at end of steel, or we'll never move a crop like this, and first thing you know there'll be no room for the next crop, and them stupid bastards will be telling us not to grow so much. Stupid sons of bitches," he added, dwelling as lovingly on each word as if he had been an Old Testament prophet.

"You talk like Smaill in Vanguard," my father said.

"And he talks like old man Larsen," Frank returned.

"I got this seed from Larsen," my father reminded him.

"Them Scandahoovians ain't just selling seed wheat," Frank replied. "They're selling seed ideas, and I don't know how clean the seed is, nor whether it's what we want on this prairie soil."

"The wheat is good and clean, anyway," my father testified. There had, in fact, been some charlock mustard in it which we had spent hours pulling up on Sunday evenings as soon as it was tall enough to be seen, heedless of the New Testament caution against pulling up tares (Matthew 15:29-30), which I had discovered while I was churning and the butter was slow in coming. Tea finished, the binder clattered off again, and we worked until the dew fell and the round moon climbed over Scott's hills to the east. The crickets fell silent, the long day was over.

We trudged back home where my brother Dick was filling the watering trough. It was, however, a losing battle against the leaks; for our united skill in carpentry had not been able to put together a watertight trough. We tried to caulk the seam with string and oakum from old ropes; still it leaked. I spelled my brother off and between the two of us we had pumped the trough half-full of water by the time my father arrived. This pleased him, for all he had to do then was water the team, give them a quick rubdown to prevent them from catching cold, and then head for the house, where we all settled down to high tea with eggs, mother's plum-cake, and last Saturday's mail.

In addition to the business documents from the departments of Education and Agriculture, the Post Office brought us treasures from the loving aunts and uncles who maintained the link with the far-off, strange, romantic world into which we had disappeared. There was the *Birmingham Post,* three weeks old, but secreting a slip of geranium swathed in damp moss, and ready to be set out in a coffee tin to lend freshness and colour to the room we lived, cooked, and ate in. There was the latest issue of *The Captain,* a curious periodical devoted to the habits and outlook of British public-school boys. It had no personal validity for me, since I had never been to a public school (i.e., an expensive private school), but it ran serially an early adventure story by John Buchan, which had fascinating side-lights. I followed these up avidly, scouring teacher's encyclopaedia for data on Zimbabwe and Prester John. It also had a good stamp corner and an indifferent editorial page which occasionally commented on the doings of British royalty. The fascination of this schoolboy chatter for my father astonished me; he devoured each number as it came in; the cricket column may have accounted in part for this attraction, but I think on the whole it was an escape into the never-never land of what might have been if his own father had not died shortly before his birth, leaving his upbringing to mother, grandmother, aunts, and twin sisters.

Arrival of *The Captain* on Saturday ensured that Sunday would follow standard pattern. Established procedure was that after break-fast and the washing-up, my father, Dick, and I went to the barn and moved a week's accumulation, piling it in a long "harrow" beside a slough. The lengthening mound of manure destroyed a pretty row of white wood-anemones which had managed to accommodate them-selves to the rigours of the treeless prairie, but could not survive the destructive habits of the homesteader. I regretted the desecration of the slough-side flora, which was the first plant association I had studied; but it was a handy place to dump manure, and that was reason enough on the prairie where the harsh elements bred a harsh insensitivity to the claims of anything else to survival.

While we were cleaning out the stable, my mother prepared a gigantic rib-roast of beef for Sunday dinner, Monday cold, Tuesday hash, Wednesday shepherd's pie, Thursday and Friday stew, and Saturday steak-and-kidney pudding. Sunday's roast was accom-panied by Yorkshire pudding and potatoes, if I had remembered to peel them or been caught before I could escape to the barn. Later there was also horseradish, once it had accepted the prairie climate and soil. It took to them readily enough, pushing roots down to surprising depths to resist the summer heat and the winter frost.

In season there were fresh peas, which my father and I competed to shell. I liked to hear the contents of a good pod rolling into the collander. Rarely on Sunday, but as a special treat some weekday, I had my favourite dessert, apple dumplings, a heavy suet concoction of which I ate so much that I spent a comatose afternoon absorbing it. On Sunday I was expected to be reasonably lively while Mother hitched up an ox, Old Billy, to the stone-boat and went for an afternoon's visit to Pearson's or Boyd's or even two miles north-west to Robinson's, although this was horse-and-buggy travel, inconveniently far for ox and stone-boat. My father settled down to his study of *The Captain,* while I worked through the latest war and astronomical information in the *Family Herald and Weekly Star.* I much preferred this occupation to visiting, for I was uncomfortable and shy with strangers and too ready to take the lazy course of withdrawal rather than struggle with unfamiliar attitudes and backgrounds which had nothing in common with my own.

While dinner was cooking, my father shaved. He used an old-fashioned straight blade by Krupp; the edge cut into the week's growth with a noise like raking gravel. I was so impressed by the ease with which he handled the "cutthroat" that when I joined the Army I used the Army-issue straight blade myself, to the intense admiration of my tent-mates.

Sunday shaving over, my father put on a shirt and tie — he wore his working shirt open all week — and added a splendid fancy waistcoat, made by his Aunt Jane long ago of green silk strings drawn through primrose-coloured canvas; it had glass buttons. In this glorious attire, my father presented a handsome figure as he whipped the carving-knife against the steel and shaved off slice after slice of red meat. He stood up to get a better purchase on the roast and delivered a brisk comment on affairs of state, province, and school district, while he carved. It was his moment. His moustache was full without exaggeration into handle-bars; his skin was fresh and clear, easily acquiring a glowing tan which too readily developed wind-burn under the sun; it was justification enough for the once-a-week shave even had there been time enough for a daily rite.

For my father, however, most of Sunday afternoon was taken up by correspondence with the Department of Education and the Grain Growers Association. He also used the occasion to make up the minutes of the last School Board meeting, recording the detail of payments to Tom Jones for janitor services — " 75 cents if we have the money in the bank"; $1.50 for a new bucket because the old one had frozen solid overnight and burst; a resolution instructing the teacher to ensure that in future the bucket should be emptied before she left to prevent recurrence of this expense. To these chores was now added the furnishing to the Department of Agriculture of statistics on the agricultural and social activities of the Rural Municipality of Glen Bain. This time was carved out of my father's Sunday afternoon sleep in the Morris chair. He gave it up reluctantly for he was always fighting for a few minutes' more sleep. When you got up at half past four, it began to feel like a long day quite early in the afternoon; it was a struggle to survive until supper-time. He went to bed a few minutes after nine o'clock, taking with him a candle on a blue enamelled holder, with a wide base as a precaution against fire in the event he fell asleep before putting out the light. He usually read for ten minutes before extinguishing it with one dexterous wave of the hand.

One of the problems with which Father had to cope was getting overdue school funds from the Department of Education. When they failed to come on time, Miss Reaman could not be paid and she could not pay Mrs. Boyd; Mrs. Boyd in turn could not pay Agar's Dry Goods; and they could not settle with Henderson's Hardware. Thus the economy of the village and the surrounding school districts were intimately connected, and so delicately balanced that a very small gap in payments produced concentric waves of economic distress.

The gap was, in fact, pathetically small. Miss Reaman's salary was only $600 a year, with a promise of raises, if she proved satisfactory and the money was available, to $800, $1,000, or even $1,200, if there was another good crop. That scale, however, was not to be reached for years to come. She paid $25 a month for her board to Mrs. Boyd. Malvern Link School District had a problem in paying the teacher's $60 a month; when the provincial subsidy was late, my father finally took his courage in both hands and resolved to send the Deputy Minister of Education a telegram to jog his memory. An extravagance such as sending a long telegram when a three-cent stamp would have done would never have received the board's approval, so my father drew it up without consulting his colleagues. It read:

> Courage, fortitude, patience of our teacher playing out. Check from your office to cover long past due and current grant monies will help restore in a tangible way the above good qualities of our whole teaching staff.

My father thought Miss Reaman would appreciate being called "our whole teaching staff". She would appreciate even more getting paid on time.

The telegram was dispatched from the railroad depot by Mr. Pilson, the station agent, when my father went to town the following Tuesday, and to his gratification the cheque arrived the very next day. Education had a reprieve.

The long warm autumn of 1915 resounded with the trilling of crickets and the low drone of the threshing machine. Mountains of wheat straw spewed out of the separator, creating a major hazard to cultivation if it was left, while if removed by burning it destroyed the fibre of the soil on which it stood. We deplored the waste, comparing this hasty threshing with the relaxed English method, in which the straw was carefully bundled up, intact save for the heads, to be used as bedding for stock. With us, however, faced with overwhelming abundance, haste was imperative; otherwise the crop would be buried under the snow. So, haste and waste became our motto.

With the bumper crop of 1915 we discarded our scruples when the money began to pour in. It financed, among larger items, my essay into photography, undertaken on the assurance of the teacher that it would not be an expensive hobby if developing and printing were done at home. I built a dark lantern to her design from two empty salmon-cans and some haywire. Illumination was by candle, screened through a window of red crepe paper. I assembled the equipment on the settle in the cellar. It consisted of three ironstone soup-plates, one for water, one for the developer, and one for the fixative.

I felt that I was stepping into a new-found land when I went down the cellar steps one morning and closed the trapdoor over my head, warning my mother on no account to open it until I gave the word. My camera was a battered box Brownie, a parting gift from my favourite cousin just before I left England.

There is nothing to equal the excitement of the amateur photographer when for the first time he watches the yellow emulsion of his film strip resolve into dark patterns in the recognizable outlines of a sailing ship passed on the Atlantic crossing; other frames produced a prairie slough with ducks, a shack, and a face!

In my excitement I shouted aloud; my mother took this as the signal to open the trapdoor; but no harm was done. The equipment was assembled upstairs in the evening, when I printed out my pictures on Velox, activated by the kitchen kerosene lamp; its low candle-power gave opportunity for variations in exposure and trick effects with masks which were hailed as great triumphs of art. Nearly sixty years later, those early prints, however faded, still thrill me.

Photography competed for a time with war fever, but the pressure of events and the yearning to take part in history were too strong. I saw myself in heroic roles, sounding amid shot and shell the charge which rallied a hopeless retreat. My father cautioned that there would be time enough for that when I was eighteen but I feared it would be all over without my having lent a helping hand or sounded a solitary bugle call.

Chapter Nineteen

Early in 1916, I persuaded my mother to drive me in to Vanguard, and to go with me to the recruiting station set up by the Royal North-West Mounted Police. There, on Saturday, March 4, I signed the blue attestation papers and she signed her consent to my becoming No. 252352, Private Minifie J. M., C Company, 209th Battalion, Canadian Expeditionary Force, for three years or the duration. I gave my true age; the recruiting sergeant said, "That's all right; they need buglers." I was in! Accompanied by a Sergeant-Major, who materialized from the livery barn where he had been enjoying a little nip, I was marched to the station and put aboard the Vanguard Mixed, with a free railroad warrant to Swift Current. A band, assembled from the cinema house, played martial music from "Intolerance", with Lillian Gish. My mother waved her handkerchief bravely, and at three o'clock on that same Saturday afternoon, the Vanguard Mixed took a deep breath and snorted out of the depot, bearing me to my assignment with destiny and the Bugle Corps. It was dark by the time the Vanguard Mixed roared at eight miles an hour into Swift Current.

I was dazzled by the five-branched street-lamps which threw golden circles of light on the snow. The Sergeant-Major marched me across the street to what seemed to my unsophisticated eyes a smart, even majestic, building, but which was in fact a filthy, decrepit small-town hotel. On the second floor, the Sergeant-Major pushed me into a dingy room — "The Quartermaster-Sergeant will look after you!" And to the Q.M.S. he explained: "Here's our catch for the day." He pushed me inside and closed the door, The Q.M.S. looked at me dourly and reached for a forage cap. It sat on my head like a tom-tit on a round of beef.

"Go get yourself a haircut," he said, "and then come back and see if this fits."

"I want to be a bugler," I quavered.

"First thing you have to learn is to do what I tell you," he retorted. "There's a barber in the basement. Get rid of that thatch!"

That was the last I heard of bugling. No bugle touched my lips in the entire three years and fifteen days I spent in the Canadian Army. It gave me a haircut and a trip to Britain and a dummy rifle. The sergeant told me to get something to eat and find a room with a spare paillasse (straw mattress) over in the Carlton. He found a uniform, shirt, underwear, and shoes, and washed his hands of me; from then on I was on my own. In the Army, as on the farm, any honest accounting would have to reckon me a net loss. However, a close haircut helped my morale, and I was "doing my bit", however insignificant that might be. I set my cap firmly on my head and strode off through those glamorously lit streets in search of my billet.

The 209th Overseas Battalion was quartered in two hotels in Swift Current in the spring of 1916, while it received preliminary drill before going off for the summer to Camp Hughes. A and B companies were lodged in the Imperial Hotel, an old wooden fire-trap, while C Company was assigned to the Carlton, a more pretentious brick and plaster building. One platoon of C Company remained in Vanguard, but for some obscure military reason I was not assigned to it, possibly because I came from the area. One unit remained at Maple Creek, seventy-five miles west of Swift Current, and was not really incorporated into the battalion until we were moved to Camp Hughes, in the sandy country between Portage la Prairie and Brandon.

The commanding officer of the 209th was Colonel Smythe, a local judge who did what he could with the material at hand. The company commanders were local men of character and ability; until they

went overseas they held acting rank of major; thereafter this fluctu-
ated at the whim of unidentified forces at much higher levels. There
was MacDonald of A Company, a solid officer whom I lost track of
after the war. There was M. A. McPherson of B Company, another
outstanding officer, who later became a distinguished lawyer and
public servant, with whom I felt it an honour to have been associated. C Company was headed by Roy T. Graham, whose untimely
death thirty years after the war terminated an honourable legal
career and deprived the bench of a potentially great judge. D Company was commanded by Sandilands, whom I lost sight of after the
war. The overwhelming number of Scots needs no emphasis. They
brought with them the clannishness, intelligence, conscience, and
compassion which make them such tough competition wherever
they go. Since my Army days I have lived and worked with many
groups, but nowhere with more respect and affection for my supe-
riors than I felt in the 209th Overseas Battalion, C.E.F. They were
men of honour, courage, and distinction.

The quality of leadership was reflected in the rank and file. Our
cannon-fodder were men of substance, farmers or businessmen,
volunteers all, many of them with records of service in the Imperial
Army in earlier wars. Most of them were canny homesteaders, glad
to be visiting the Old Country at the King's expense, but anxious to
get back as soon as possible to civilian life before they became
strangers there. An exception to the general run was a group of eight
Japanese who had joined the fortunes of C Company. I came to
know them fairly well, but never found out what led them to enlist
in the Canadian Army. I might have been more curious had I known
of the infamous treatment to which Japanese had been subjected on
the West Coast, chivvied and harried as if they were enemies. But I
knew nothing of that and they said nothing about it, so presumably
they had enlisted, like the rest of us, to defend the little man against
the tyranny of big government, in support of his right to be considered innocent until proven guilty, and to be safe against seizure of
his property without due process, and all that. Privately I had hoped
that by associating with Tanaka and his friends Kubota and Kubo-
dira I might pick up the rudiments of jiu-jitsu, which appealed to me
much more than the bayonet drill through which we sweated with
dummy guns and sacks stuffed with straw, urged on by Sergeant
Patrick Donovan's command to "hate that fellow". I simply could

not visualize conditions under which a bayonet charge by me could be successful. The brass in their wisdom thought otherwise. Fortunately, we were never forced to put our divergent views to the acid test of performance. I was amused many years later when other brass in another war discovered judo, and insisted that the saviours of democracy be initiated into its mysteries, along with karate cuts, as basic to the defence of peace with honour, or whatever we were fighting for this time.

I learned no jiu-jitsu. My fighting effectiveness was brought to combat pitch by Sergeant Donovan. As a veteran of the Boer War he believed in the efficacy of cold steel, without ever using it; he had been indoctrinated in this by a veteran of the Crimean War, who had never used it either, but had himself been trained by a veteran of the Napoleonic campaign, who had had the good fortune to be in hospital at the time of Waterloo.

As a good Irishman, Sergeant Donovan was conventionally disaffected to the British Crown, but proudly wore the Boer War ribbon — Queen's medal, course — which meant that he had received it either for active service in South Africa or for guarding Boer prisoners in St. Helena between April 14, 1900, and the death of Queen Victoria. He was a model drill-sergeant, although he never demeaned himself by resort to traditional drill-sergeant language. There was no need to. His commands were intelligible and delivered with timely precision on the correct beat. Off duty he was companionable, which to my mind was no merit, since the yearning for company usually overcame him late at night, impelling him to forgather for talk at a time when I ached for sleep. Like my father, I needed my full ration of sleep and resented deprivation.

My first military role was as a casualty. After two weeks I came down with scarlet fever. Along with half a dozen comrades in arms I was evacuated to an empty house across Swift Current Creek, where we lived the life of Riley, waited on by a pleasant nurse, who also thought she was waging "war for peace". I came out of hospital ten pounds heavier and was promptly granted ten days' sick leave and a railroad pass half-fare to Vanguard and return. This took me home for a brief family reunion and a satisfactory chance to show off my new uniform, and a one-dollar wrist watch which I had bought with my first pay cheque.

I found nothing changed on the homestead. I willingly maintained my fitness for hand-to-hand combat by forking ammoniated straw and cow-dung out of the stable, and establishing a minor record for loading and unloading the stone-boat. My father was amused and gratified by this display of combat readiness and by the conclusion he drew that, once the war was over, I might be ready to come back to the farm. I was happy enough to exchange Army rations for my mother's cooking, and a rifle for the pitchfork, especially since I was being paid $1.10 a day for my time and saving money, there being nothing to spend it on.

I returned to duty avid for the coming transfer to Camp Hughes, and what was billed as "summer field training". It turned out to be much the same as we had been doing in the streets of Swift Current, except that we stamped about in sand instead of snow, and slept uncomfortably on the ground in a tent, instead of equally uncomfortably on the floor in a room. However, my cash in hand and pocket increased so rapidly, since I neither drank nor smoked, that I was able to buy another wrist watch, this time a Waltham, in a silver case, for $16.50. This was my pride and joy for twenty-five years, until I lost it in a New York subway, through my negligence in not replacing the strap in time.

My tent-mates were agreeable, though not stimulating; they looked after me in a friendly, avuncular way, urging me to embrace learning and eschew wine and women. One of them was a printer who could recite Kipling endlessly. I retaliated with Tennyson, but "The Lotos-Eaters" did not make much impression, although I could spiel off reams of verses and kept a thin copy in my right breast pocket for handy reference. In the left-hand pocket I stowed a thin India paper Bible, with the vague idea that, placed over the heart, it might deflect a bullet.

A thunderstorm provided one adventurous night, flattening the tents and drenching all our clothes and blankets. The following night I was listed for guard duty. It was a twenty-four-hour stint, two hours on guard, four hours off, in four reliefs. I particularly disliked the watch in the morning hours. I left my nest of warm blankets in the middle of the night; for two hours I paced back and forth along the battalion perimeter, guarding crates of Coca-Cola stacked behind the mess tent, fighting the temptation to pry off a cap with the bayonet which was carried mounted on the rifle, making it awkward and out of balance, and, as it turned out, worthless as a pop-bottle opener. At the conclusion of the watch, I marched back to the guard tent, where my blankets, lying outside, by that time were drenched with dew, a small misery perhaps compared to being flooded out, but one which cancelled out my enthusiasm for the sight of the winter constellations glowing like jewels in the eastern sky in the early hours of a summer morning.

I stood guard the following day in a semi-comatose condition which produced shockingly unmilitary reactions when the brigade-major and the commanding general approached my post. Instead of turning to face them and presenting arms, I halted sideways on, and started to give the low-ranking salute of slapping one hand across the rifle stock. Then I caught sight of the insignia on their epaulettes; without turning outwards as I should have done, I transformed the smart low-ranking salute into a sloppy present arms, omitting even to draw my left foot back in the regulation manner. The ranking officer returned the salute in a half-assed way, and the party went on, snickering — at my expense, I felt.

Cumulating lack of sleep led me to drop off for a few minutes even in rest periods on the parade grounds. I awoke from these naps dizzy and dopy, to go through the routine of squadron and platoon drill like a zombie. I do not recall that I ever had occasion to use these marching skills. Army movements were just beginning to be motorized; it would have been more practical to have taught us the care and maintenance of mechanical transport, and how to drive a "lorry". However the military mind was still obsessed with the picture of a solid mass of infantry, moving as one man in close order, a perfect target for machine-guns, of which the Germans, who were not fighting like gentlemen, had an abundance.

At Camp Hughes, however, I had no convictions about the military virtue of precision marching, so I welcomed the first chance to get away from that hot, dusty camp, and the everlasting sand in food, in clothing, in the tea, in bedding. The Army had drained off the farm-hands and these were needed in August to help harvest a rust-ridden but still valuable crop. I applied for and obtained harvest leave, happy for once at the thought of stooking endless rows of wheat-sheaves, but eating sandless food.

I took home with me my prized belt encrusted with thirty battalion badges which I had laboriously collected from units quartered near by. It weighed five pounds or so, which, at the end of a morning's stooking, felt like thirty; by dinner-time, sweating and aching, I gladly hung the trophy belt on the wall. Our own badge was no great shakes, but some of the others displayed a good deal of ingenuity in combining the maple leaf, the battalion number, and an appropriate motto into a readily recognizable design. The 124th, raised in Moose Jaw, had no difficulty in working out a graphic if obvious solution. I was proud of the sample which I had removed from a cap placed carefully on a neatly folded pile of uniform pants and jacket that I had stumbled over in one of my walks out in the bush near camp.

It had obviously been discarded by a deserter. I twitted the next 124th officer I saw about this, but he indignantly denied that the 124th had lost any men by desertion. As he also denied that any of his men had lost or disposed of their uniforms, I was bound to conclude that the officer was misinformed, since I had the evidence of the badge. This shook me, for until then I had regarded the word of an "officer and gentleman" as gospel; if that could not be trusted, what could?

I found that very little of the war propaganda churned out by the Grit spokesmen and printed as news by the editors of Montreal and Winnipeg had much more validity. It lacked credence both in Vanguard and on the farm, although the war was not unpopular, since it kept Russia out of the British wheat market. Prices were high in consequence and farmers happy, despite an honourable reluctance to take advantage of the Old Country's hunger by racking prices out of sight. Prairie farmers showed a degree of enlightened self-interest in this respect which their detractors in the military-industrial complex might well have imitated. They received little immediate recognition, but the renunciation of several hundreds of millions of dollars paid off in the long term in goodwill, a non-marketable commodity but one which nations, industries, or individuals neglect at their peril.

I contributed to my district's fund of facts by denying widespread rumours of massive desertions to the United States, supporting this by disclosing the single desertion I knew of in the 124th, and another in the 209th itself, which came to my knowledge when one of the men who had been with me in the fever hospital at Swift Current disappeared from the nominal roll. After being carried A.W.O.L. for three weeks, he was formally listed as a deserter — and where else would he go if not to the United States, where a friendly welcome existed for escapees from the "imperial system", with better pay, better prospects, and, if desired, a billet in the U.S. Army, which, of course, was democratic and moral, untainted by effete and corrupt Old World ways, and not too hampered by discipline.

I was happy enough to display my uniform and my "inside knowledge" around Vanguard, but I steered away from arguments over responsibility for the war. For verbal controversy I had little taste and less talent; I did not think on my feet, and the crushing rejoinder never occurred to me until the next morning. After three weeks of stooking, during which I developed primary and secondary blisters the size of the palm of my hand, I was happy enough to return to Camp Hughes, elated at the prospect of early shipment overseas.

The day I returned, however, Sergeant Donovan informed me with a grim smile that he had been waiting for me. I fell in, prepared for a dreary morning stamping up and down the parade ground. To my surprise and relief, however, Donovan marched the platoon into the bush, past sloughs now choked with weeds, to a tent and marquee assembly occupied by the Dental Corps. Five minutes later I was lying back in a dental chair, sweating with fright, while a Dental Corps captain went over my teeth, dictating ominous incantations to his sergeant, who tut-tutted sympathetically at the appearance of my oral chart. My only earlier encounter with a dentist had been in Vanguard, when a visiting "dental surgeon" had drawn two molars after "freezing" the gums with an external application of "painkiller".

I would have scrambled out of this Dental Corps chair but for the fact that the captain in charge had authority, and he used it. The ordeal began a course of dental care which lasted the rest of the summer, and for which I have been ever since grateful whenever I bite into an apple, or munch blackberries, without having to bother about the pits getting under my plate. With his pedal-operated drill, in that hot tent, my R.C.D.C. captain and his sergeant scraped, bored, filled, and polished so conscientiously that almost sixty years later I can still eat what I please. Let me pay this grateful tribute to the Canadian Army Dental Corps. I hated dentistry at the time, but welcomed the respite from platoon drill.

Another agreeable change came with target practice at the rifle butts. We had been issued Ross rifles, a heavy weapon with a straight-draw action which jammed unless it was kept cleaner than could possibly be effected in sandy Camp Hughes. Sergeant Donovan instructed us in its use, praising its accuracy for a war in which precision fire could not possibly be indulged in except by snipers, for whom the Ross was too large. I learned to withdraw the bolt without skinning my knuckles, and did creditably on the range at three hundred yards. The Ross rifle had a peep sight and wind gauges, which Sergeant Donovan advised us to ignore, since as soon as we reached England Lee-Enfields would be issued to us. The Short-Magazine Lee-Enfield had a Vee-sight, a raise-and-draw bolt action, and a smaller magazine which was quite tricky to refill, requiring a special charger if the magazine was to work smoothly; otherwise, the rounds caught by the rim and had to be ejected unfired. The S.M.L.E., however, was a lighter weapon, which was in its favour, but it was still two or three wars out of date.

My dental and rifle courses had no sooner been completed than the contingent at Camp Hughes was inspected by the top soldiers, if they could be so described — the Duke of Connaught, then Governor General of Canada, and Sir Sam Hughes, the Minister of Militia and Defence. It was an impressive occasion, I thought, as 20,000 men massed, wheeled, and marched past the reviewing stand in column of companies, one hundred men broad and two deep. As we saluted "Eyes Right", passing the reviewing stand, I was dismayed at the appearance of our company, which looked like a broken-backed snake. I also noticed a quick movement among the officers attending the Duke of Connaught, who sat, correct and handsome, on his charger, returning the salute. I thought I detected a ripple of laughter among his staff. It occurred to me much later that one of them might have repeated Wellington's remark: "I hope your appearance frightens the enemy, because by God it frightens me!" I wouldn't have blamed anyone for saying so at that moment.

This was my last public appearance with the Canadian Army as an infantryman. Soon afterwards I joined the staff of the Orderly Room, which had come to my attention as a result of obtaining No-Parade chits to cover my visits to the dentist. The Battalion Orderly Room was set up in a pleasant marquee, with tables, chairs, typewriters, and ready access to the coffee urn in the canteen. I spent my time agreeably, filling out parade states, ration and clothing indents, passes, charge sheets, and training reports for forwarding to brigade headquarters. I learned to peck at a typewriter, a skill which I thought might be useful to me after the war, and I became adept at military diction. From this command post I could perceive, and to some extent control, my military destiny, and I was subject neither to fatigues nor to guard duty. It was a splendid haven, in which, once installed, an alert private could avoid most of the perils and hardships of the military life while at the same time making sure he was not forgotten for promotion. Moreover, it was a self-perpetuating post which brought me into contact and friendship with the best of the battalion officers, and ensured good billets and early access to special supplies when they arrived at the canteen.

Since at that time I did not smoke, and drank nothing stronger or more costly than Coke, I was always well supplied with money. I tried to improve my cash position one Sunday afternoon when I happened across a poker party in full swing out in the bush. I knew the words but that was all; after half an hour I was $1.65 down and decided that poker was not for me. I gathered later that it was an inexpensive lesson. At all events it lasted; I haven't played poker from that day to this. With nothing else to drain off my surplus capital, I was free to spread it over chocolate bars to supplement rations, another watch — I never could resist them — and slim pocket volumes of poetry, or at least verse, by Robert W. Service, Omar Khayyam, and Tennyson. I was particularly attracted to "The Lotos-Eaters", and could spiel off verse after verse, chanting the lines to myself as I stumbled through the chokecherry bushes on my Sunday afternoon hikes. My tent-mates regarded this as a worthy characteristic. Soldiers today are as fond of the rhythm and imagery of poetry as they must have been in Homer's day; it was a point of honour in my tent to be able to recite Kipling or even Swinburne, who had a touch of mutiny in his lines which appealed to a bored Sunday audience, whose thoughts were with the flesh-pots of Portage la Prairie or Brandon.

From my vantage point in the Orderly Room, I could detect the toll of those flesh-pots as paybooks floated across my desk with deductions in red ink for pay forfeited by hospitalization for preventable diseases. This information reinforced the lectures given by the M.O. to Other Ranks about to go on leave to the local Sodom and Gomorrah, if Portage and Brandon will accept the tribute.

Our next major move was coming up. We were to be transferred to England to receive final infantry training before being shipped to

France for the acid test of all these months of intensive physical and spiritual hardening, designed to transform us from peace-loving homesteaders into fighting men capable of engaging and defeating the world's best-trained, best-led army nurtured in a long tradition of victory.

The Sunday before entraining, we were marched off to a pleasant dell for a farewell spiritual goosing by the senior Chaplain, who ranked as a lieutenant-colonel in the Canadian Army and as a bishop in the Army of God. With the band at our head blaring "Onward, Christian Soldiers", we marched through the bush, heavy with the fragrance of saskatoon berries. In a green glade fringed with rustling aspens and glowing with wild orange-lilies, we were ranged on a hillside facing an altar created out of an up-ended drum, draped with appropriately coloured bunting. A little slough in the centre of the dell was fringed with rushes and arrowhead, and laced with bladder-wort which sent precarious blossoms up to the surface. Our arrival disturbed a family of coots from its Sunday morning frogging; when they left, the frogs resumed their chorus, as if they too were trying to render

Jesu, lover of my soul,
Let me to thy bosom fly.

Our buttons were bright with spit and pink polish — "The Soldier's Friend"; our spirits were bright with the ecclesiastical spit and polish of the Psalms of David. The senior Chaplain thought it would be fitting to omit the hackneyed "Soldiers' Friend" Psalm: "a thousand shall fall on thy right hand and ten thousand on thy left hand . . ."; he felt that would strain credulity among this group, many of whom, he knew, had friends in the casualty list. He substituted, perhaps innocently — for few men are as innocent as Army chaplains — Psalm 103;

He read: "Bless the Lord, O my soul, and forget not all his benefits";

We replied in antiphony: "Who forgiveth all thine iniquities; who healeth all thy diseases."

At this I looked hard in the direction of two privates and a lance-corporal whose paybooks had recently come under my notice with their bright red-ink notations; they wore red bars on their epaulettes, too. Their iniquities might be forgiven, but they would not be forgotten unless they got new paybooks. I resolved to send a chaser after our indent for pot. permang., which had not been filled. This kept my mind pleasantly occupied throughout the service, and I only gave half an ear to the Chaplain explaining that the different accounts of the Crucifixion and Resurrection of Christ in two of the Gospels were testimony to their truth, since no two witnesses ever describe the same event in identical words. I remembered the variations in the narrative from my churning days; the Chaplain's remarks made me decide to read the accounts again and see what my tent-mates thought of them. We marched back to the strains of Schubert's "Marche Militaire", which the band had been working on in a nearby copse throughout the sermon. The very blackbirds had red bars on their wings, as if they, too, had been weekending at Portage or Brandon.

My tent-mates thought poorly of the sermon. The printer figured that in the earliest manuscripts someone had not followed copy as carefully as he should and mistakes had been made worse by people trying to correct them and "justify" lines to fit the page. Old Garrett, who was suffering from a gumboil, said that he did not like to think of the number of people who had been boiled in oil for the sake of a few typos, and, so far as he was concerned, doubt one and you doubt them all: read with your mind, not your emotions. The discussion was ended by a loud report and a shout from the printer. He had been stuffing a revolver into his pack and when he banged it on the ground to settle the contents, the shock fired the weapon, sending a bullet through the pack and his foot too. We hustled him off to the M.O.'s tent, and I marked him down as a casualty, so that he would not lose any pay, while we could draw a ration for him as long as he remained on battalion strength. I took care that he did.

Old Garrett said that it was a direct intervention of providence which had saved the printer's life, for he would probably be graded C3, unfit for combat duty, if he took proper advantage of his accident. It possibly could be considered a self-inflicted wound, but the tent agreed that it was accidental, and we were prepared to testify to that effect if called upon. I said that I would see to it that his record sheet was properly filled out and endorsed, so there would be no trouble from Brigade. Feeling very important, I consulted the printer as to whether or not he wanted to go overseas with the unit. He said he wanted to get back to his job and out of this crazy business where everybody was thinking in terms of two wars back; so I managed to get him invalided out a few days before we received orders to entrain for Halifax and shipment overseas.

There was great flurry and excitement in the Orderly Room as we prepared to move — papers boxed, typewriters crated, baggage assembled, and a truck rounded up to take Orderly Room personnel and effects down to the depot. The battalion came behind on foot, a long straggling column, to be packed into antique railroad coaches, one hundred men to each, with rifles, canteens, and packs stowed under seats, and the upper compartment made reasonably comfortable with paillasses.

We had been warned for reasons of military security not to tell our kinfolk that we were leaving. It was a pointless caution, since few of us knew until the day before. But everybody along the line had received the word, and knew not only the day but the precise hour and minute when the train would arrive. Every level crossing had a little knot of onlookers, waving flags and cheering as we passed. Before leaving Camp Hughes, facetious warnings to Kaiser Wilhelm to beware the 209th O.B. had been chalked on the coaches, a breach of security which advertised both our name and our destination. It was encouraged as a contribution to morale. Security was forgotten, and our arrival, telegraphed ahead from town to town, brought a swarm of sightseers to the station. Most of them were girls or young women, attracted, I suppose, by the uniform, the glamour of soldiers off to the battlefield, or perhaps just by men, one thousand of them, a miraculous draught of fishes, some of whom might be hooked or netted before they swam away, forever out of reach.

At Oshawa we detrained and marched through the town. The parade was designed to stir up enthusiasm for their work among the munition-makers who were too valuable as producers of ammunition and equipment to be allowed to enlist. The march through Oshawa was also a useful antidote to constipation, which was a problem in a trainload of troops huddled together without exercise day after day; it did something also to allay the boredom which was sapping our enthusiasm, and to break up the poker games with which we beguiled the time. Snaking our way in low gear, side-tracked for expresses, we took a week to reach Digby, Nova Scotia, where we were to await our transport within easy reach of Halifax. Digby was a pleasant interlude for troops after the treeless, waterless prairies, and we made the most of it. Our tents were filled with spruce boughs, in the hope that they would make comfortable mattresses. They did not; spruce boughs are for the birds! It was pleasant, however, to ramble through abandoned apple orchards, or to essay the perils of the tide-rip through Digby Gap, through which the waters of the Annapolis Basin hustle into the Bay of Fundy.

Chapter Twenty

The crowning joy, however, was receiving orders to embark for England. We had a smoky, uncomfortable, overnight journey to Halifax; but by noon we had detrained and marched to the quayside where H.M. Transport 345, in peacetime the 20,000-ton Cunarder *Caronia*, was berthed to receive us. I noted that the 209th were assigned to the lowest deck. The portholes were eight feet above the waterline, which argued for stuffy quarters on the voyage, and no chance of escape in case of emergency; we would have been drowned like puppies in a bucket if H.M. Transport 345 had been torpedoed, for there were 4,000 troops on the decks above us. With this in mind, the Orderly Room staff managed to find office space on an upper deck. I arranged a series of guard duties which would keep me on deck for the greater part of the voyage.

Guard duty on the troopship *Caronia* was something only the military mind could have thought up. Four posts were established on the boat deck, each manned by a private with a machine-gun. This was the first machine-gun I had ever handled, and I had not the faintest notion how to use it. In fact, I was scared stiff of the thing, which was perhaps as well; if I had fooled about with the weapon I would probably have shot somebody, as likely as not myself, and been a "casualty", like the printer at Camp Hughes.

At dusk we cast off. The barrier nets were swung open and we filed through the Narrows and out to sea. I paced up and down the boat deck, with orders to check for lights and to report anything unusual. However, as I did not know what "usual" was, I kept my own counsel, and enjoyed the romantic pattern of four liners filing out to sea, where two more vessels, converted merchantmen each equipped with a gun, which I suspected was as incompetently manned as our machine-guns, awaited to escort us through the perilous passage. Our convoy included the *Empress of Britain*, the *Caronia*, and two Allan liners, slower than us. They held the group to a dreary crawl through November gales which made life miserable. Down on E deck, the portholes had to be kept shut, for the waves slapped against them with every roll. We slung hammocks from the beams, or whatever rafters are called in nautical jargon. Underneath them, long combination tables-cum-benches were bolted to the deck. Here we ate, wrote letters, and played cards; it was too dark to read. We lined up in a long corridor to get our food at the mess kitchen, and took it back precariously to the tables.

It required agility to arrange the Army blankets and climb into the hammock; it was virtually impossible if the occupants on either side had retired first. It was well to get into the hammock early, although this condemned one to lie listening to the interminable poker games which went on below far, far into the night. Lights Out was a principle honoured chiefly in the breach. However, these discomforts had the enormous advantage that swinging with the motion of the ship, as the hammock did, warded off seasickness. We all acquired sea-legs and made our way about the ship or waited in stuffy, smelly corridors without noticing any discomfort but hunger. I doubt if our military masterminds had planned it that way, but even their oversights were sometimes useful; I never afterwards suffered from *mal de mer*.

We were fortunate in having relatively calm weather for the first two or three days, which gave us time to get used to the ship and the food. Perhaps the fact that the lighting on A Deck was strong enough to play cards by but too dim to read by helped to build up our resistance, for one had to abandon oneself completely to the swing of the ship. The hammock, slung fore and aft, was essential to the process, and by the time the really rough seas built up, just off the Irish coast, my immunity to sickness had also built up. We wore cork life-jackets day and night, except in the hammock, when I used mine as a pillow. I do not recall any boat-drill; it would have been an exercise in irrelevancy, since there would have been no hope of any systematic launchings with the ship listing and lurching after a mine or torpedo explosion, and five or six thousand men fighting their way up from the lower decks. Their best contribution and hope for survival would have been to jump overboard and hope to be picked up before they perished from exposure.

A day west of Ireland the storm raged violently. This cheered us, for it made U-boat activity unlikely. I was amazed at the power of the storm to toss the 20,000-ton *Caronia* about like a coastal ferry-boat. She plunged downwards as if she would never come to the surface, quivering like a jelly as her screws beat the surface into froth. We could see the same thing happening to the *Empress of Britain* on our beam, and to the two Allan liners ahead and astern. I was thankful for the hammocks then, for we might have been badly knocked about in bunks. Our tin mess-dishes were unbreakable and so was the water-bottle in which we carried coffee or tea. We cared tenderly for our very breakable limbs, and the only casualties which came to my attention in the Orderly Room were two typewriters, against which we planned to obtain a new issue of better machines.

As the storm died down we moved closer inshore as a precaution against U-boats. In the end we followed the indentations of the Irish coast so faithfully that we could watch farming operations in detail, which nourished our innate feeling of superiority to old-world, old-fashioned ways of doing things. Only the Irish element, supervised by Sergeant Donovan, insisted that the Ould Sod could do no wrong; but among the men of English descent, and to a far less degree among the Scots, it was almost a ritual to scoff. So, when we landed at Liverpool, after ten days at sea, English trains and their little peep-peep whistles became an object of derision; nobody commented on the obvious reality, that six men were travelling much more comfortably in a third-class compartment than they had been in a first-class section on the Canadian train. It was impossible not to notice how smoothly the carriage rode, but this made little impression on the mood of contempt with which we greeted everything in England.

This attitude, which was really an inverted snobbery, infected all our relations, and particularly the military connection. Canadian troops either discarded or, as irrationally, embraced British military practice; thoughtful appraisal or perspective was lacking. The British

— whom we referred to as the "Imperials" — had webbing harness; we had to have webbing, discarding our perfectly good leather rifle-slings, pack straps, and belts. The British had a different cut of tunic, with pockets inconveniently placed; we had to have British-type tunics, and invented a rigmarole about how the pockets were much more significantly placed for carrying Mills #5 hand grenades. "But don't let me catch anybody carrying Number Fives in these pockets," Sergeant Donovan commented; "you'll loosen the pin pulling them out, and blow everybody to pieces." This was mutinous talk, but it came as near as anything in the Army to making sense.

The British had a mania for blancoing, which was the real reason they preferred web equipment. Orders were issued that we should blanco everything, including rifle-slings. This display of military genius, however, was undermined by Sergeant Donovan, in collusion with the Regimental Sergeant-Major, a magnificent personality with a rainbow display of campaign ribbons. As the latest contingent to arrive in Shorncliffe, we were inspected by the Canadian General Officer in Command — I forget who it was, and it doesn't much matter; brass is brass the world over; stuffed shirts are international. It had been raining, as usual, and on the review day, the R.S.M. marched us to a parade ground which had not been surfaced. It was inches deep in mud, and Donovan took care that C Company was drawn up in platoon formation in the muddiest part. We shouldered arms, marched out, brass glowing, webbing rifle-slings blancoed blinding white. Just as the C.G.O.C. and his staff stepped from their cars, the R.S.M. gave a stentorian command "Order Arms", which brought the rifle butts down on the ground with a muddy squish. Then "Shoulder Arms" brought rifles on to shoulder, steadied by a hand under the muddy butt. "Present Arms" in salute to the G.O.C. with muddy hand slapped against the blancoed sling, which was then turned outwards, so that the G.O.C., marching down the ranks, had the impression of a thousand dirty palm prints on a thousand rifle-slings offered for his inspection. The G.O.C. suspected a studied insult; the blancoing regulation was rescinded. "Even that stupid S.O.B. could see it didn't work," Sergeant Donovan commented. "But we sure had to rub his nose in it."

This victory cheered us up, and we were ready and anxious for the next step of intensified infantry training before going to France. This was preceded by a medical inspection. The fit would go on to the Ninth Reserve Battalion for further polishing, after which they would be fed into the grinder which was insistently calling for more meat. The unfit would be transferred. I had invented for myself a post as battalion runner. This kept me out of the drudgery of fatigue duties, guard, and parade, which made such a hell of life at base. Being a runner involved hanging around the Orderly Room stove until a message had to go to headquarters about a mile and a half away, at which point I put it in a pouch, strolled off, delivered and obtained a receipt for my message (we were not yet sophisticated enough to call it a "signal"), and strolled back by way of Shorncliffe Church, which had an inscription over the porch which seemed to sum up my post quite well: "A haven from the storm and a shadow from the heat".

As messages averaged two a day, this meant that I walked six miles daily, which was tiring in the unending rain and mud. At one point, at the end of my second trip, I was so tired that I lay down between the mounds of two graves and slept. When I got back to camp, I found the medical inspection in full swing. Sergeant Donovan, bellowing from the nominal roll, had reached the M's. I fell in, answered my name, and stripped. An R.A.M.C. major peered into my mouth and muttered something I did not catch. I asked him what he meant. At my tired, piping voice, the Major looked at me again and asked: "How old are you?"

As I had never lied about my age, and knew that the facts were on my attestation papers, I said, "Sixteen."

The major shouted, "Out! Over there!"

I wandered in the direction of his gesture, gathered my clothes, and sat down among a group of depressed rejects, most of them kids like myself, culled from the bugle corps. By evening we had rounded up our kits and entrained for an unknown destination.

As the train was heading westward, I hoped that we might be bound for an embarkation port for the voyage to France, but we detrained at Shoreham-on-Sea, a fishing village on the south coast between Brighton and Worthing. Instead of marching to the quays we swung inland, at which point someone volunteered the information that we were destined for the 34th Battalion, quartered near by.

As Army camps went, Shoreham was not too bad. The 34th Battalion was housed in forty single-storey wooden huts built in orderly rows on a chalk hillside that was part of the South Downs. Each hut held between twenty and thirty youths, for the 34th was a concentration camp, or dump, for kids under eighteen, who had been weeded out of units destined for France, as I had been the day before. Having nothing to do but drill, and nothing to look forward to or work for, they got into mischief. They got drunk, for publicans assumed that since they were in uniform they must be of age; they broke into tobacco shops and, allegedly, assaulted innocent young women, and perhaps others not so young. Being old enough to get into trouble but not wise enough to take care of themselves, they contracted venereal disease at an appalling rate; we isolated them in two or three huts until they could be transferred to Boulogne, where a floating population of some 40,000, older but not wiser, waited out the war with a red strip on their epaulettes — heroes of amatory actions.

My orderly room training served me well in the 34th. Since I was skilled in the mysteries of making out the daily parade state in such a way as to obtain the maximum ration issue, I was promoted to corporal and assigned to duty as perpetual Orderly Sergeant. This meant that I was first up and last to bed, since I had to call the roll in the morning and again in each hut at Lights Out, ten o'clock. I also had to be within earshot of our bugle, ready to answer, on the double, any call for Orderly Sergeants. Most of the time, however, I spent, comfortably, beside a stove in D Company Orderly Room, reading or filling out charge sheets and parade states. A quarter-mile away both the Salvation Army and the Y.M.C.A. had huts and a little stock of books which I could borrow. I used to slip down there after mess to buy a couple of penny bars of chocolate to ease my hunger for sweets.

One day we received a complaint from the Shoreham Police that two of our soldiers had been arrested for breaking and entering, and what did we want the police to do with them: send them up for a jail term or turn them back to us for appropriate action? I suggested to Major Metcalfe, our Company Commander, that we had better collect them, read them the riot act, and see if we could not straighten them out. Metcalfe was a conscientious officer and a thoughtful man from London, Ontario. I suspected him of often wondering how in hell he came to be fighting the war to end war here in Shoreham in charge of this gang of thugs. He suggested that we send them up to Battalion Orderly Room on a reduced charge which could be handled by the C.O. without making it a court-martial offence. The C.O. could give them twenty-nine days, which would mean they would be sent up to Stafford where there was a military jail which tried to rebuild warped careers and characters, rather than to the Glass-house at Wandsworth which aimed to break them ("they come in lions, but they go out lambs").

This was arranged with the C.O., who duly handed out the maximum twenty-nine days' confinement, and I was given orders to escort them to Stafford. I felt sorry for them. They wore a hang-dog look; long pendulous arms sagged down to their knees, terminated by knobby hands which seemed to have no function or capability other than to dangle at the end of those stringy arms. Their buttons were dull, their tunics shapeless, their trousers baggy and wrinkled, their faces hopeless. I gave each of them a packet of cigarettes and we entrained for Stafford. I put them on their honour not to escape, for I would have had no way of recapturing them if they bolted. I pointed out that with the number of military police about they were sure to be asked for their passes and picked up, which would mean a spell of rigorous confinement in the Glass-house with pack-drill. They appreciated this and we sat in glum silence as the Underground rattled and screamed its way to Euston, where we settled into a comfortable third-class compartment and dozed our way to Stafford. I noted that the express stopped briefly at Lichfield Trent Valley, which was only about three miles from my Uncle Ted's house, where there would be white table-cloths and sparkling glass and silver, instead of a mess-tin of slum on a dirty table in barracks. I longed to get out and let my wards deliver themselves to Stafford Jail, but they had been signed out to me and I would have to produce a receipt for them when I got back, or face a court-martial myself. But I kept in mind the possibility of a stopover once my charges were delivered.

I turned them over to a hard-faced grey sergeant-major in a grey office in a grey stone building, stuffed the receipt for "two prisoners" into my pocket, and picked up two days' rations for three before scurrying back to the "Up" express for the return trip. For a packet of Players the ration corporal obliged a colleague (I was wearing corporal's stripes in virtue of my job as permanent Orderly Sergeant) with an extra issue of tea and sugar, for I planned to sweeten an unannounced appearance at Uncle Ted's with a useful offering. As I had not myself begun to smoke, I always had a supply of cigarettes, which were becoming auxiliary legal tender — none the worse for deteriorating quickly enough to ensure fast circulation and a high gross purchase before they became worthless through fraying and loss of content.

The side-trip from Lichfield Trent Valley to Hammerwich was a nostalgic return to schoolboy memories. I sat at the carriage window reflecting on how few signs of change appeared in the five or six years since I had known every field, hedge, and Dutch barn on that line. I felt that the lifetime of adventure which lay between me and the Lichfield Grammar School must have changed the landscape as much as I thought it had changed me.

When I arrived at Uncle Ted's I found that the unchanged surface veiled deep and disturbing alterations in the comfortable pattern of middle-class Midland life. Economically it was feeling the pinch; wages and prices were sky-rocketing in what was later to be known as "inflation", although at that time the authorities had not tried to exorcise the demon by giving it a name nobody understood. The gardener was demanding wage increases so outrageous that Uncle Ted reluctantly let him go, and attended himself to his sweet peas and his orchard of Cox's Orange Pippins, which were a prized novelty.

Business was booming after a fashion. Orders were flooding in from abroad, but metal was rationed so closely that they could not be filled, although the government urged more exports to obtain foreign exchange to finance the fantastic purchases of munitions in the United States, who were winning the war to end war by ensuring that their allies would be too poor to wage another. Uncle Ted felt gloomily that the dislocation of markets caused by the price rise, and the loss of them occasioned by the rationing of supplies, would create post-war difficulties which the small manufacturer might be unable to survive, with consequent unemployment and unrest. These forebodings presented a new and darker picture of the future than anything I had heard in camp; the economic picture was coloured in more sombre hues by estimates of the prodigious debt which war spending was piling up for the next generation to assume. Economic and financial gloom was intensified by growing doubts about the ability of the military leaders to conceive and execute any really significant strategic plan for piercing and rolling up the static lines of trenches which now stretched from the English Channel to Switzerland. Doubts about the military leadership had been fostered by visits from Uncle Ted's two sons. One of them had been in the Navy Division in Gallipoli; he brought home chilling stories of incompetence in the conduct of that campaign. The other had already been wounded in some futile attack on a useless strong-point, the capture of which cost lives but brought no compensating military advantage. He reported that there was dangerous discontent back of the lines in France, and that British units were buzzing with rumours of massive mutinies among the French troops on their right flank. My cousin told me that he had no idea how well-founded those reports were, or if they had any foundation, but they certainly bore no relationship to the press assurances of happy French co-operation until the war had been brought to a victorious conclusion. Among themselves, my cousin said, the French were saying that perfidious Albion was determined to fight to the last Frenchman.

Uncle Ted's two sons both volunteered in 1914. The younger was dispatched to that bungled operation in the Dardanelles, where he was fortunate enough to contract dysentery for which he was invalided home and later discharged. The elder son was less fortunate. He was sent to France as a subaltern of infantry. After recovering from a wound suffered in one futile operation, he was committed to the next aimless fumble and, predictably, slaughtered. The girls fulfilled their destinies more happily, went to university, married their peers, and lived for many years in quiet and content. Another cousin, the only son of my mother's only sister, was allowed to go up to Oxford, where he was admitted into Oriel College, and soon afterwards rode off on a bicycle down the dusty autumn roads with the Artists' Rifles, to his appointment with death in another blunder near Cambrai, two years later. I inherited his college and his blazer.

My mother's brother's son, who had been sent to Hamburg on business, spent the war in a civilian detention camp, from which he emerged in 1919 several pounds lighter with long hair and a regrettable tendency to accept the German viewpoint as reasonable. He was an advance guard of the Beatniks and much too intelligent for his years.

These gloomy reflections did not make my routine as D Company Orderly Sergeant back at Shoreham any more attractive, but I got through it automatically, and even pleasantly, thanks to one of the C Company officers, a dour Scottish major who appeared on parade with a corkscrew walking-stick and tartan trousers. It may have been this taste for eccentricity which had occasioned his transfer from his regiment to the 34th. He made the most of his opportunity to support this reputation, and was delighted to learn that he had been nicknamed Johnny Walker. He came around to the Orderly Room one day while I was sitting by the stove reading *The Pickwick Papers*, and used the book as an excuse for a talk. It wandered around until we got to local antiquities, when he delivered a lecture on flint construction and stone facing in the local churches, following it with a brief survey of the characteristics of Roman and Early English architecture, the Norman arch, and the Gothic ogive, and concluding with an offer to accompany our company route marches to local points of interest which would illustrate his talk. I welcomed this suggestion, which would give some point to the dreary, aimless marching which was supposed to keep us physically fit and mentally stagnant, ready for the grinder.

In this way we visited Shoreham Old Church and admired its Norman arches, then trekked across the valley to Lancing College, a rather poor imitation of Early English architecture, but a dominant monument in the landscape. I have always been grateful to "Johnny Walker" for an introduction to what became an enduring interest which mitigated the boredom and squalor of life in an Army base in wartime. He also increased my ardour to get to France, where I longed to see some of the architectural splendours which he described so lovingly. "Johnny Walker" rates a place high on the list of inspired teachers I have been fortunate enough to meet.

Failing Rouen or Amiens, I decided to have a better look at Lichfield Cathedral when the occasion returned at the end of twenty-nine days to escort our prisoners back from Stafford. So, from my command post in the Orderly Room, I appointed myself as escort, drew my extra rations and a travel allowance, and entrained for Stafford, where I signed for my two delinquents. Stafford had smartened them up noticeably. True, they still shuffled their feet, and their hands still hung loose as if on strings, but at least their buttons were polished and there was a suggestion of a crease rather than creases in their trousers. Their shoes were not ostentatiously shined, but at least they were not daubed with mud; their hair had been cut by the prison barber and looked it, but for once it did not hang in their eyes, and I was not as reluctant to be seen in their company as I had been on the way in. They did not seem to have been scarred by their experience, but I did not feel that I could thrust them as well as myself on the hospitality of Uncle Ted's household at Hammerwich. So I decided to trust them, feeling that this would arouse their better natures, dormant within. Thus, when we reached Lichfield Trent Valley, we all detrained; I thrust ten shillings at each of them, told them to meet me on that same platform next morning, glanced briefly at the Cathedral, noting some features "Johnny Walker" had mentioned, and climbed aboard the Hammerwich local. I enjoyed my evening at Uncle Ted's, sitting cosily before an open fire and snuggling into clean sheets for the night. My aunt was so alarmed at my rashness in turning my prisoners loose that she infected me with her doubts, so that I returned rather nervous and apprehensive to the Trent Valley station next morning. But my eyes were gladdened by the sight of my delinquents, forlorn and hopeless-looking as ever, but intact and not in custody of a policeman. I could have embraced them. They actually seemed as glad and relieved to see me as I was to see them, for they had spent their cash on a drink, and bed but no breakfast, and they were happy to be back in my custody, assured of their next meal. We journeyed amicably back to Shoreham, where I turned them over to the Orderly Room for re-integration into the military machine, to fight for God, country, and peace.

I picked up my duties as Orderly Sergeant. Nothing had changed. I hustled together a few parade states and drew rations for the company. At ten o'clock, I made the round of D Company huts, calling the roll. In the last hut, No. 38, there was no answer when I got to the names of my delinquents. "Where are they?" I asked. Someone replied with muffled voice from beneath a blanket: "They've gone to the can." This was a common excuse for failure to answer roll-call, but I had a conviction that it was not true. However, I accepted it, for to have reported them missing so soon after their return from Stafford would have ensured them a long visit to the Glass-house at Wandsworth and a future of escalating offences. So I went back to the company Orderly Room and reported D Company as "All present and correct" for the night. Just before noon next day the bugle shrilled a call for Orderly Sergeant — D Company — On the Double. That usually meant trouble, and this was no exception. With a face of thunder, the Regimental Sergeant-Major asked me how I reconciled the fact that my Lights Out report had declared D Company to be All Present and Correct, whereas a call from the Shoreham Police had reported two members of the Company as incarcerated at that moment for breaking and entering a tobacconist's shop. With sinking stomach, I waited for the R.S.M. to reveal the names; but I knew them already. Sure enough, they were my warriors. They had not been in the can, they had been in the tobacconist's; and they were now facing a serious charge as recidivists, burglars; and I was facing a serious charge of making a false report of company strength, which, the R.S.M. suggested, his dark face burning with a hellish glow, was a court-martial offence.

At this point Major Metcalfe took a hand, pointing out that the reputation of D Company was poor enough already without having a court-martial hung around its neck. He fell back on that military garbage can, Section 40 of the Army Act, "Conduct to the prejudice of good order and military discipline", in that accused did blow his nose in a disrespectful manner at the regimental sergeant-major. The R.S.M. looked bleak at this irreverence, but he agreed to substitute appropriate language. So I was marched up to the battalion Orderly Room, where the C.O., tipped off by Major Metcalfe, said that I appeared to be promoted above my competence. He ordered me reduced to the ranks, and I was marched out again, tears streaming down my face, with my military career in ruins. Still sniffling, I removed the corporal's stripes which I had so lovingly sewn on my sleeve a few weeks before. When Mickey, a little Irish hooligan from an eastern regiment, taunted me on my tears, I kicked him in the face and he ran off howling that I had murdered him. Before that incident could develop, however, the bugle sounded Fall-In for Picket, and I was glad to take my place in a rear rank, to be marched away by some unfortunate corporal who was sweating out his tour of duty as Orderly Sergeant.

For the next few days I shovelled coal, piled lumber, filled sandbags, and stood guard with an enthusiasm which led my messmates to accuse me of bucking for promotion. So I was. While I was thankful to be rid of the wearisome grind as permanent Orderly Sergeant (without sergeant's rank or pay) and the daily blizzard of parade states, ration strength, and equipment indents, I yearned for the comfort of the Orderly Room stove and the few tranquil hours of reading which N.C.O. rank made possible.

Major Metcalfe, in turn, wanted to be relieved of his paper chase by a competent orderly sergeant; and the Company Sergeant-Major wanted to give the Regimental Sergeant-Major a black eye for his arrogance in the Sergeants' Mess. So in a few days' time my name appeared in Battalion Orders under *Promotions:* to A/Cpl with pay, as of 7/2/17, #252352 Pte. Minifie J. M. So that was it; I was reinstated. Once again a career of military glory opened before me. I drew my stripes, sewed them on in my hut, and gave Mickey a week's Kitchen Fatigue as a lesson in manners.

It was a miserable winter, cold, wet, and comfortless. In the 34th we waited for spring, doing nothing and doing it badly. Little by little our strength declined, worn down by draughts to reserve regiments, jail, venereal disease, and repatriation. The bad winter was followed by a flowery spring bringing an irresistible temptation to scramble over the South Downs. I assigned myself an appropriate duty, and spent hours sitting in the sunshine, gazing out over the Channel, listening to the diminished rumble of guns laying down barrages for another turn of the meat-grinder. It rolled in like distant thunder; or, in visual terms, like a sea-fog enveloping the land in its embrace. To me, it sounded very romantic; it was the nearest I ever came to the actual battle, for all my efforts to transfer to active units. They ended with the spring when a draught on which I was listed was cancelled owing to an outbreak of mumps, for which the hut was quarantined for three weeks. On the nineteenth day another case was detected; a further three weeks' quarantine was imposed, and with a view to eradicating the source of infection the occupants of Hut 38 were moved to a vacant group on the other side of the valley. I was still in charge of the hut but there was little to do except maintain some sort of order, which was difficult enough, since I had no authority but my stripes, and no enforcement apparatus.

To mitigate boredom, I went to Brighton as often as my funds permitted. On one of these forays I picked up a *Flora of the British Isles* and a pocket telescope; these treasures enabled me to spend the daylight hours studying and identifying the South Downs flowers, and my evenings watching Jupiter's satellites.

I was able to enforce the rule of ten o'clock Lights Out by pointing out that violations would bring the Military Police to the scene on the double; but that did not mean that the hut got a good night's sleep. At one end Corporal Fetterley, a kid from a London, Ontario, battalion, had set up his paillasse. He had a good voice and liked to sing in bed. He had a repertory of English ballads which he said he had learned from his father. I had a great fondness for ballads, so I hadn't the heart to stop him; in this way I picked up the best version I know of the Gypsy Davy ballad, which Professor Child collected in an inferior rendering.

My passion for ballad-singing was not shared by others in the hut. One night shouts of "Shut up", being unheeded, were followed by Army boots. One of these went so high it shattered a window; a volley followed, until there was scarcely a window left intact. Next morning I pointed out that the cost of replacements would be deducted from pay; then I left for a ramble over the Downs. When I returned every window was glazed, without even a crack. My satisfaction at this miracle was tempered by the discovery that the huts on either side had been raided to provide new panes for our own. The operation was so successful that it was bound to be repeated. There was a renewed blizzard of boots that night; and the following afternoon another hut was cannibalized for its glass.

The routine might have continued as long as there were huts available had not a Medical Officer turned up to conduct a routine inspection before lifting quarantine and returning us to active duty. He was accompanied by the Assistant Provost-Marshal and the usual raggletaggle of N.C.O.s. The M.O. discovered one suspicious swelling, and, to my great disgust, decreed another twenty-one days of quarantine; then he peered into the mouth of a young fellow standing next to me, but started back in astonishment when the lad said: "That swelling ain't mumps; that's syphilis." My horror at this self-diagnosis was increased by the fact that the fellow had proposed only two days before that he bunk in with me, pooling our blankets. The M.O. ordered the victim to the V.D. Hospital for treatment, and requested the A.P.M. to see that the woman who had transmitted the infection was removed from the area. Our records showed that the youth had been discharged from one V.D. Hospital as cured. On his own showing he had returned to the same woman, who had re-infected him. As a parting tribute to the hut, the A.P.M. confined us to barracks, which was an act of supererogation, since quarantine should have restricted us to our lines. However, he atoned for this by sending around his sergeant with a football, a baseball bat, a baseball, and a catcher's mitt. It was a civilized thing to do, and I regret to have to report that it failed. The A.P.M. paid a surprise visit to us a few days later. I was alone, asleep on my pallet; the football and the catcher's mitt hung in an elm branch and the baseball bat was nowhere to be seen.

Chapter Twenty-one

The situation was so plainly out of hand that the A.P.M. broke up the hut, sent two patients to receive appropriate medical care, and transferred the rest of us to the Canadian Forestry Corps's Base Depot, which was happily isolated at Smith's Lawn in Windsor Great Park. Somewhere in the neighbourhood another C.F.C. unit was sawing trees into railroad ties, to be used for light railways servicing the front in France. It would have made more sense, it seemed to me, to establish the unit with its sawmill in France, where native timber could be felled and the ties used on the spot. Ultimately, this reasoning reached the upper levels, and a unit was set up, but it was so close to the front that the great German offensive of the spring of 1918 overran it.

The C.F.C. Base Depot at Smith's Lawn was a pleasant place, but it was plagued with rats, which clawed at my head as I slept, awakening me from dreams of being attacked by birds whose talons I could feel in my hair. However, we did not stay there long. A composite group of about two hundred was put together, baptized No. 64 Company, Canadian Forestry Corps, and marched down to Sunningdale, where we entrained for Aviemore, a tiny village in the Spey Valley, not far from Inverness. Without further delay we marched some seven or eight miles through romantically beautiful country, heavily wooded and criss-crossed with streams, to the Sluggan Pass, where still another C.F.C. Company had recently started operations, reducing Scotch pine into the inevitable railroad ties, and Sluggan Pass into a desolation such as it had not seen since the Roman general Agricola pacified the area, giving the historian Tacitus the chance to write *"Ubi solitudinem fecit, pacem appellavit"* — "He made a desert and called it peace".

This apt passage in the classical historian was pointed out to me by one of my tent-mates, a tall youth who had been weeded out of a British Columbia unit because of his age, but had been posted directly to the C.F.C. without passing through the preliminary purgatory of the 34th Battalion. Edward T. Applewhaite was a year or two older than I, and he had had much better schooling, as witness his knowledge of Tacitus, who was not even a name to me at that time. But he was still an adolescent, a youth rather than a young man, imbued with the romantic idealism of a Victorian family, and an innate conviction that the Christian duties were the only valid pattern for living. We spent long lazy afternoons lying on our blankets, guessing at the motives of whoever had given our tent its camouflage job. He surmised that he must have been a frustrated artist, possibly a drunken house-painter whom the Army, with its odd sense of what was fitting, had set to splashing daubs of colour on white tents to make them, hopefully, less conspicuous to any hostile eye that might be in the neighbourhood. Working with a tar-brush, the artist had daubed on our tent a rainbow, a bird, and a huge rum-jar or demijohn. Our tents were best hidden by the pine trees among which they were pitched; the uncamouflaged tents had been pitched near by in the open, in orderly and obvious ranks which clearly established the number of men in that unit. This prime example of the logic which governed military practice induced in Ted Applewhaite and me some doubts of the value of our own contribution to the defence of democracy and the ending of war. We decided that the best thing we could do for the common cause would be to fit ourselves to make a living if we ever returned to civilian life, which at that point in the war was hard to envisage. In 1917 we still expected another four or five years of war, and we were signed up "for the duration".

Since Ted came from Nelson, B.C., where fruit-growing and

lumbering dominated employment, he determined to get as much experience as he could in the mill our company was building. I opted for the Orderly Room, for two reasons: it would get me out of the physical labour of logging and mill-work, and it would give me a chance to help win the war by learning to type well and use short-hand. I was teaching myself an easy system, adapting it as I went along; back of my mind was the thought that I might find work as a secretary or office hand after we had won the war. Somewhere in the background was a vague shape calling itself Khaki University, but it never materialized sufficiently to interest me. The name put me off, because I was not university material at that point; I had hardly started Grade VIII studies when I enlisted. Had Khaki University taken any interest in me or made any effort to find out and fill my needs, it would have been very helpful in starting me off academic-ally without the handicap of the empty years wasted on parade grounds; but it did not do this, so the hell with it. I made my own way, no thanks to Khaki University.

The 64th Forestry Corps Company initiated me into the war effort as a railroad construction worker. Ted Applewhaite and I, along with Victor Deakin, another volunteer for freedom and demo-cracy, worked on a gang laying track for a light railway intended to link the camp at Sluggan with our railhead supply depot at Avie-more. We struggled with the heavy ties our mill was vomiting out, laying them on the moors with a minimum of grading, on the theory that the weight of the ties would ensure that they settled level. They did nothing of the sort, of course. However, we slammed light rails on to the ties and spiked them down. Somewhere or other we acquired a narrow-gauge steam engine, a wood-burner, believing that it could burn up slabs and butt-ends to maintain steam pressure as it hauled us to work at the end of steel.

It did not work out that way; green slabs are not recommended fuel for keeping up steam on a narrow-gauge locomotive. On the rare occasions she could muster enough pressure to turn the wheels, she ran off the track, and by the time we had pried and levered her back on the rails, the steam level had dropped almost out of sight. After a couple of weeks of off again, on again, away again, it became obvious that the light railway would never be able either to supply the camp or to remove our output when we began operations. The Command-ing Officer faced up to reality, stopped work on the railway, and expanded his Table of Organization to provide for a three-ton lorry, a Studebaker staff car, and a truck-of-all-work. The lorry proved to be as difficult to start as the steam locomotive had been; but on the assumption that its performance would improve with experience, we were put to work grading roads and building bridges to link up with the highway at Halfway House. Applewhaite and I thought that the mechanical transport would facilitate our trips to Aviemore, Boat o' Garten, or any other roaring metropolis, but we found that this was a mistake. The M.T. was reserved for the Commanding Officer and staff. We could use our two feet, or a bicycle if we could borrow or steal one. However, about that time 64th Company was transmuted into 121st Company and transferred to another site near Loch Morlich where there were neither roads nor bridges. Here we were accommodated in orderly rows of white, uncamouflaged tents in a green, open meadow while the pioneers built a new camp, a mill, and bridges over the stream.

It was romantic to fall asleep to the roar of a mountain torrent as we tried to recollect appropriate lines from Tennyson; but it was chill and damp, and our equipment grew a coat of furry mildew. The move to Loch Morlich involved a transfer of records, which may have brought to the attention of the accounting department the fact that it had omitted to increase my pay when I was restored to corporal's rank the previous February. When the Paymaster came around to dole out our pay and allowances, he discovered that I had some twelve pounds due to me from this source. A quick check with the base depot confirmed this, and I soon had more money in my pocket than I knew what to do with. Since there was nothing to spend it on in camp, Ted Applewhaite and I walked down to Aviemore, which proved equally sterile. With money burning a hole in my pocket, I marched into the Post Office and bought a £10 5% War Bond, thus initiating a fund which ultimately financed me, with the aid of scholarships and occasional work, through seven years of high school and university.

While we were negotiating this investment, Ted and I noticed an invitation to soldiers at Sluggan or Loch Morlich to attend Rothie-murchus United Free Kirk next Sunday and call on the Minister afterwards. We welcomed diversion on a long, boring day and determined to march to Rothiemurchus, which was only eight miles away, if we could not get any M.T. It was, as we had suspected, reserved for more important military missions than taking enlisted men to church. However, we covered the eight miles in two hours, dozed through the evening service, and went on to the manse as soon as it was over. The Reverend William Fraser and his wife and daughter welcomed us with Highland affection. They were touched by the small offerings of sugar and tea which we brought with us, and we enjoyed presenting them almost as much as we had savoured wheedling them out of the ration clerk. The Frasers, learning that neither Ted nor I took alcohol, produced cocoa and scones. We sat around for a pleasant hour, chatting and munching, priming ourselves on the schism between the United Free Kirk and the Wee Frees; the one had all the grace and the other all the gold, it appeared. At ten o'clock we said good-night and trudged back to camp, checking in at two minutes before midnight, and rolling up in our blankets without bothering to undress, which would have been awkward in the dark, crowded tent.

The Frasers had pressed us to return the following Sunday and we gladly accepted the invitation. Thereafter, we marched down every Sunday evening, rain, shine, or snow, for the warmth of a little cocoa and humanity, and the consolations of Presbyterian philosophy as distilled by an enlightened pastor. The romantic scenery of the Grampians, and the beautiful shore road beside Loch Morlich, held our attention as we mulled over the ideas we had picked up at kirk and at the manse. The march never seemed long, although it had an eerie quality on moonless nights when the road plunged through deep forest and our footsteps aroused a slumbering deer to crash through the undergrowth. The shores of Loch Morlich posed an additional hazard, for the track was said to be haunted by a White Lady expiating some romantic delinquency. We both hoped and feared to catch sight of her, particularly as one of our company swore he had done so; but he was a logger of such mendacity that his testimony only cast doubts on the legend. A vaguer tradition of a haunt clung to Glenmore Lodge, a rather pretentious shooting box belonging to the Duke of Richmond and Gordon, whose trees we were destroying, whose deer and trout we poached, and whose lodge was made use of for officers' quarters.

The Lodge was a two-storey brick and stone job with a rough-cast finish; a ground-floor wing of wood rambled off at an angle. I managed to allot myself a billet in this section, preferring even constant association with the officers to my damp, mouldy blankets in the camp tent. I secured a room to myself in the wing, as far removed as possible from the officers' mess. It had a fireplace which gave me great joy. The wing was full of rustling and creepy noises which gave an eerie tinge to my evenings. I passed the time well enough, working on my shorthand and grinding my way through a good but dull botanical handbook I had bought in Brighton. By ten o'clock the creakings and rustlings combined with stories of the haunt to become too much for my nerves. I laid out my paillasse and blankets under the table, where the legs gave me a sense of security such as a four-poster might have offered; and I fell asleep watching the flickering firelight. I roused early, dressed, and hurried down to camp for breakfast, my appetite sharpened by the chill mountain air.

Soon after I had transferred to the Lodge, the mill began operations, first priority going to boards for huts, and then more of those interminable railroad ties. We ground out 20,000 feet, board measure, every day until the hillside above the lake began to show signs of our murderous activities in mangy, bald patches which appeared in the forest. We did nothing about reafforestation; that would have taken manpower which we needed to turn out ties which would never reach any railroad, and slabs which we used to give a glamorous veneer of rusticity to our huts. We assumed that nature would restore the forest, as it had done after the previous savage assault during the Napoleonic Wars. We hewed down the hundred-year-old trees to save democracy by turning them into 5x10x9 sleepers to rot in our stock-pile. As soon as the mill began to function the engineer ran a steam-pipe into a water-tank on top of a rough shelter, and we had a hot shower! It was high time, for washing in a cold mountain brook had produced an alarming tally of bronchitis and scab, and most of our clothing was lousy.

The futility of this operation spurred me to renewed efforts to transfer to a more significant unit. My hopes centred on the Royal Naval Air Service, which I favoured because two cousins in Australia had received commissions and decorations therein. But the bureaucratic hurdles to exchanging from the Canadian Army to the Royal Navy were so alarming that I modified my plans and settled for the Royal Air Force, in which there was already a substantial Canadian enrolment.

Months dragged by as the slow procession of documents crept

between our Orderly Room and Canadian military headquarters in London. The only obvious result of the paper-chase was that I was summoned to Cromarty to be looked over, a perfunctory operation carried out by a young man with flight-lieutenant's bars whose vapid questions quite discouraged me. However, I cheered up when I noticed a cottage by the roadside with a sign declaring that it was the birthplace of Hugh Miller, author of *Old Red Sandstone.* I had not heard of either the book or the author until that moment, so I made a point of buying it on my way through Inverness. I found it disappointingly boring, and even Ted had to report defeat in his effort to work through it.

I must have made a better impression on the R.A.F. than its officer had made on me, for word came through from H.Q. that as soon as the R.A.F. had recovered from its birth-struggle with the Royal Flying Corps, I was to report to No. 2 Cadet Wing for training as pilot. My exhilaration at this release was shadowed by the regret that I should be leaving Ted, who was philosophically resigned to remaining with the C.F.C. for the duration. However, the wheels were turning and there was no retreat, so, as summer of 1918 drew to a close, I packed my kit, bagged a ride on the lorry to Aviemore, and said good-bye to Loch Morlich and my friends in 121 Company C.F.C.

No. 2 Cadet Wing was stationed at Sandling, a dreary headland on the coast of Kent, with fewer amenities even than Shoreham. It was run by a Colonel Lamb who disliked "colonials", reportedly owing to having been ducked in a horse-trough at St. Omer by some Australians who disliked "Imperials" — particularly Imperial colonels with old-fashioned ideas about discipline. These were exemplified by insistence on blanco and quick-step. We had to blanco belts, harness, and rifle-slings; I wondered how Colonel Lamb came to overlook shoes: the Air Force had not got around to issuing spats, or they would have been blancoed too. Our drill, for reasons which are still mysterious to me, was supposed to be modelled on the Guards. We skipped along at 120 to the minute, swinging arms shoulder-high, exhausting ourselves with martial futility, but winning the war, unquestionably.

The Commanding Officer encouraged boisterous fun in barracks as fostering *esprit de corps.* This took the form of night-time raids on neighbouring huts. The raiding party ran down the line of exhausted sleepers, tipping up the beds as they ran. The beds were constructed of two independent segments, which could be swiftly dismembered. This ensured that nobody got a full night's sleep, ever. Consequently we turned up on parade next morning, sleepy, surly, and sullen, with our equipment soiled by the night's raiders.

The "colonials" were collected in the fourth platoon of each company. The colonel rode slowly along the platoon ranks, eager to spot and punish any deficiency. Bless his heart! He knew how the war should be won! In what time remained we were given instruction in map-reading and mathematics, rudimentary even for Saskatchewan Grade VII. I longed to go up in a plane and get the feel of flying; but we were never so much as shown a plane. I never set hand or foot inside an aeroplane while I was in the R.A.F.

My only military activity was to raid the fuel dump for coke, since our huts were miserably cold. Instead of raiding each other, we took a big wash-tub as soon as darkness fell, and while one party held the guard in conversation, another group scooped up the coke and scurried off with it to the hut. We must have stolen a ton in the eight weeks of our purgatory. I hope the Colonel was not charged for it. I mitigated this misery by the hope of going on at the end of eight weeks of "ground training" to more advanced instruction at the School of Aeronautics in Cambridge, for which I ardently longed. On November 11, with only a week or ten days to go, we were paraded in wing formation. Precisely at 11 o'clock, the Colonel read a proclamation that the Armistice had been signed. The war was won! Then he added: "There will be no rowdiness or disorder. No celebration in town! No. 2 Cadet Wing will be confined to barracks! Wing: to your quarters. Dismiss!" So now they want to call it Remembrance Day. O.K., I'll remember that! I spent the evening shining buttons and blancoing my webbing, for the last time.

The Armistice destroyed my hope of going to the School of Aeronautics at Cambridge. A vague desire to remain with the R.A.F. perished when a career adviser warned that aspirants for a permanent commission should have a private income of at least £400 a year. I had no expectation of even $400 a year, so I thankfully discarded the R.A.F. and began to think of getting back to Canada. In the meantime we stole more coke, polished fewer buttons, blancoed less webbing, and adopted an attitude of contemptuous disregard for authority which verged on mutiny. The C.O. read the symptoms and broke up the unit. I was marched to the station, entrained, and disembarked again at Sunningdale for another tour of duty at the C.F.C. Base Depot, pending repatriation. This proved to be a tedious wait; shipping was in short supply, and priority was given to the Americans, who insisted that, as they had been the last overseas, they should be the first back; and they were. It was a winter of supreme boredom, mitigated somewhat by the fact that I had picked up another stripe by virtue of my rank as a cadet, which gave me the run of the Sergeants' Mess, and a handsome increase in pay. Having nothing to spend it on I bought more 5% War Bonds.

With money still burning a hole in my pocket, I felt it becoming to cultivate a few vices; I selected smoking as probably the least dangerous. Remembering the satisfaction Ted Applewhaite had derived from a cigarette I invested in a pack of Bull Durham and a packet of Zig-Zags and spent hours learning to roll my own. Fortunately I also learned to blow smoke-rings which limited the amount of carcinogenic smoke I inhaled. My only other diversion was a nip of cherry brandy in the Sergeants' Mess. I read and read all day — the light went off at night, although the war had been won. I read Pickwick again and memorized long sections of Tennyson's "Lotos-Eaters". I had no particular friends in this outfit; Applewhaite was still in the Highlands and there was nobody to exchange ideas with. I used to wander down to Egham and Sunningdale, but there was nothing much to do there, and there was no kindly Scottish major who might have organized an expedition to Windsor, which was too far to march to alone.

On January 29, 1919, there was a bit of a dust-up outside the Sergeants' Mess when the beer in the men's canteen gave out. Someone threw a snowball through the window and there was a halfhearted attempt to rush the Sergeants' Mess. When that died down the men went back to crown-and-anchor boards set up outside their own canteen, and played by candlelight until nine o'clock.

There was nothing else to do because the electric power had been cut and reading by candlelight was trying. It was cold, muddy, and dismal, with dirty snow everywhere. The C.F.C. Base Depot was a nothingness with rats and rumours of sailings which added to frustration. In the middle of a forest we had no fuel, and the Q.M. Stores refused to issue axes. I "borrowed" one from the Q.M. and cut down an oak a foot in diameter. It was not easy, as the axe was light and blunt, but in time we chopped it up and piled logs in the hut. We were nice and cosy for a couple of nights. After that the camp commandant, who was warm and cosy enough himself, put a picket on the copse with orders to stop further felling of trees. It turned very cold again, so that evening I wandered off with a French Canadian from our hut who was fairly congenial. We talked about smashing into the Commandant's quarters and chopping his head off, but we turned in our axes instead and walked down to Englefield Green, where we took a room for the night, bathed, and climbed in between clean sheets. I have subsequently wondered whether we would not have made a greater contribution to the future of Canada if we had chopped the Commandant's head off. We could have acted out our frustrations with Argyll House, the Canadian Headquarters in London, instead of taking them back to Canada to vent on Ottawa.

We had a comfortable night at Englefield, but got up at six in the morning to be back in camp by breakfast-time in case orders to move came through. They did, as we had guessed. The war was over, but the Army saw no reason to change on that account. We were sitting around the stove at about 10.30 when an orderly burst in shouting that we were moving right away. In fifteen minutes all ten of us were stowed in a Ford with our kits, and on our way to the railway station. We were homeward bound! It was a scramble, chiefly because headquarters had failed to alert us the day before. It chilled me to think how close I had come to missing the movement. When we reached London we found that the Underground was on strike, but we got as far as the Bank and then commandeered a lorry to take us to Euston. We roared through London, disregarding policemen, and just caught the 2.20 boat-train, arriving at Liverpool about 7.30 p.m. We were met by a Transport Officer with a long face, who wanted to know where the hell we had been. "You've missed the boat!" he laughed.

What to do? Nobody knew. When would there be another sailing? Nobody knew, but the *Royal George* might be sailing Monday, and there might be room on her for us, if we were aboard. It would have been too simple to put us aboard then and there, so we had to scatter. It was Sunday, February 9. February in Liverpool is a low point; Sunday in February in Liverpool is vanishing point.

There were ten of us and we had to sleep somewhere. I found

berths for seven in an American Officers' Y.M.C.A. With two others I went to a nearby hotel for the night. The next day we moved to temporary billets at Kirkdale Hospital. It was as cheerless a place as could be imagined, but it offered some assurance that the Transport Officer would be able to find us if he got another fifteen minutes' notice to embark. He told me that arrangements had been made for us to board *Royal George* that very day, although there was no assurance she would or could sail, since she had engine trouble and the artificers were on strike. I told him we would be aboard early, and let nobody try to stop us, or there would be another Rhyll to explain away. There had recently been a serious military riot at Rhyll. In our then state of anger, frustration, and disgust, any impediment to our return home would have brought on a crisis.

We hustled our equipment together, commandeered a lorry, and roared down to the docks, where, sure enough, a fat liner, bright in peace-time black and white and red, was tied up. Avoiding the Transport Officer, I marched my squad up the gangplank, prepared if necessary to force our way aboard. It was not necessary. We boarded at noon, and by one o'clock were installed in comfortable staterooms — very different from the *Caronia*'s accommodations on the eastern crossing. My quality as cadet and rank as sergeant entitled me to first-class accommodations and food. The others were stowed below, but we all spent most of the afternoon peering down at the dock, wondering whether we were to sail or just sit there and wait until the engine was functioning, by which time the dock might be strikebound and the *Royal George* unable to cast off. About five o'clock she pulled out into the Mersey and anchored to await the tide. At seven we moved gently down the estuary, while I stood on the aft deck, watching Liverpool disappear into the dusk. It was Monday, February 10, 1919, and I had been overseas two years and three months without ever getting to the front or doing anything significant for the war effort except tally the lumber vomited out of our mill to be piled in the yard at Loch Morlich camp.

Chapter Twenty-two

The weather, which had been so cold and filthy for weeks in camp at Sunningdale, now turned clear and mild. There was a bright moon in a cloudless sky. I checked over the familiar constellations and then reviewed my own situation before going below. I had a pocketful of money, expectations of a good deal more on discharge, and nearly three years' deferred pay which had been accumulating in my savings account in Vanguard. I could type, after a fashion, but I had not mastered shorthand. Educationally I was an elementary-school drop-out, for I had left Malvern Link School just before starting Grade VIII work. As we hit the swells of the Irish Sea, I went below, wrote up my diary for the past few days in Army Book 136, and went to dinner, where I demolished a large helping of fat roast duckling and returned topside to consider my future.

We expected to reach Halifax in six days, which gave me hopes of being home by the end of February. I determined to patch up the gaps in my education, for it had become obvious that I could not do much with my life unless I had college or perhaps even university training. The Army gave me this perspective and sound physical condition to carry the load of intellectual work I would have to assume to make up these lost years. The paymaster pushed another cheque for thirty dollars into my hand and I longed to go ashore at Halifax and spend some of it. I compared the splendour in which I travelled as Cadet-Acting Sergeant, the smart uniform I had put together in London, and the luxurious food in the main saloon, with the miserable accommodations and food I had endured in the holds of the *Caronia* on the way over. I read the object lesson as a stimulus to endeavour.

Even the bugle calls pealed out the message that the good life went to the upper crust. Thus the popular words to the call for Officers' Mess declared:

> *The officers' wives have pudden and pies,*
> *The sergeants' wives have skilly;*
> *The privates' wives have naught in their lives*
> *Except a big pain in their belly.*

As the *Royal George* staggered down St. George's Channel and into the Atlantic, it became clear that she would not make the crossing in less than ten days. This was annoying, because now that we were on the home stretch every delay became exasperating; also, I knew that I had no time to lose if I were to write my Grade VIII exams this summer, and I did not want to add still another year to the three I had dropped in the service.

Late in the evening of Wednesday, February 19, we sighted the light marking the entrance to Halifax Harbour. It was an emotional moment; I went forward and stayed on deck as we nosed through the narrow harbour neck and dropped anchor for the night. At ten o'clock next morning I went ashore, feeling proud to have my feet on Canadian soil — or sidewalk — again. Some of this nationalistic fervour evaporated after I had spent two hours trying to find out what the military proposed to do with me. When it was established that they would discharge me in Regina, it took another long wait to obtain a travel warrant, and by then it was too late to get a berth to myself. I shared one with a Sunningdale hut-mate, who seized the occasion to borrow ten dollars, which I never saw again.

It was warm enough for us to stroll around Halifax looking for signs of the great explosion in 1917 when the ammunition ship blew up in the harbour. An occasional church window blown out was all we noticed. Most of the damage was in the north end of town. We had little time for strolling, as we wanted to catch the train for Montreal. It arrived four hours late, causing us to miss the Imperial Limited on which we had hoped to head west that evening. I stayed overnight at the Windsor, thanks to the recent thirty-dollar pay-cheque. The next day I roamed aimlessly about Montreal with a second lieutenant, R.A.F., with whom I had struck up an acquaintance. In the evening I got aboard the Imperial Limited, cheered by the huge signs picked out in electric lights which assured us that Montrealers remembered Ypres, Hill 60, Festubert, the Somme, Hill 70, Vimy, Passchendaele, Cambrai, Valenciennes, Mons. I did not remember any of these. They said nothing about Sunningdale and Loch Morlich; they forgot Argyll House, Shorncliffe, Sandling, and Shoreham.

It seemed to my R.A.F. friend and me that they were remembering the wrong things for the wrong reasons. There would be no medals for ducking Colonel Lamb in the horse-trough at St. Omer, for stealing coke, or for blancoing rifle-slings in Sandling, though who could doubt the importance of these contributions to winning the war? There should also have been a mention in dispatches, I felt, for capturing coke in Sandling and for deer and salmon slain in Glenmore, as well as weekly advances on the United Free Kirk at Rothiemurchus. These activities cost me much time and the tax-payer much money — we had been assured that they were important actions in the war to end war, save democracy, and get safe and sound back home again. Well, all that was now forgotten and could be wiped from the slate of memory as soon as we had turned in our equipment. There would be medals for killing men but not for slaughtering fish and game; promotion would go to those who followed King's Regulations and Orders closer than the Book of Common Prayer.

At Regina it was twenty below and blowing; my ears froze before I reached the end of the platform. As soon as I could get to the Hudson's Bay store, I bought a muskrat cap and mitts, took my papers, and got transportation to Vanguard, two weeks' leave, and my Discharge Certificate, signed, sealed, and on linen. The leave was a technicality which ensured a fortnight's extra pay and allowances and a discharge dated March 19; three years and fifteen days after enlistment.

After an uncomfortable overnight ride I detrained at Swift Current and caught the Vanguard Mixed about seven o'clock, effecting one of the rare connections between express and local which the C.P.R. afforded. The Vanguard Mixed ran three times a week, taking four hours and fifteen minutes to cover the forty-odd miles in slack times. As nine of its ten units were boxcars, the schedule was extended between harvest time and the end of the year, when cars loaded with wheat had to be picked up at each village along the line. The final car, reserved for passengers, had a coal stove at one end which provided reasonable warmth and a focus for neighbourly gossip about who was going or leaving home and why; it served to pass the time and spread the news throughout south-western Saskatchewan; the state of business registered by the drummers in spring reflected faithfully the sales and price of wheat during the previous fall and winter. Politics were dominated by the farmers' and merchants' distrust of the old-line parties, the eagerness of the farmers to get their own party afloat, and the determination of the business and professional men to tag it pre-natally with a red label and post-natally, should it ever be delivered, with the sobriquet of Socialism.

I listened to those aphorisms with some amusement when they were delivered by a stout Mennonite whose overcoat was secured with wooden pegs like a sailor's duffel-coat. He moved easily from a charge of Socialism to one of Communism, on which he claimed to be an authority by virtue of having lived in a Mennonite settlement in the Volga Valley before emigrating to Canada long before the October Revolution. However, chronology did not diminish the authority with which he damned all efforts at curbing the profits of "vree enderbrize" in the interests of the producer or the consumer as steps down the slippery slope which would end with the destruction of the poor along with the rich in a murderous class war. I recognized this as commentary on Karl Marx, whom I had found as unreadable in his *New Red Building Blocks* as Hugh Miller was with his *Old Red Sandstone* when I tried to get through both of them at Loch Morlich. However, I was unwilling to get into a controversy with the stout farmer, as my father had received a kindly welcome in the Mennonite village near Wymark when he had been forced to stop overnight there as he was hauling girders from Swift Current for the Steel Bridge then building over the Notokeu Creek, south of us. The Mennonites, also, were good farmers, who, for all their antagonism to the Communist Party, practised a sort of Biblical holding of everything in common which was difficult to distinguish from the Marxist doctrine of control of production and distribution. The farmer fired up at my suggestion that there was little to choose between Menno and Marx, as if I had committed the ultimate blasphemy, which no doubt it was. I was glad when he bundled off at Blumenhof, still fulminating against militarists, of whom, from my uniform, he assumed me to be the mouthpiece.

To be damned as the voice of the military was a new experience for me. It was so surprising that I did not know how to refute the assumption. In any case, before I found words he had bounced off the coach, and the train was backing up to move some car-loads of farm machinery to the freight depot. Glancing back I noticed a pretty girl in a red dress and fur cap, looking after him with amusement. She seemed also to be aware of my uniform, but I was too shy to take advantage of this interest and we both jumped off at Vanguard without having exchanged a word.

I had wired from Regina that I hoped to arrive home on the Thursday train, February 27, but knowing the fragility of the thread of communications, I did not put too much emotional commitment into my expectation of being met. I was therefore agreeably surprised to find my mother and Dick waiting for me on the platform. Dick had developed a deep bass voice in the three years since I had last seen him. He assured me that the Vanguard Mixed had built up such a reputation for punctuality in covering the forty miles in four hours flat that they had had no hesitation about coming into town just in time for my return.

After this we turned up our collars and headed down Main Street for the Carlton Cafe, where a hardy Chinese still served the best meal in town for forty cents. There was not much news. Father had built a beautiful new barn, with a hayloft and a cradle for ease in stowing hay and oat-bundles. The cow had calved, but again a bull—no heifer. Father had bought a few yearlings at a good price in a recent auction, and we now had twenty head of cattle, mostly short-horn, give or take a point or two of residual poll-Angus. Father planned to buy a short-horn bull, and had registered his own brand Bar-P-Bar (-P-). (Good grief, I thought, he must have been reading the Westerns.) We would be branding the younger stock in a few weeks' time, as Father planned to pasture them for the summer on an open range in the Wood Mountains to the south of us near the border, where there was good grass and water and the summer-feed rent was low. If the market held, there should be a good profit by the fall in their weight and hides, and they could get plenty of shelter in the straw-piles in winter, and some feed, too, from the grain which the thresher had blown out with the straw.

This venture into mixed farming sounded attractive; riding herd on a few cattle was much more interesting than joggling about on the seat of a disc all day, behind horses which the flies were driving crazy.

There would still be plenty of that, Dick assured me, as Father was going to buy the school section and put the plough into it; it was good land on a north slope, and very few stones. He had already bought out Frank Boyd's half-section, so that meant we should be working two sections, or 1,280 acres, which, Dick assured me, was the least you could make a living from, these days. I asked how the trees, which we had planted with such labour and love six years before, were doing. Being used to seeing trees jumping up in the Highlands almost before the logs were in the mill, I envisaged a verdant grove of willow and Manitoba maple, laced with pine and spruce, sheltering the shack from the summer storms and the winter blizzards. Maybe even some fruit trees in the garden?

Dick shook his head.

"Not too good," he said. "Except the caragana and the Manitoba maples, they're bushing out; but there's only one pine left of the others, besides some willows. They couldn't take the dry years."

"There's no shelter-belt, then?"

"No. The only shelter-belt anywhere thereabouts is at E. P. Walker's. He planted poplar and watered them in summer, so they're twenty or thirty feet high now."

My mother cut in to observe that after getting too much rain in '16, there had not been enough in '17 and '18 when the prices had been high. The last good crop had been '15 when the prices were low; "You can't win on the prairies," she said. "Everything's against you. We ought to move out to B.C., where at least the climate is livable. And you can raise a garden without frosts in May and August."

She looked very tired and discouraged; but she was wearing an ankle-length muskrat coat, so things could not have been entirely negative. The failure of the shelter-belt depressed her almost as much as the failure of the crops, for it meant there would still be no shelter from the everlasting wind, nothing to look at but the rippling sea of khaki-coloured grass, right up to the horizon; not a bush, not a shrub, not a tree. Nothing but the wind, blowing snow in winter, blowing dust in summer; and dust, dust, dust everywhere, seeping into cupboards, sifting into clothing, on to the plates, into cups and cans, filtering into cracks in the floor, sifting under the door, piling in drifts against the tumbling mustard caught in the barbed wire fences. It was marginal land at best, which was why Father was going into cattle to diversify, although it might be too late even for that, since there were few open ranges any more, and renting them for summer feed would take all the profit out of beef.

This recital of woes went on until John Lee came with the apple pie. By then I was so discouraged that I wanted to get out and get back to the shack. Even if it was cold and blowing, which it was, I figured my fur cap and mitts would keep me snug for the two hours it would take us to travel twelve miles in the cutter with old John in the shafts.

I had forgotten about the wind. It picked up the snow and lashed our faces with it. If we turned our heads it sifted around to the lee and melted, freezing again when we tried in desperation to face the blast. My feet, too, cased in smart leather brogues which I had proudly purchased in London, ached with cold. I was so uncomfortable that we had to turn in to Miracle's to get warmed up. Sitting in front of a glowing stove, I remembered that I had left my good haversack in the office of the Red Livery Barn in town. It contained my R.A.F. cap and shaving kit, including a new self-sharpening safety razor which I had also picked up in London — the latest fad at the time. I decided to take a chance on its being stolen rather than face returning seven or eight miles into the wind and back again. My mother said that if the wind had dropped by Sunday, she would drive in to town for it, but she too quailed at the thought of unnecessary exposure that afternoon. By the time she next went to town, my haversack had been stolen. Welcome back, soldier!

As soon as we had warmed up we jogged on a bit further, but the wind was sharper than ever, so we stopped three miles short of Bill Turner's place, where we were welcomed affectionately by my former teacher, Miss Reaman, who had married Bill a year or two after leaving her post at Malvern Link. I was disappointed that she was not still teaching, for I knew that with her guidance I should have no difficulty with my Grade VIII certificate. We had a long talk while we warmed up; she gave enthusiastic support to my ideas of educating myself, and rounded out my hazy concepts by clear plans for Grade VIII, for which she saw no problem, and high school. She undertook to find out firm dates for the Vanguard exams, and I left feeling that I was doing well.

We made slow time the rest of the way as the snow was moving and drifting badly, so it was dark by the time we reached home, and I missed first sight of the new barn, carpenter-built of new lumber and painted red with white trim. It was roomy and warm. There were four stalls for two horses each on either side of a wide central aisle; there was a cow-stall with a step so that they did not sleep in a cow-pat and get dung caked all over their udders; there were two loose-boxes, one for a mare and foal, the other for the bull which father was hoping to buy in the spring. There were pegs for harness, and boxes in the mangers for oats, all in heavy two-inch timber, carefully planed to eliminate splinters. You could push hay and oat-bundles down a chute from the loft and stuff the mangers and feed-boxes quickly. A layer of tar-paper between the walls kept out draughts and conserved the warmth generated by horses' bodies.

The barn, as my mother observed crisply, was a good deal more commodious and conveniently arranged than the house. However, this looked good, too, when we went up the hill and found my father sitting before an open fire, which was roaring into the chimney — brick — that he and my mother had laid the summer before, finally finding some use for the lime and sand he had assembled so many years ago.

It was warm, cosy, and home, so when my father asked me what I wanted to do with myself, I replied that if I could go to collegiate for a couple of years at his expense, I would be quite happy to settle down on the homestead. In this way I thought I should have the best of both worlds: education and the big cosy barn, which at that moment appeared much more substantial than the ethereal vision of some distant uncosy university which would probably be out of my reach financially. This quick reversal of the grandiose design which I had been discussing so ardently with Mrs. Turner only a few hours before stirred me emotionally to the point where my voice thickened and my words came out in a jumbled torrent, so that my father understood me to say that I proposed homesteading on my own. Later in the evening he urged me to give up that idea. Homesteading was much too exhausting for what it returned either in money or in satisfaction; and as for staying on the farm, I had better not unless I was sure I liked it. The fact was that I did not like it; I hated the wind and blowing snow, but I was moved emotionally by the cosy house and the big, commodious barn, added to a sense that I owed it to my father to stay with him, and that this offered security and permanence. I think my father divined this; it must have corresponded to some emotional crisis in his youth when he left the cosy farm-house at Coton for the uncertainties of the great world as an apprentice miller in Brownhills or a corn factor in Burton. But he had risen to the challenge and broken away, and he encouraged me to do the same. I only dimly realized at the time, for all my emotion, how important a cross-roads this was.

It was much later before I recognized this occasion as a turning-point or watershed, determining irrevocably the direction of my life. It appals me now to reflect on how critical are the decisions adolescents have to make on such inadequate foundations of experience and understanding, and how susceptible these decisions are to the winds of chance and circumstance. I have been forever grateful to my father for the prescience he showed in extricating me from my emotional urge to sacrifice my future on the altar of bucolic domesticity, and family solidarity.

Throughout that summer the barn competed with the school. On rainy days my father, Dick, and I sat around mending harness, riveting traces, and sewing reins while we listened to the horses snuffling in their mangers and the rain drumming on the roof. There is no more comforting melody in a country which for three years past had been seared by drought. It was fun at night to hear the rainwater from the roof trickling into the cellar cistern which had been installed while I was away. It was a notable improvement, because it gave us soft rainwater to hand immediately through a pump on the sink instead of trudging outside through mud to get a bucketful from the rain-barrel at the corner of the house. It was one of many amenities which the good crop of 1915 had permitted. Another was an extension of the cellar, doubling its size, and the installation of a central heating system which took the curse off getting up on winter mornings. My father had also built a two-room addition to the house over the cellar extension. He had built without a spirit-level, trusting to his eye, and the result was that the flooring had a decided gradient, which caused the table and anything loose to sidle towards the wall. One could get used to this, however; it made for novelty, but the cant on the floor combined with the slope of the ceiling-roof to make paper-hanging a very tricky mathematical problem. It led my father to the philosophical conclusion expressed from the depths of the easy chair after a day's paper-chase: "By the time you know enough to get through life reasonably well, it's too late to do much about it."

The exhilaration of a well-watered prairie spring was tempered by the realization that, with the best will in the world, I could not qualify as a competent hired hand. I never succeeded in properly milking the cow; to be sure, I did not put my heart into trying. I could assemble and hitch up four horses to plough, disc or harrows, but I had no fast reflex to cast loose when the plough struck a buried stone. By the time my reflexes had functioned the horses had put their weight into their collars, and the hardwood evener which distributed their traction had splintered, ending ploughing for the day and racking up a twenty-dollar charge for a new evener. In fact, as a farm-worker I was not only not worth my keep, I was a net loss. My father accepted this and encouraged my hopes of leaving the farm.

The winter snow lasted well into March, so we moved either by cutter or on horseback, spending the evenings at one of the neighbours' — Annis or Pearson, playing cards — rummy or nap — and belting home about midnight when the horses were keyed up with the crisp air, the snow, and the sky glowing with the Northern Lights. The new teacher turned out to be Marjorie Pelletier, the pretty girl I had noticed on the train from Swift Current a few weeks before. This added a new dimension to Grade VIII and I worked hard to overtake teacher, which was not too difficult, since she was only a lesson or two ahead of me. I arranged to get kept in after school, when I pursued other studies eagerly. The spring passed in a golden glow so pleasantly that it was with a twinge of regret that I saddled the grey mare and rode into Vanguard in June to write my Grade VIII examinations. The papers were not difficult; I felt that I had done them justice, and the local teacher who monitored the room kept a close eye on me so that he was able to tell me with some assurance that not only would I pass, but pass well.

I do not recall that the Department of Education bothered to let me know the results officially; I went to Regina to find out from the listing in the Regina *Leader*. I used the occasion to tidy up details of my discharge from the Army, which was dated March 13, 1919, and to make sure that I received whatever monies I could obtain, under whatever terminology the bureaucracy saw fit to use — re-settlement, rehabilitation, or whatever was current cant. I did not care what they called it so long as I got the money, so I filled out acres of vari-coloured forms with my number, rank, dates of enlistment and discharge, and what I proposed to do with the money I was asking for. I did not mention going to school or college, which I sensed would not be acceptable. With the guile fostered by three years of orderly-room training in stimulus and response in the military mind, I wrote down "re-establishment into civilian life". I thought that would do.

I must have struck the right note for the funds came through with commendable dispatch and I prepared to take up my re-establishment. The first thing to do was to buy a suit of civilian clothes. This was a trying procedure for I had no clear idea of what I wanted. I settled on a grey three-piece with two pairs of pants, for $57.00. As prices went in those days, it was expensive raiment. The Regina *Leader* was advertising tailored suits at $9.95 with "odd trousers" $1.95 to $6.00; shirts were 69 cents; with French cuffs, 79 cents; Oxford walkovers were listed at $2.49, but I had mine already; ties 39 cents; Stetsons $2.95, which seemed odd, since shoes were fifty cents less. Fortunately on my trip to London I had bought a good officers' trench coat with oiled silk rain-proofing and detachable fleece lining, which would take care of both summer and winter wear. It was serviceable and radiated prestige, although I neither knew nor cared about prestige. But I had a coat, so I wore it day in, day out, for the next four years. I had brought back from England, as part of my cadet equipment, a walking-stick; it went well enough in Regina but it was not well thought of in Vanguard. Returning to the farm, I spent the rest of the summer in a delightful daze which contributed little to agriculture but tempered my family's reluctance to see me return to Regina for the opening of the college year in September. I chose Regina College because it was the residential college with the best faculty in the area, and recommended by Mrs. Turner, my former teacher.

Chapter Twenty-three

Just before term opened I stood in my splendid civvies in front of Regina College on a clear, crisp fall day envying the assurance with which similarly attired young men sprang up the steps two at a time and swung through the doors with such intimate confidence. Would I ever be able to match that casual approach to the holy of holies? I wondered. It was hard to imagine. Regina College was a battlemented brick building, with stone facings and pinnacles, which reminded me of the flint and stone construction in Shoreham. I tried to identify the architectural style, but it did not fit into any of the patterns outlined by old Major "Johnny Walker" when he was taking D Company, 34th Battalion, out for a route-march. It was, however, vaguely reminiscent of the dormitory buildings at Lancing College, so I concluded that it might be classified as Tudor academic. Regina College was supported by the Methodist Church. Its staff were overworked and underpaid, recruited mainly from Victoria College, Toronto, which carried a good reputation, as my first teacher had assured me. The R.C. staff carried on the tradition. They were dedicated, and they spared no effort to transmute hayseeds and threshing hands from the Soo Line or the Vanguard spur into God-fearing, informed citizens. It had what I wanted, as Mrs. Turner had divined.

The Rev. Dr. E. W. Stapleford, who had put himself through college by selling books door to door, drove his staff and students as hard as himself. He took a class in education, preached on Sundays, and doubled in brass as a fund-raiser from local businessmen who profited by the influx of students and faculty into their small enclave. They were invited annually to a dinner at the college, from which they counted themselves to have emerged unscathed if they contributed no more than twenty-five dollars. In my first term I was assigned to open the main door and escort them to the reception room for this occasion, which led Dr. Stapleford to observe that I would make a good butler. I replied that this was not my ambition, but that it would be useful if I could get a job on staff as a waiter the following year; otherwise I might have difficulty returning. Dr. Stapleford recognized a good sales pitch when he saw it, and turned me over to his sister, Miss Marion Stapleford, who ran the Commissariat. She signed me on to wait on three tables of eight boys for my board and room. I considered this a very good deal indeed, for it meant that I would have to pick up only a couple of hundred dollars the following summer to ensure my return for senior matriculation, a most desirable springboard into university.

That first year at Regina College was one of the busiest and most profitable of my whole life (reversing the judgement of Gibbon on his fourteen months at Magdalen College, Oxford). I found that I had a compendium of unorganized information on topics ranging from astronomy to zoology, but a three-year gap on the educational ladder which the province's bureaucracy had devised. This gap had to be filled. I set myself to this task with diligence; I got up at six o'clock, which was luxury to a farm boy used to getting up at five, and got in two hours' work before breakfast, at which we were supposed to appear bright and shining at eight-thirty sharp. I still did not need a daily shave, so I managed to squeeze in a very quick wash before classes at nine. They went on, with a fifteen-minute break, until noon; then lunch and classes again from two until five. Dinner at six. I split my evening home-work into half-hour sections, carefully preparing work two days ahead, so that I was never pinched by emergencies. I rolled into bed at eleven and fell asleep before I hit the pillow. Somewhere or other I worked in a half-hour at tennis, and on Saturdays played soccer. On Sundays I had a long afternoon sleep, which brought my reserves up to par.

The really tough period of each weekday was two to two-thirty in the afternoon, which was usually scheduled for Latin or Greek. These classes were taken by the Reverend E. R. Doxsee, a silver medallist in classics from Victoria College, who also dealt with ancient history. In his spare time he filled the office of dean. I used to fall asleep in my place after a few minutes, as the hour, the warmth, and the droning voices of my class-mates construing Virgil, overcame me. Mr. Doxsee, bless his heart, could not have missed what was going on, but he never embarrassed me by calling attention to my slumbers. When it became my turn to construe, he always gave me time to collect my wits by announcing at length the initial words of the passage, its place on the page, and its general tenor. I bulled my way through well enough, thanks to my grounding in Latin at Lichfield, but I could not do that in Greek. Mr. Doxsee tried hard to give me elements of grammar and a vocabulary which might compress three years' work into one, but the time factor was against him. Greek texts, it seemed to me, together with notes and vocabulary, were arranged on the theory that spending as long a time as possible over a word or a passage ensured that the student would grasp and remember it. It was poor psychology, for it led to frustration and exasperation which aroused an antipathy and made certain that what was learned in the effort would be wiped off the slate of memory. Also, few students have unlimited time at their command; I had not, and I refused to let my command of the other subjects I was trying to master be imperilled by denying them the time consumed pointlessly through unimaginative editing of the classical texts.

After a particularly frustrating encounter with Xenophon's *Hellenica,* I was forced to pocket my pride and trot down to Mr. Doxsee's office one evening when the good man was working on his correspondence and tell him sadly that I simply could not catch up, and would have to drop his Greek class. He was sympathetic but regretful: "I thought of you as Rhodes Scholar material," he said. This startled me, for while I had vaguely aspired to this honour, I was too modest to think I merited it. But for Mr. Doxsee, this modesty might have ensured my missing it. From that moment I actively planned and worked for it, using every opportunity offered by the immolating devotion of Regina College's faculty.

Edith V. Phillips took the senior class in English, and imbued me with a passion for Chaucer which still glows. She also served as Dean of Women, for Regina College was a co-educational institution. She was responsible for some 150 nubile females, particularly to see that they were given opportunities of associating, at arm's length, with nubile males. I used to creep over to her office in the girls' wing once a week to ask if I might take Miss Blank out to church, or a movie, or whatever was going. I was sternly enjoined to be back with Miss Blank at or before ten, and my name was jotted down in the book.

John W. (for Wesley, of course) Ansley, took care of the boys' (Men's) residence when he was not teaching physics, chemistry, and biology. I was better acquainted with prairie fauna and flora than most, so biology was a gift. Unfortunately there was no slot on my crowded schedule for chemistry, so that had to go by the board.

Treliving, a bustling young man struggling against obesity, ground in the elements of mathematics and tried to make us approach problems in an orderly manner and solve them by logic. He made it clear that formulas were only tools of the trade; if we forgot them, it was not too difficult to fashion a new tool on the spot. I found this helpful in tight squeezes. Someone must have "done" history, but I cannot remember who; Gertrude Stangways did her best to discipline her class in French, but she was not by nature a martinet and her class was often too unruly for its own or her good.

During my first term I was startled to hear from Dr. Stapleford that I had won the Governor General's bronze medal for leading the Grade VIII examinations in Southern Saskatchewan in that year, and was warned to be sure not to skip chapel lest I louse up the presentation ceremony. The medal was a bronze plaque three inches in diameter, with a likeness of the Duke and Duchess of Devonshire on one side and the armorial bearings of the Dominion of Canada on the other. It encouraged me to believe that with careful organization and economy of my strength and talents, I might go a long way in the academic world, which even then showed an excessive regard for the outward symbols of learning.

Knowing that mathematics was my weakest subject but also one in which it was possible to score 100, I concentrated on that field. I was guided in my approach by L. C. Walmsley, a gentle man with the courage to work out mathematical problems on the blackboard before a critical class, whose help he was not too proud to seek at need. Walmsley used mathematics as I did, as a means to an end. He subsequently went to China where his gentle industry gained him renown and respect and ultimately a post as an Oriental expert with the University of Toronto. My other mathematical mentor was Blake Harper, a youth from Rouleau, on the rich Soo Line, who came to Regina College with a pork-pie hat and a pair of dice. He taught me how to use quadratic equations, and the theory of probability. Both quadratics and galloping dominoes, he pointed out, worked out on a plus or minus formula, whereas the theory of probability was a one-way street. The best way to learn crap-shooting, he held, was to lose twenty dollars betting on probability.

From my room on the third floor, south side, I could look out on fifty miles of wheat, covering the Regina Plain to the foot of the Dirt Hills, a faint blue smudge on the horizon. In the foreground, Wascana Lake, a small artificial pond, offered romantic attractions of water and willows, with the architectural glories of the Legislative Building rivalling, however remotely, the Taj Mahal, in the background. By dint of constant watering, rolling, and mowing, a lawn of impressive size and vigour had been created, while hedges of luxuriant caragana provided secluded nooks where students from co-educational institutions could pursue their researches, with only an occasional discreet interruption from the sparrow-cop when the pursuit of knowledge appeared to be getting out of hand.

I was fortunate in my room-mates, and particularly in William B. Milburn, son of a pioneer law officer in Swift Current and brother of one of the 209th Battalion's officers. Bill respected my odd working hours and I respected his odd devotion to the clarinet, an erratic instrument, much given to jumping an octave without notice, like a boy's voice at breaking age.

Bill and I were pillars of the dramatic society, with roles in the student production of As You Like It, he as the Melancholy Jacques, I as Duke Senior. We founded a lifelong friendship on our mutual recognition that neither of us was meant for the stage. Bill went on to study dentistry in Toronto and to practise it in Victoria, B.C. In due course I arrived there too, to study the incidence of red-tape-worms among local and mainland bureaucrats, and develop sound procedures for worming them. There are plenty of specimens across the water in Vancouver where a good vermifuge should merit the Canada Medal.

At the end of my first academic year I had established myself as head of the Junior Matriculation Class and looked forward eagerly to moving up into the Senior Class if I could find the price — what was left after deducting my benefits as waiter and scholarship holder. A summer stint at teaching would cover my needs. I had no certificate or normal school training, but my father took the view that my army training would ensure discipline and the rest could take care of itself. So, as secretary-treasurer of School District 717, he took me on for the summer at $100 a month. As I ate and slept at home, and had nothing else to spend the money on, this was net profit. I had an easy task. There were ten little tads ranging from six to ten years old; some of them rode to school, three to a horse, bareback; some drove in a broken-down buggy held together by haywire. All brought their lunches in lard-pails; all but the little girls smelled of old gopher tails, and most of the little boys tried to extend lavatory privileges to the time needed to snare another gopher. The classroom in other respects was unchanged since Miss Reaman had presided over it, so I called on my recollections of her methods, and soon had the entire school reading, writing, and figuring, and in their off hours observing local fauna and flora. They used their pencils, reserving inkwells for wild-flowers, which I encouraged them to draw, name, and conserve. It was all wrong by later educational fads, but when the inspector paid a surprise visit, he was impressed to find how informed and subdued the little stinkers were. He gave me a good report, which set my father's mind at rest, for his conscience had been pricking him about nepotism.

I had hoped to redeem my failure to master Greek at Regina by working through Xenophon after school. But by four o'clock, after a day in the schoolhouse, heated by the sun to greenhouse temperature, I was too weary to concentrate; I fell asleep in the Morris chair and Xenophon dropped from my hand.

Just before returning to Regina College, I put in a short hitch with Cooper's threshing-gang, working on stacked flax. This is the most brutal of the various brutalizing threshing operations. The bunches of flax settle down into the mass of the stack, and herculean efforts are required to pull loose each forkful. I developed secondary and tertiary blisters across the entire palm of my right hand and finger calluses on the left. However, I needed the money. As soon as I decently could, though, I hustled back to Regina College, to add waiting on tables to my already rigorous schedule.

To save time, I stimulated my three tables to competitive eating. First table out got a bigger helping next meal. This reduced the time I had to cut from my schedule of studies. It may not have been the best for my charges' digestion, but nobody complained. I staggered through the crowded dining room with a tray piled high with dishes, and learned how to carry eight cups of coffee at once. My one catastrophe came when I was entrusted with an extra shift with the College's fanciest china for an afternoon tea designed to put the bite on the Ladies' Auxiliary. With a tray loaded with the special china tea-service, I slipped on a wet patch, and crashed in a heap of shards, bread and butter, and jam. Miss Stapleford, whose account would have to absorb the damages, uttered no word or whisper of reproach; but it was months before I could meet her gaze again.

Despite the dining hall job and the fifty-dollar scholarship, I had to pinch and scrape to get through the college year. There was nothing left over for extravagances. Fortunately, Regina offered few temptations. On Saturday evening, however, I had a night on the town, but it always ended in a harrowing decision to be made. Should I blow sixty-five cents on Boston cream pie and coffee, or should I go two blocks further to the drug-stationery-bookstore opposite the Union Station and blow it on an Everyman? At nineteen the alimentary canal speaks with a commanding voice; I was always hungry, but the number of Everyman volumes on my shelves today is witness to the triumph of brain over belly. It might not have been so complete had I not had the reserves offered by the waiters' table at College.

There were eight boys waiting on tables that year. We used to eat before the others, at a small table in one corner. We saw to it that we got the pick of the menu, and always had a half-gallon pitcher of milk on the table. This proved a disaster for those of us who had not had army experience, for the milk supply was tainted, which led to a virulent outbreak of typhoid fever, hospitalizing the entire student body and many of the staff. The waiters had drunk more milk than anyone, but the four who had been in the Army, where they had received anti-typhoid injections, escaped the infection, while the others went down with it, two of them acutely sick. I bear in mind this escape as well as my good teeth when I think of the three years I devoted to the Canadian Army. I needed all my strength to carry the work-load; but I put in extra time during the Christmas holidays, for I did not want to risk infecting my family by returning home before every chance of transmitting the germs had been eliminated. I put in much time carrying blocks of ice up to the sick bays on the third floor and doing some practice shots on the tennis court in intervals of mugging up Cicero and Virgil. The result was that I roared through the last two terms, sweeping the board of prizes and capturing a scholarship to the University of Saskatchewan for 1920, which in those days was awarded by a faculty committee, without reference either to undergraduates or to political necessities.

Fifty years ago, under Dr. Walter Murray, the University of Saskatchewan was a free institution which attracted scholars from all over the continent. A reputation for scholarship and independence brought in men like Thompson in biology, Thorvaldson in physics, Sullivan and Ramsey in classics, Underhill, Morton, and Simpson in history, Richard Wilson in English, Rutherford in agriculture and Sharrard in philosophy.

Most of the teaching staff were graduates of Dalhousie or Oxford; only Sullivan was from Trinity College, Dublin. These elements made a unique amalgam of Canadian and Oxford lectures and tutorials, a ductile compound which moulded readily to fill educational caries resulting from earlier neglect or mischance. Teddy Muller used to conduct informal French sessions over tea at home. Dr. Manning liked to have chats over a late supper in his rooms in Qu'Appelle Hall, which I had learned to enter with that gay insouciance I had so envied in sophomores and juniors when I stood in the driveway on my first visit to the university. Muller was an Alsatian whose accent and views were tinged with border emotions which I recognized long afterwards as dominating attitudes from Vienna to Virginia and from Toledo to Tennessee. Remembering Muller's poetic evocation of the glories of Strasburg Cathedral, I later made a point of visiting Alsace. With an early miniature camera, I took a picture of the Main Portal which was so sharp that I had it blown up. Then I discovered, well in the foreground, a man admiring this same portal, while thoughtfully scratching his backside. For years the picture had a place of honour on my mantelpiece. Muller, who was an agnostic, enjoyed elaborating on the themes decorating church portals; imbued with the scepticism of Voltaire, he, no less than Underhill's

220

history lectures, encouraged in us a spirit of uninhibited inquiry and conscientious reporting of our findings; they set the tone of the university, and the Class of 1924 lived up to it.

The University of Saskatchewan brought me a world where reality was to be sought and, possibly, discovered. To be sure, Dr. Sharrard publicly and privately questioned these assumptions and urged his students to do likewise. He scoffed at the pretensions of the Faculty of Science that their discipline could indeed know and identify phenomena floating across the field of their microscopes as surely as if they were salmon climbing a fish-ladder. The Department of Philosophy, it seemed to me, had not advanced one step beyond the Department of Classics, where Ramsey and Sullivan were still pondering questions *De Rerum Natura* to which the Roman poet Lucretius had given much thought and many verses some two thousand years ago. Can we indeed find answers to the basic questions: "What does it mean to know?" and "What is knowable?" Was it not frightening to realize that Science had thus far outstripped Philosophy, by assembling a mass of data which we assumed to be knowledge and dared to use as an implement for further inquiries, without any philosophical doubts about the soundness of our assumptions or the wisdom of using them, first to define the Good Life, and then to impose our conception of it on our associates as a "scientific" certainty?

The limitations with which Muller, Underhill the historian, and Manning the biochemist insisted on qualifying these conceptions spurred me to contemplate widening my own area of knowledge; they did not destroy my confidence that ultimately this accumulation would afford spiritual content, even wisdom, and with it a good living, which I defined as a well-paid job, and the intellectual companionship and stimulus of my peers; but I assumed, over-rashly as it turned out, that appropriate academic degrees would assure these benefits automatically; the alternative was to slump into a chair at the end of a long day on a plough or at a blackboard, teaching kids how to teach more kids how to teach yet more kids to be unmotivated and unknowing inhabitants of a vast ant-hill. The great German thinkers might have found some answers to this problem, but I was unable to adjust my schedule to include German. This distressed me at the time and has caused me vain regrets ever since, for I have never been able to fill this gap.

I found the university atmosphere so stimulating that I did not mind long hours of study, and I finished my sophomore year with 4 A's, 2 B's, and the vice-presidency of the Class of 1924. These successes encouraged me to think seriously about applying for the Rhodes Scholarship, although my athletic performance, which carried equal weight with scholarship and leadership, was negligible. To remedy this I played tennis, which did not carry a "letter" but which I liked; soccer, which I detested, although I cherished the "half-letter" it offered; and indulged in indoor track, trotting and jumping in a gymnasium pungent with sweat. During the year I succeeded to the presidency of the Class organization when the elected president was removed by misadventure.

Finally, encouraged by Teddy Muller, I wrote out my Rhodes application, delaying it until the ultimate minute, since I was uncertain whether this scholarship could be granted in the junior year (there was no precedent for this and Oxford University regulations discouraged creating one); however, in another year I would be too old under the regulations then obtaining, so after long hesitation I put in my bid. I had a moment of panic just after I had dropped my letter in the post-box, when it appeared that I had waited too long and overshot the deadline for application. Had it not been already in the Royal Mail, I would have withdrawn it. However, my concern was unnecessary, for I discovered that the current issue of the university paper, *The Sheaf*, had been by mistake ante-dated by a week; I was well within bounds. The unusual journalistic error took on the appearance of fate, so I was not too surprised when, after an unpleasant game when the Class of '24 Soccer Team had performed without distinction, a fellow class-mate burst into my room, pushed me over with a shout on to my bed, and yelled that I had been chosen Saskatchewan Rhodes Scholar for 1923. It was many years before I discovered that my informant had himself been a strong runner-up for the honour, which may have accounted for his exuberance, as a reaction to disappointment. I was glad not to have known that at the time, for it would have tarnished somewhat the blazing glory of my triumph.

I passed the remainder of the term in a daze, dropped soccer, and soft-pedalled studies while I sought advice on how to conduct myself in this strange new world which lay ahead. The consensus was: Don't be conspicuous! I began conforming before I left the West. I was gratified to overhear a campus conversation as I passed one windy morning: "He hasn't let it go to his head; same old trench-coat, same old muffler blowing loose!"

With Underhill in mind, I put down Balliol as my first choice, although I was somewhat daunted by its reputation for high thinking; as second choice I selected Oriel, since it had welcomed one of my cousins; it was also Cecil Rhodes' college and the home of A. H. Clough. Oriel accepted me. My happiness was complete.